I08181O3

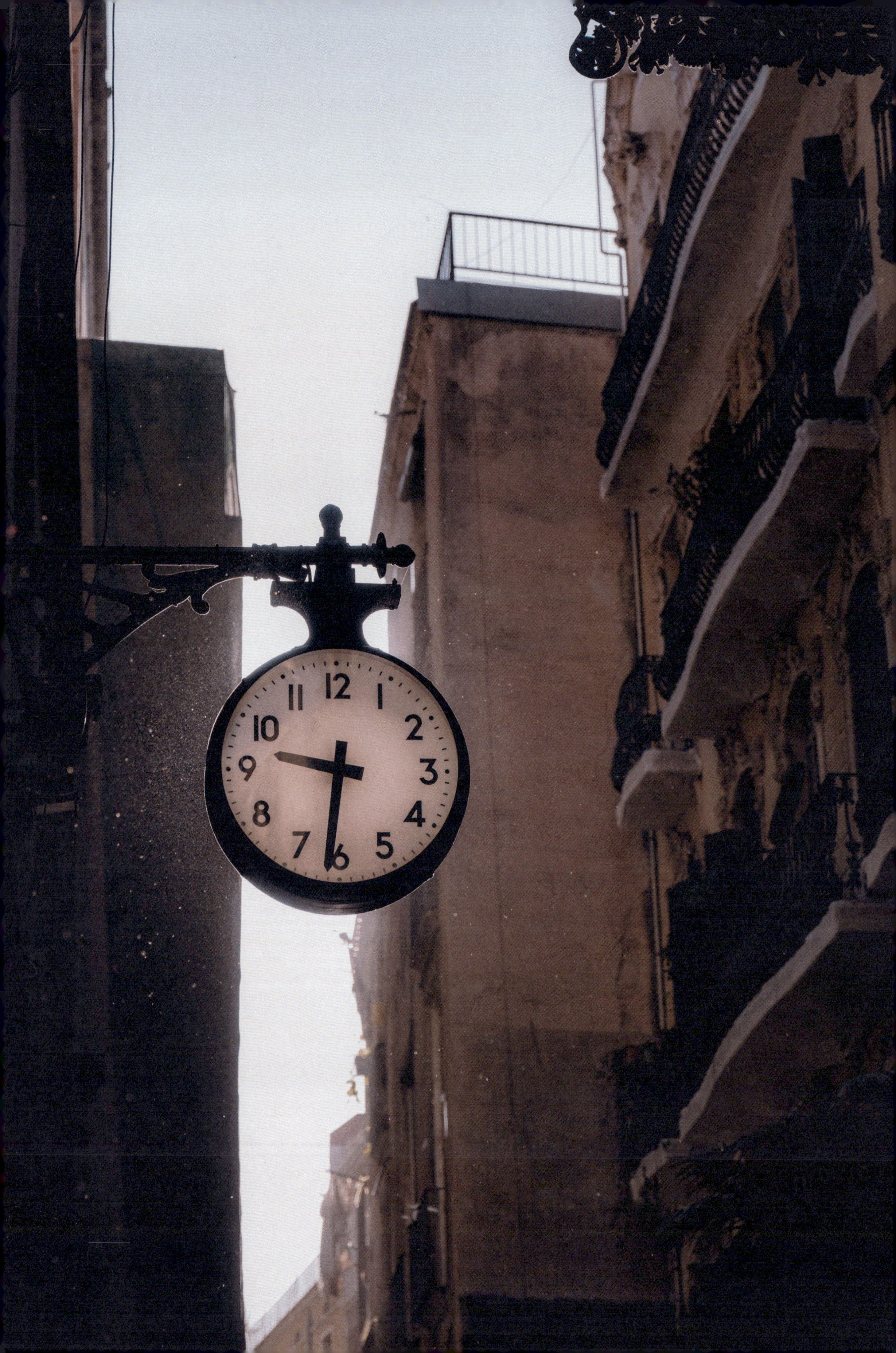

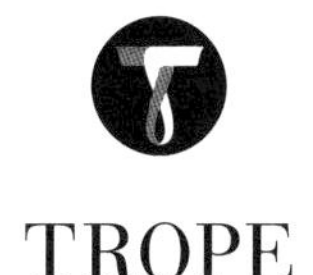

TROPE

BARCELONA DREAMING

PETER JONKER

TROPE PUBLISHING Co.

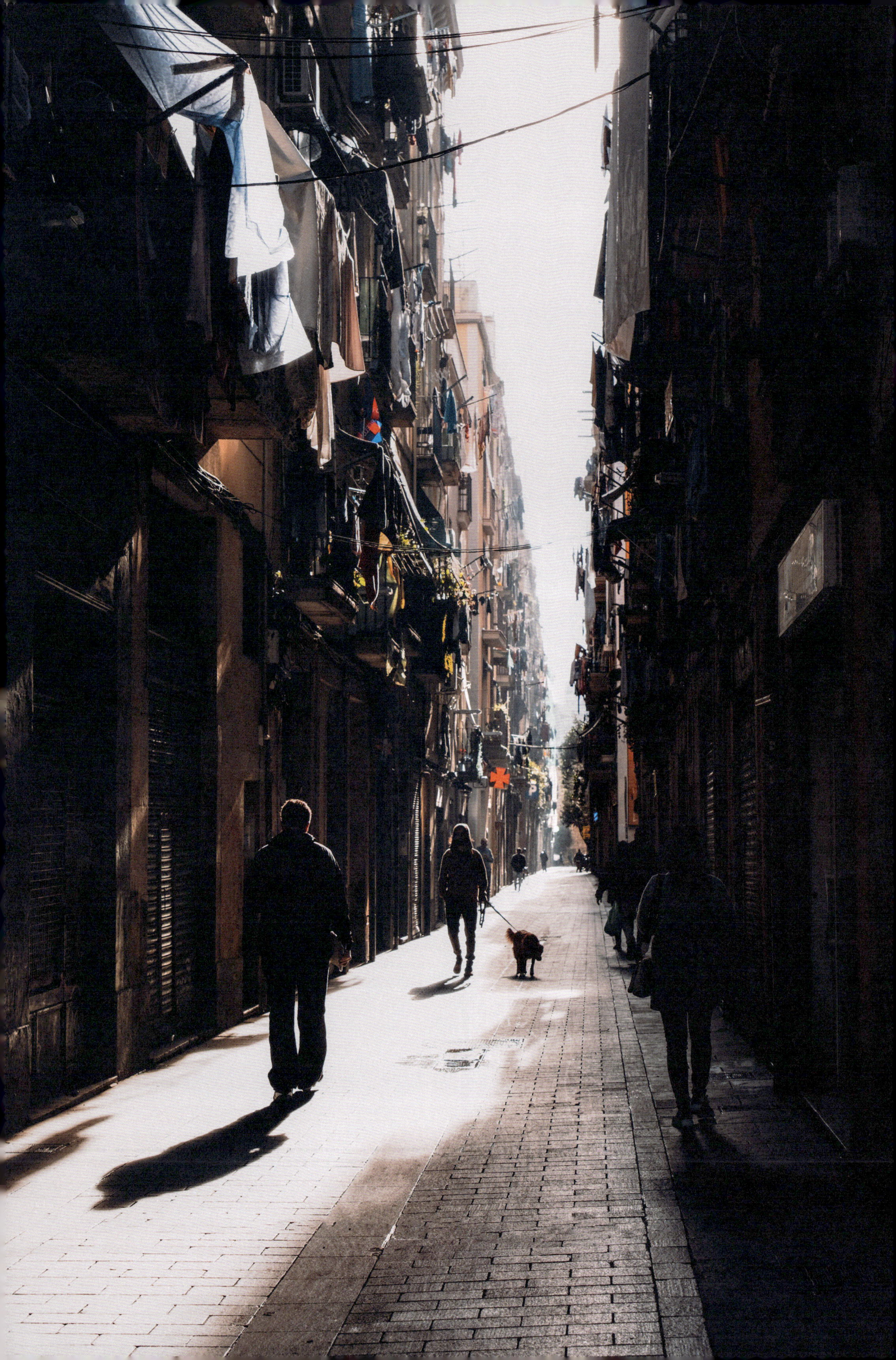

INTRODUCTION

There's something magical about Barcelona. It's a city that defies definition, with a deep-rooted sense of identity. It's a place where ancient Roman walls hide behind modernist façades, where centuries-old traditions collide with cutting-edge innovation, and where every narrow alley or sun-drenched plaza hides a story.

Founded as a small Roman colony around 15 BC, Barcelona, then known as Barcino, served as a strategic military and trade outpost. This Roman influence is still visible in the city's layout, remnants of ancient walls, and archaeological sites integrated into the modern city planning.

Celebrated worldwide for its architectural heritage, modern Barcelona is in many ways synonymous with architect Antoni Gaudí who transformed Barcelona. His innovative designs like the whimsical and colorful Park Güell and the modernist Casa Batlló are instantly recognizable. But Gaudí is perhaps best known for the Sagrada Familia, the remarkable unfinished Catholic Basilica famous for its distinctive Gothic and Art Nouveau architectural styles that has been under construction since 1882.

In *Barcelona Dreaming*, photographer Peter Jonker gives the reader his view into the city. His is a vision of shadows and light, a journey through arches and avenues, towers and terraces. It is the everyday Barcelona: the man walking down the cobblestone streets of the Gothic Quarter; the couple sitting on a park bench; the group of men playing dominoes along the Mediterranean. He expertly captures the warmth and magic of Barcelona through his images.

Whether you're familiar with the city or are experiencing Barcelona's layered charm for the first time, Jonker shares an intimate portrait of the city, taking you beyond the landmarks to the very soul of Barcelona. Enjoy.

MICHELLE FITZGERALD
Editor

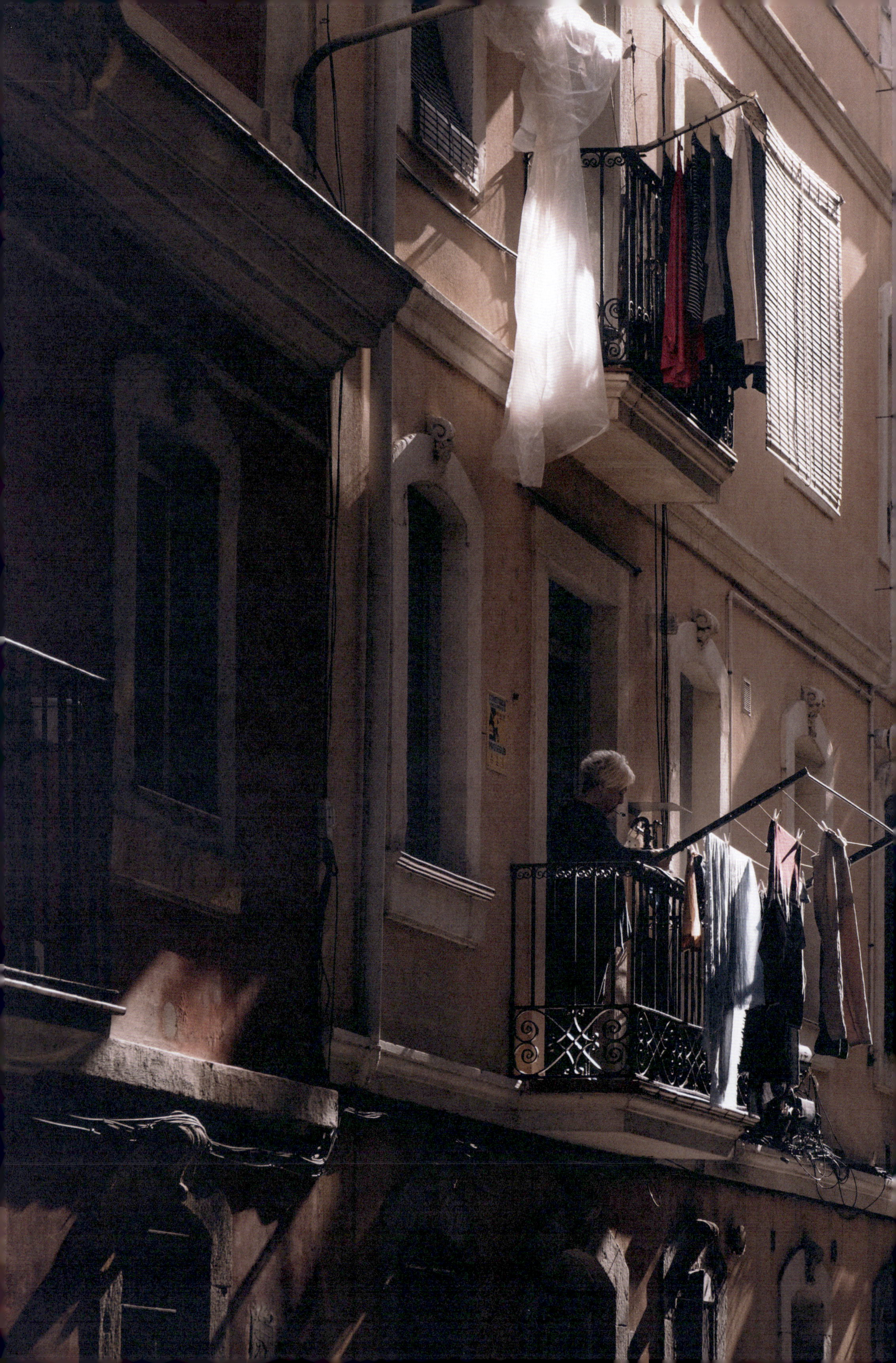

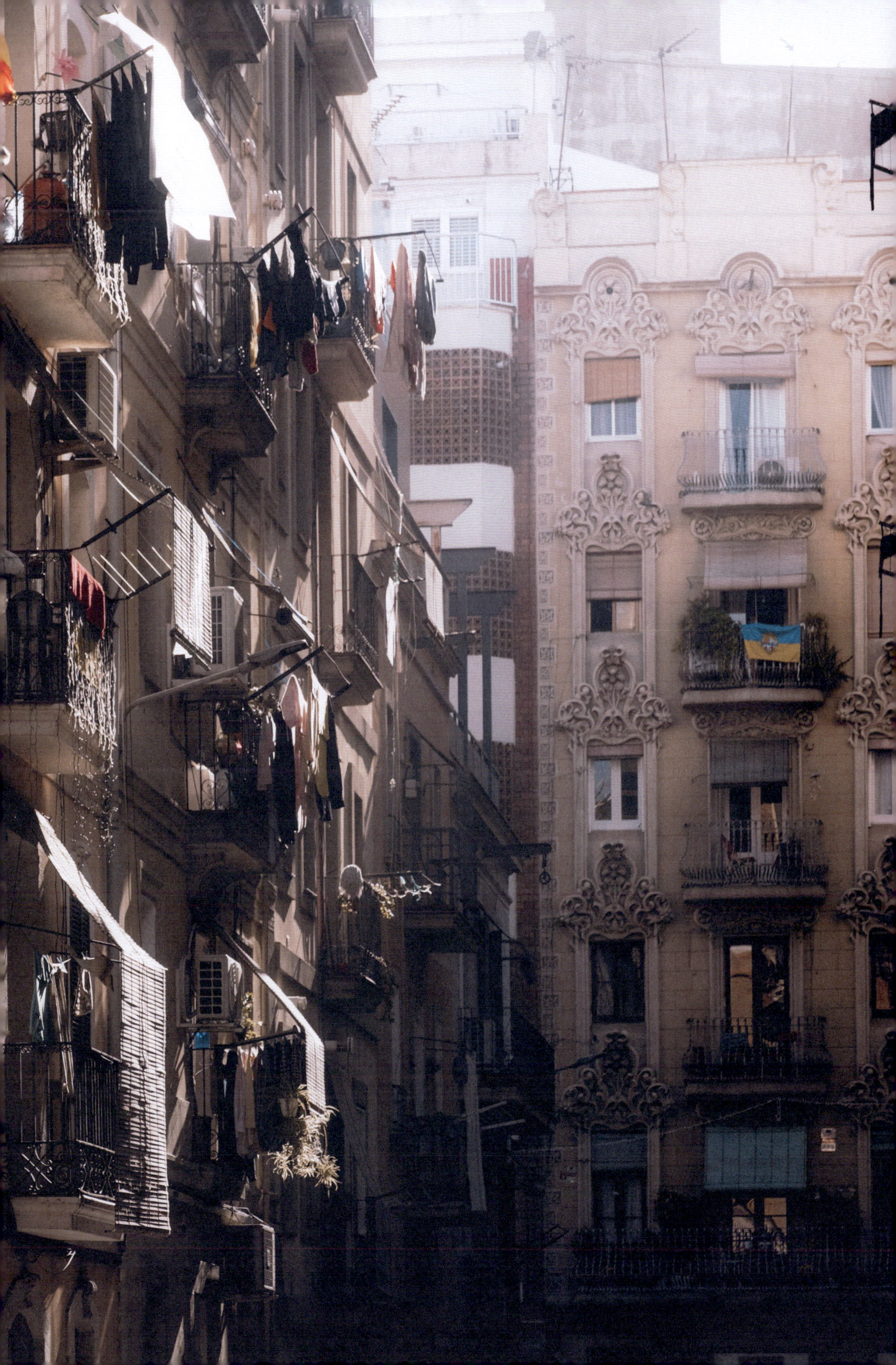

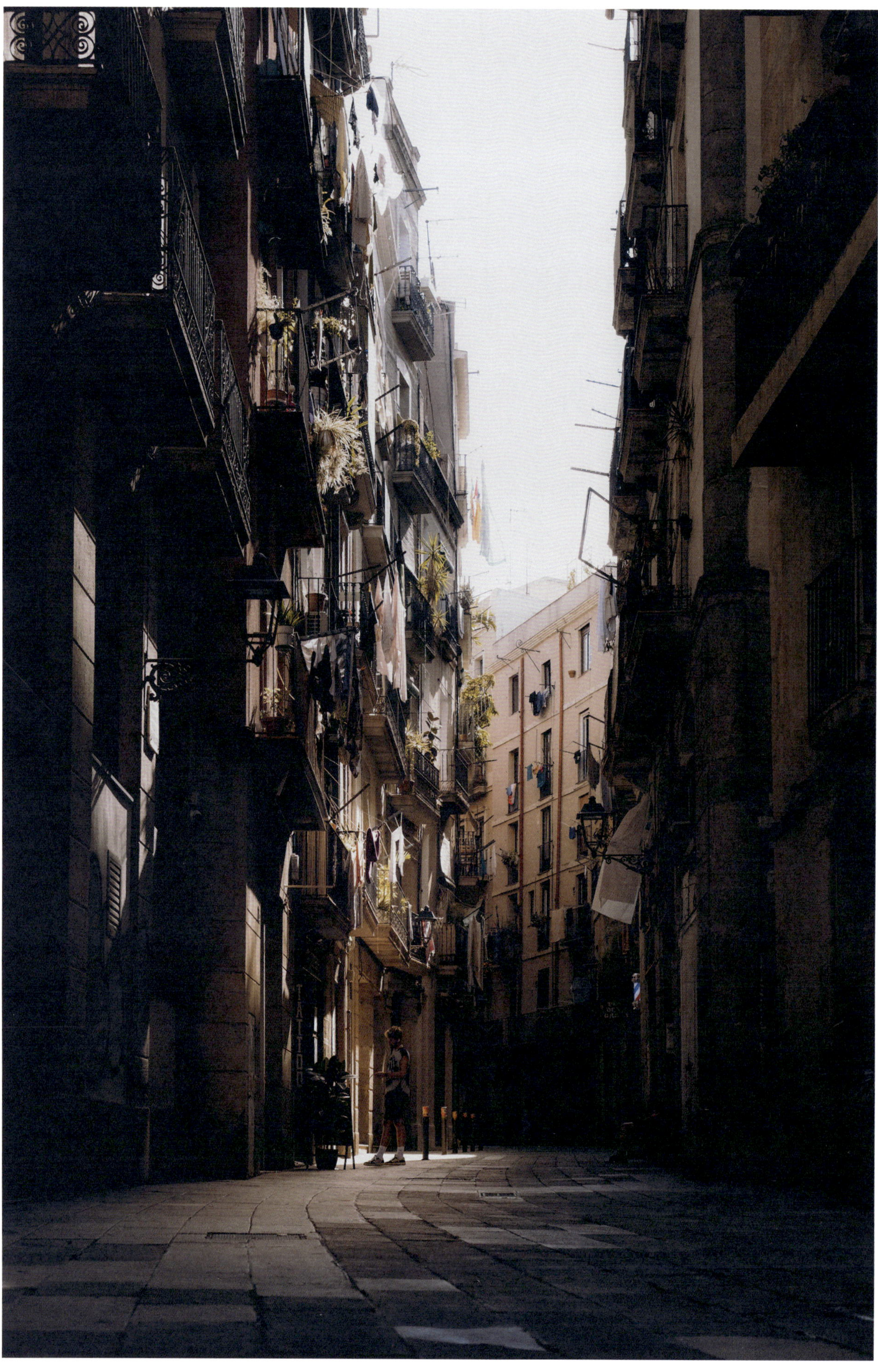

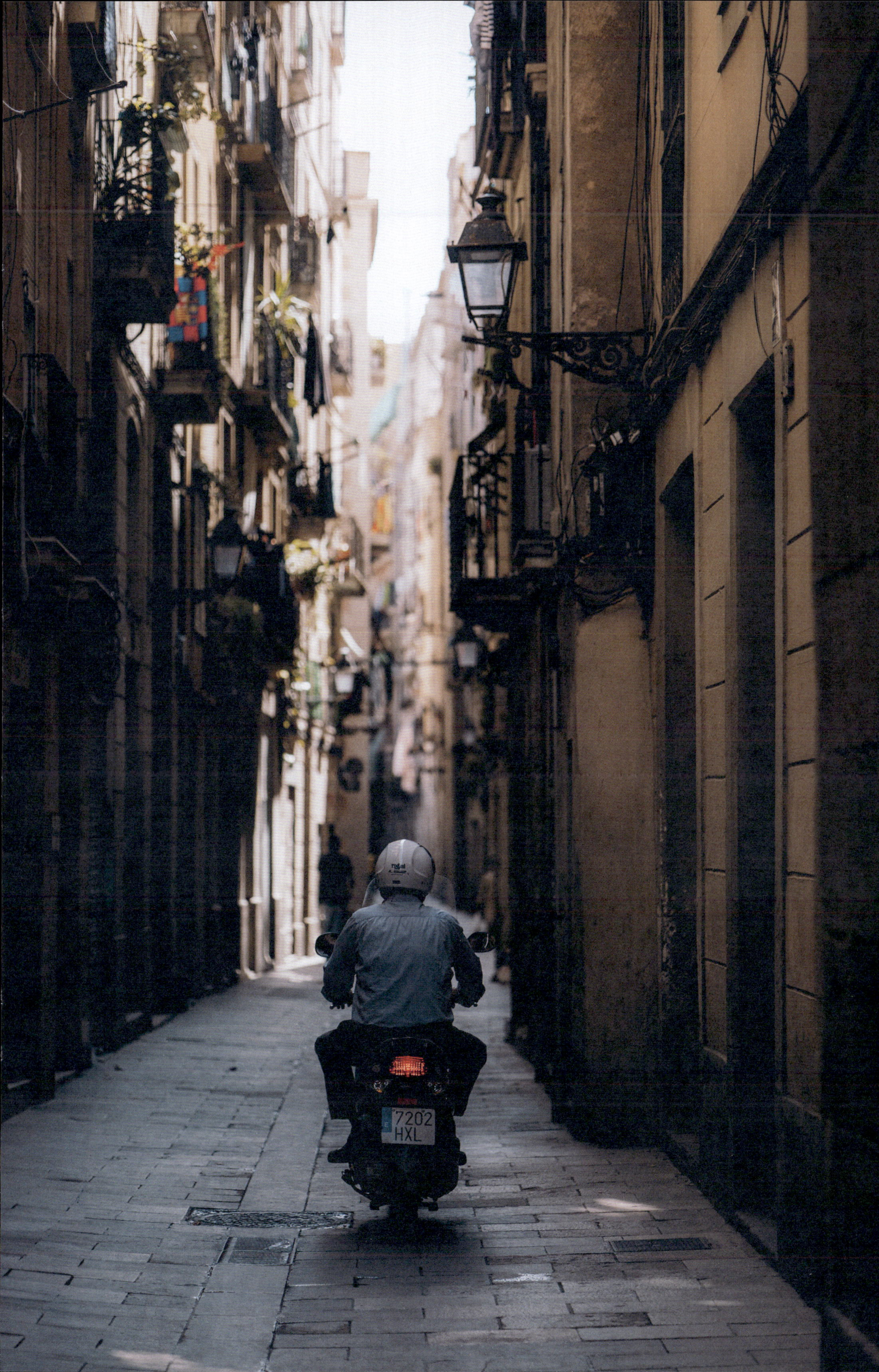
7202
HXL

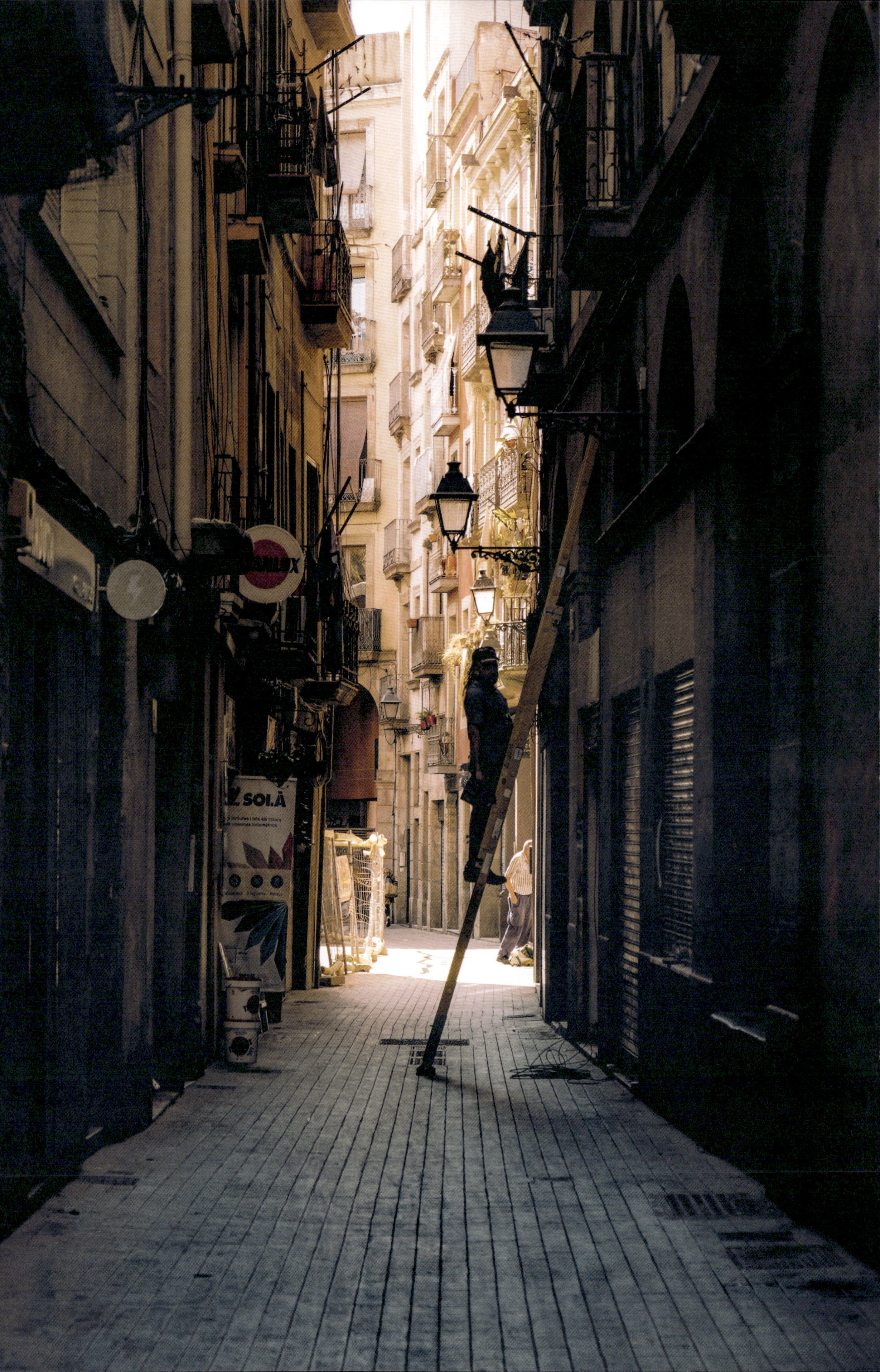
SOLÀ

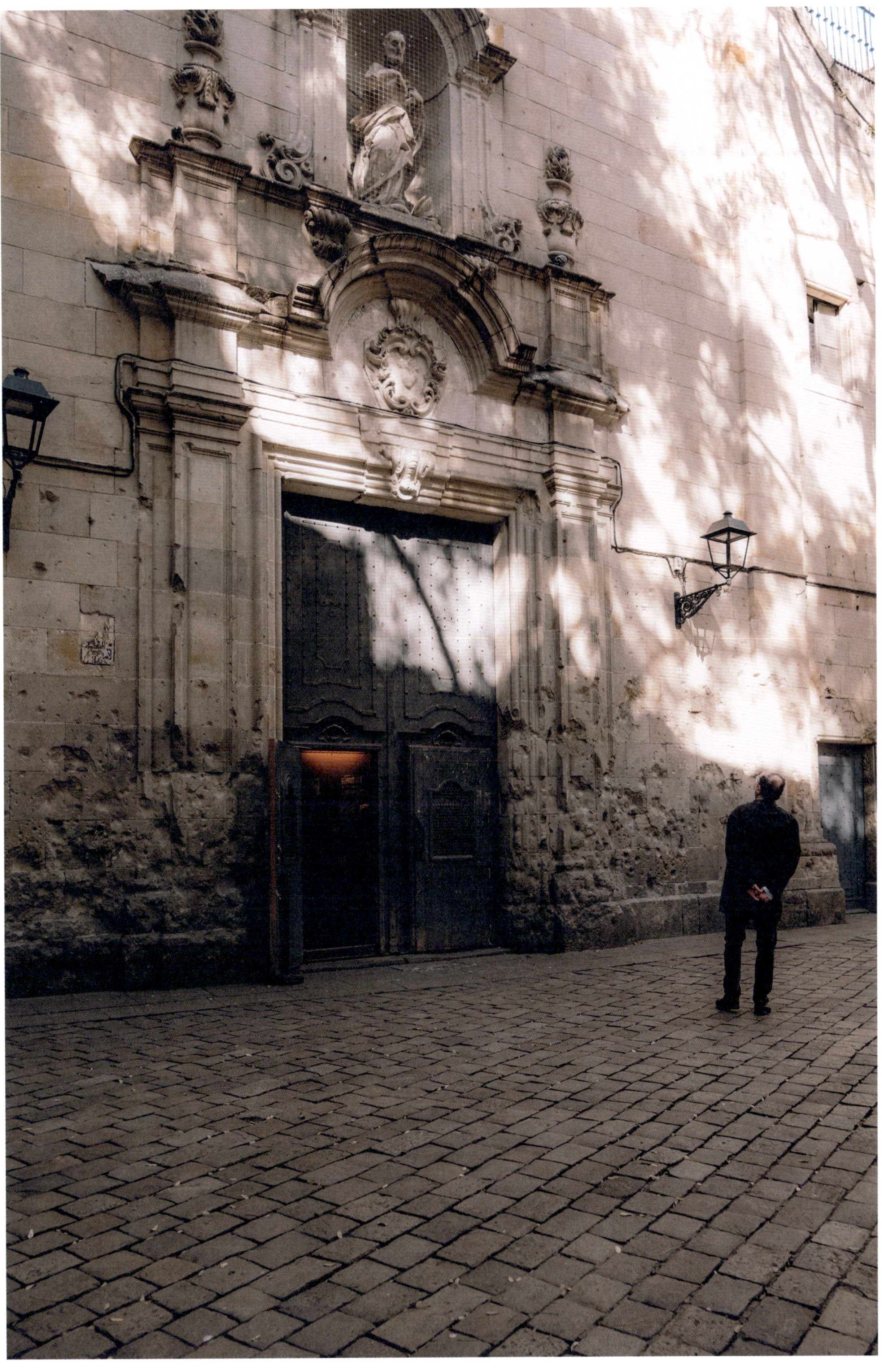

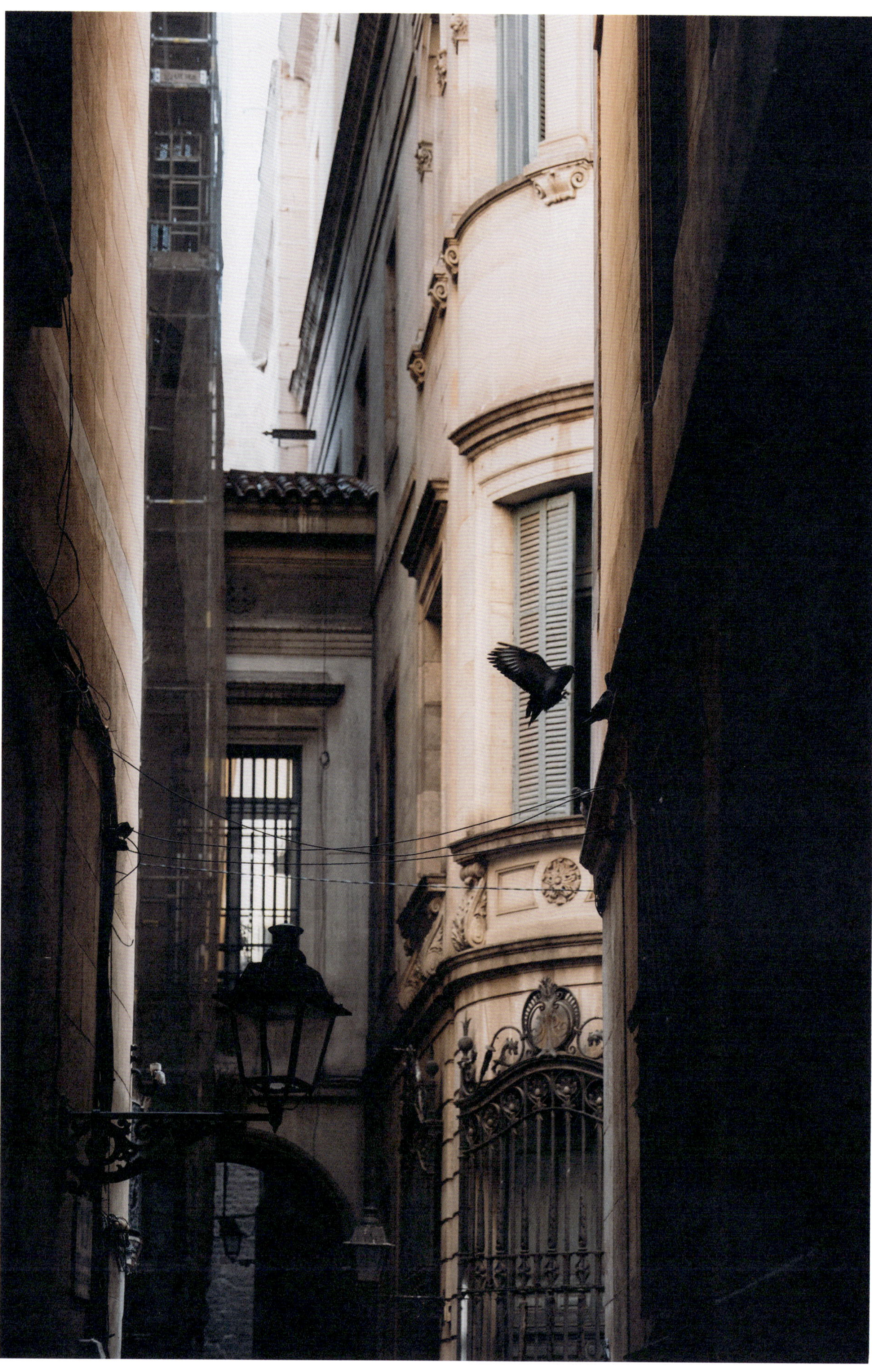

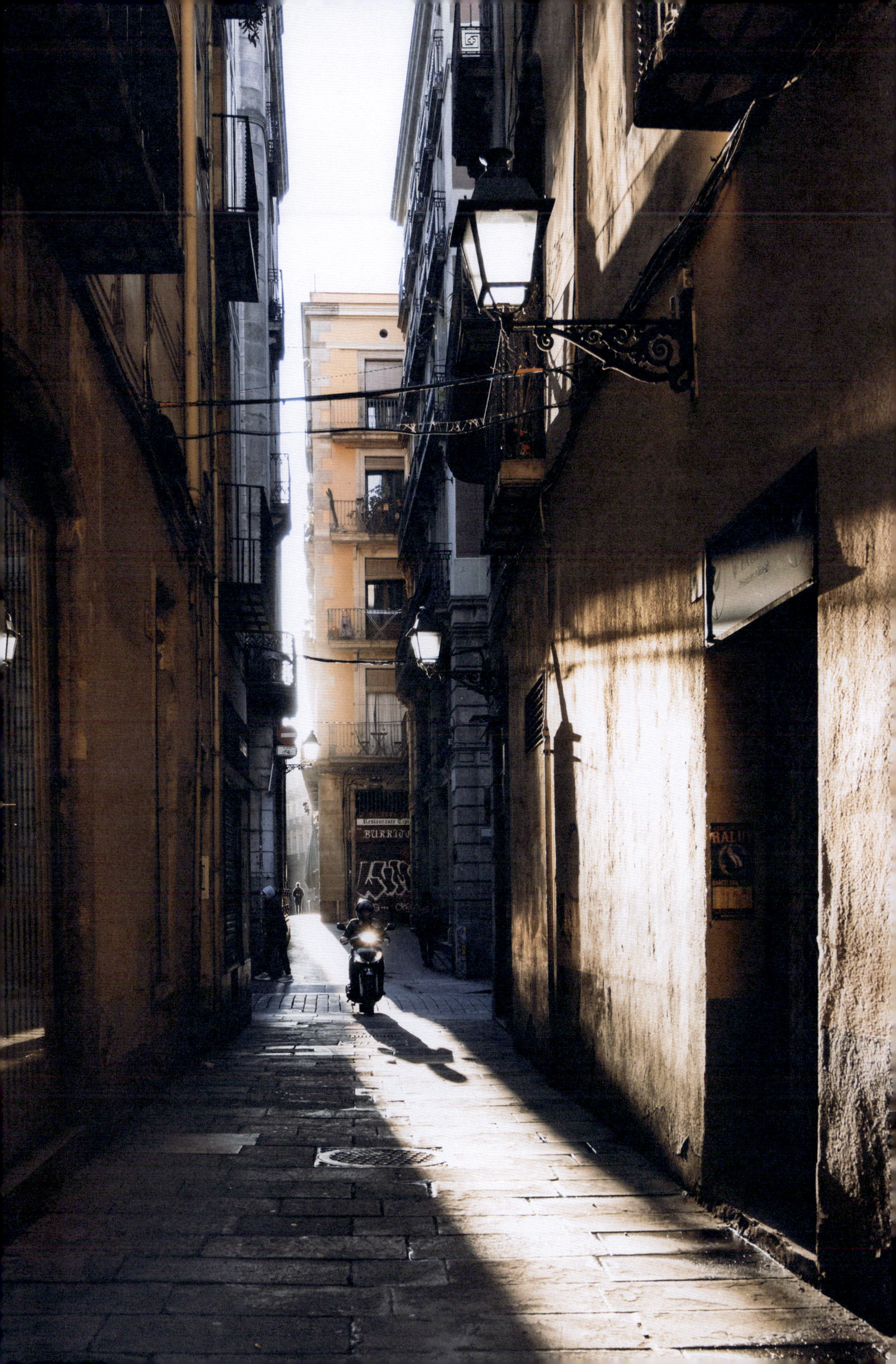

Barcelona is a very old city in which you can feel the weight of history; it is haunted by history. You cannot walk around it without perceiving it.

CARLOS RUIZ ZAFÓN

Spanish Novelist

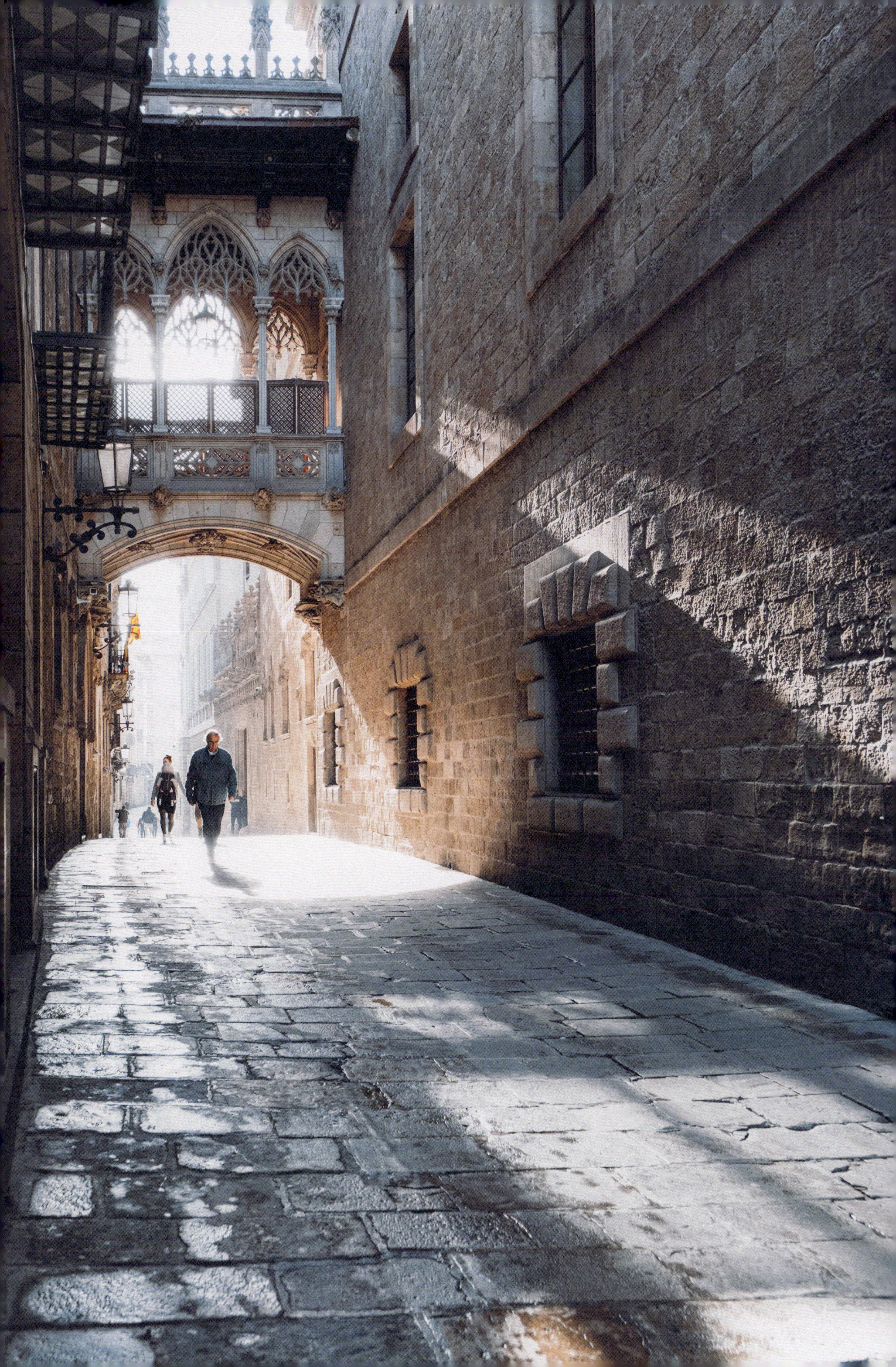

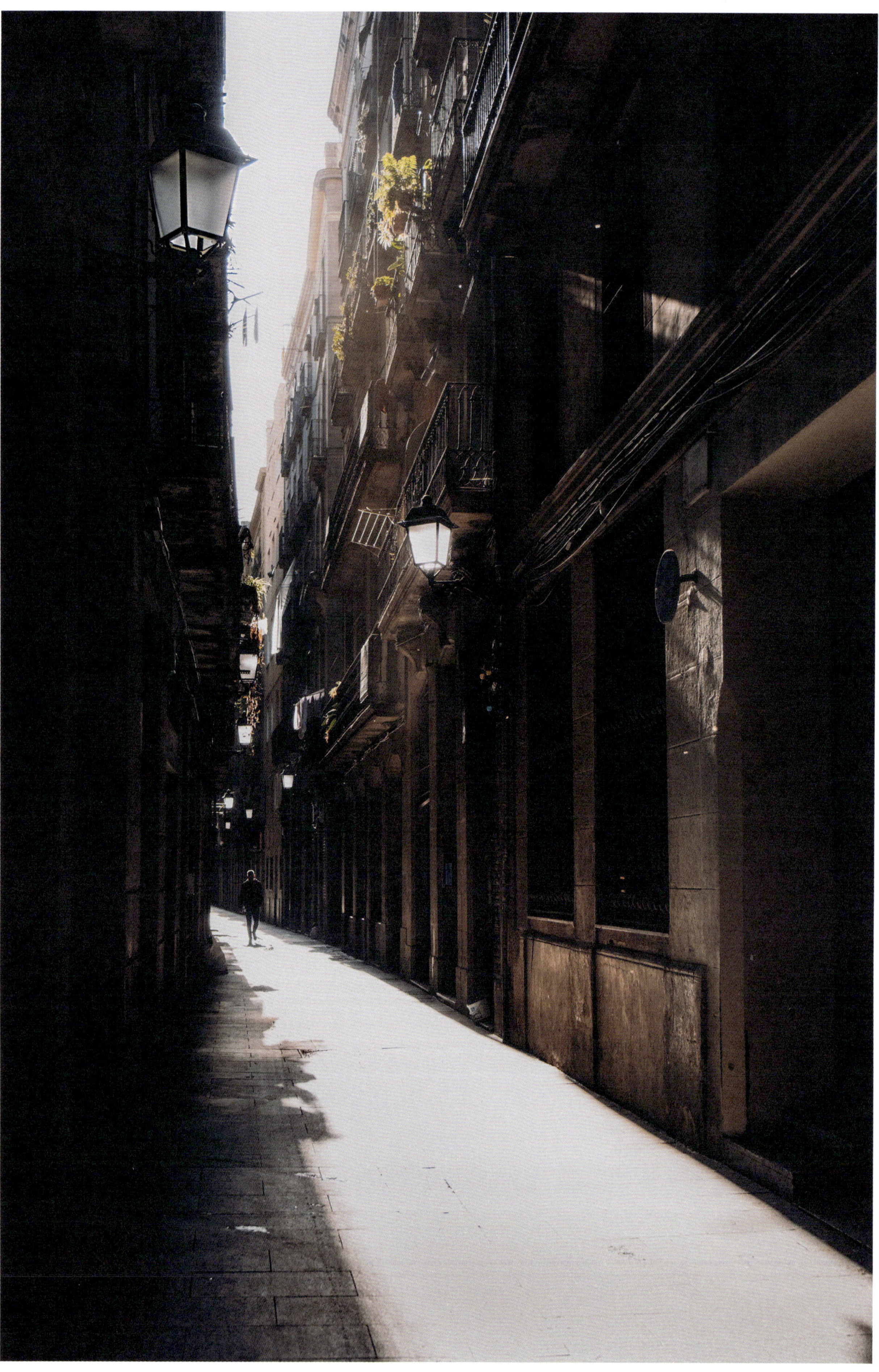

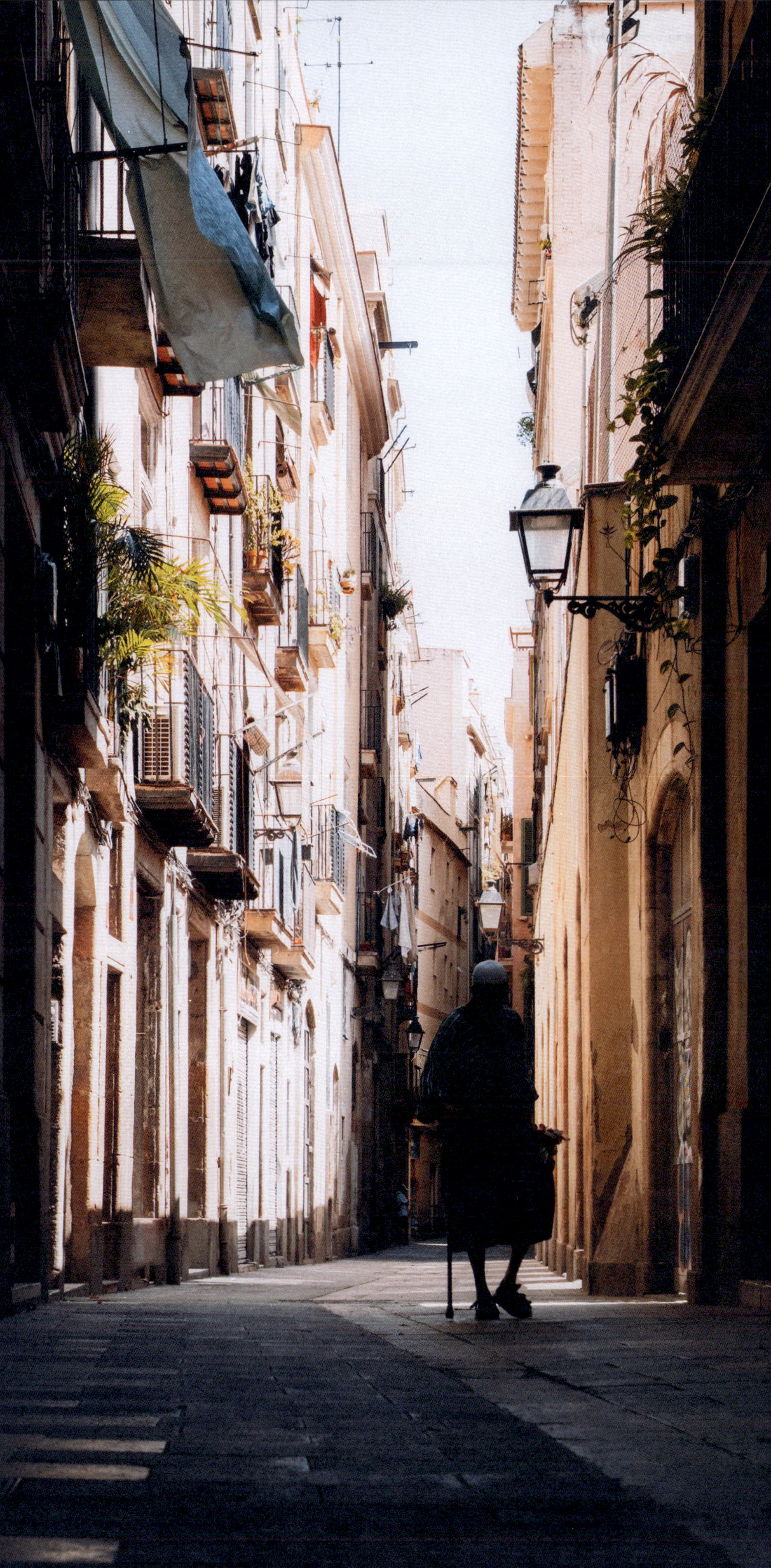

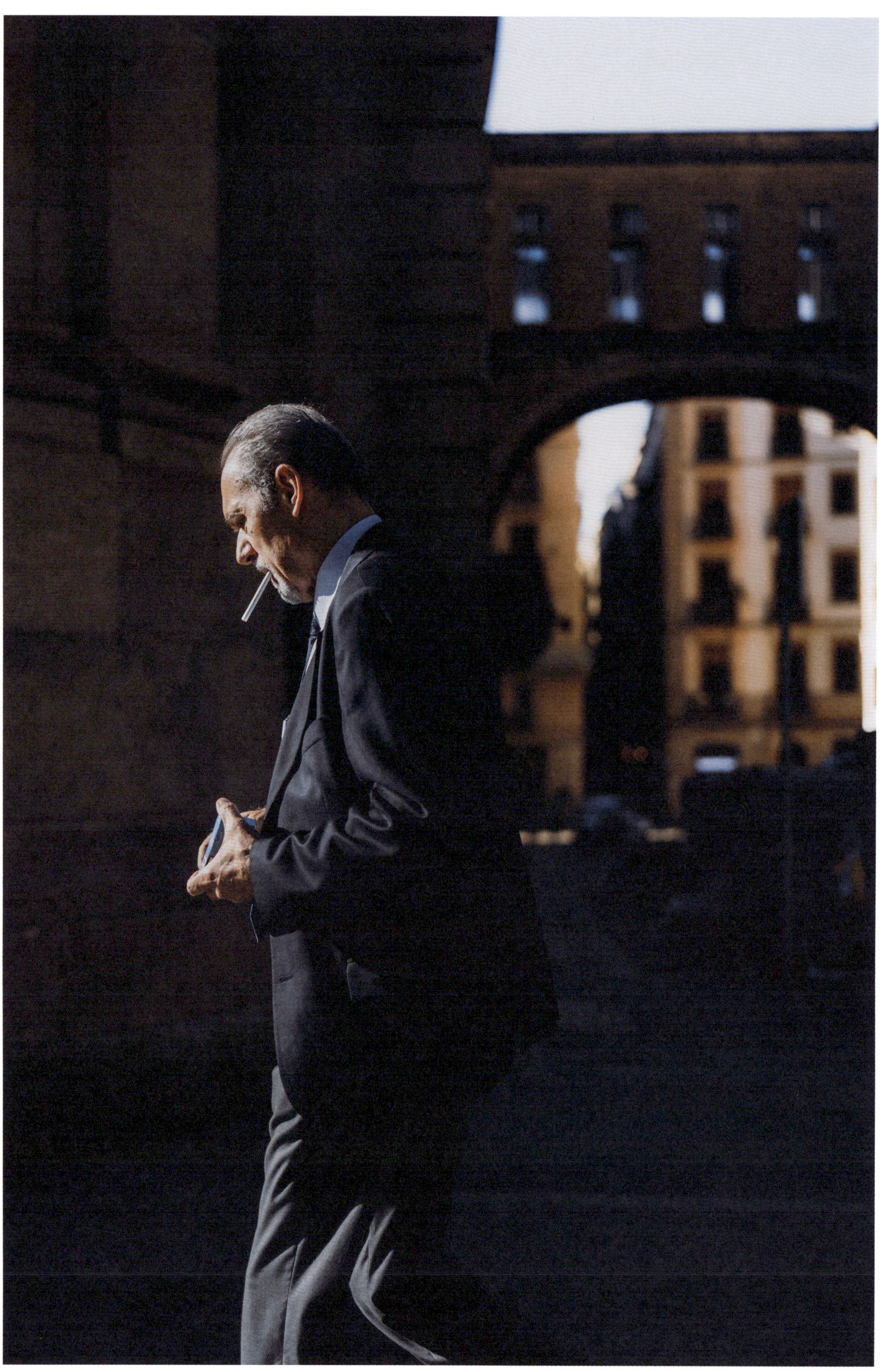

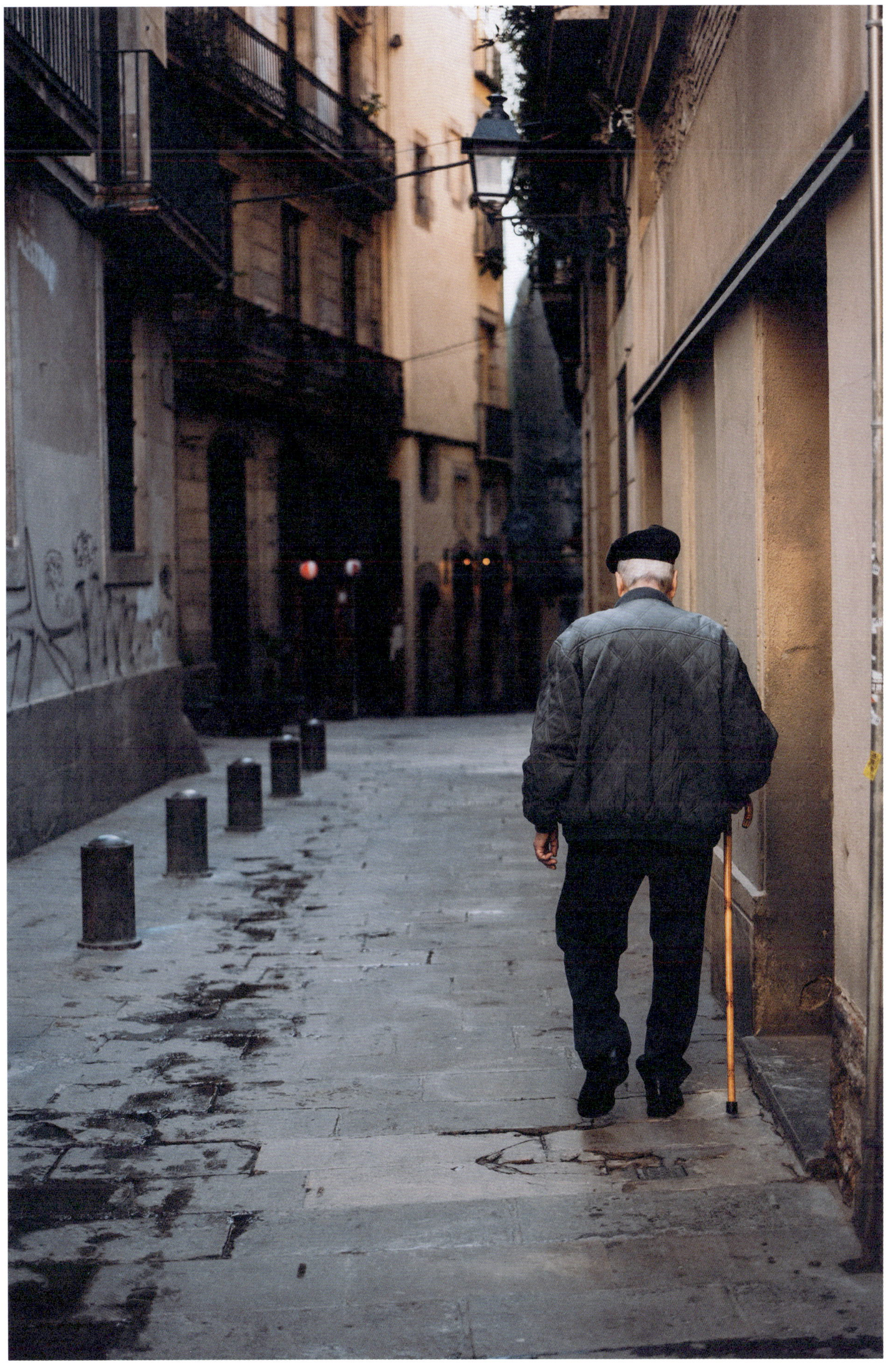

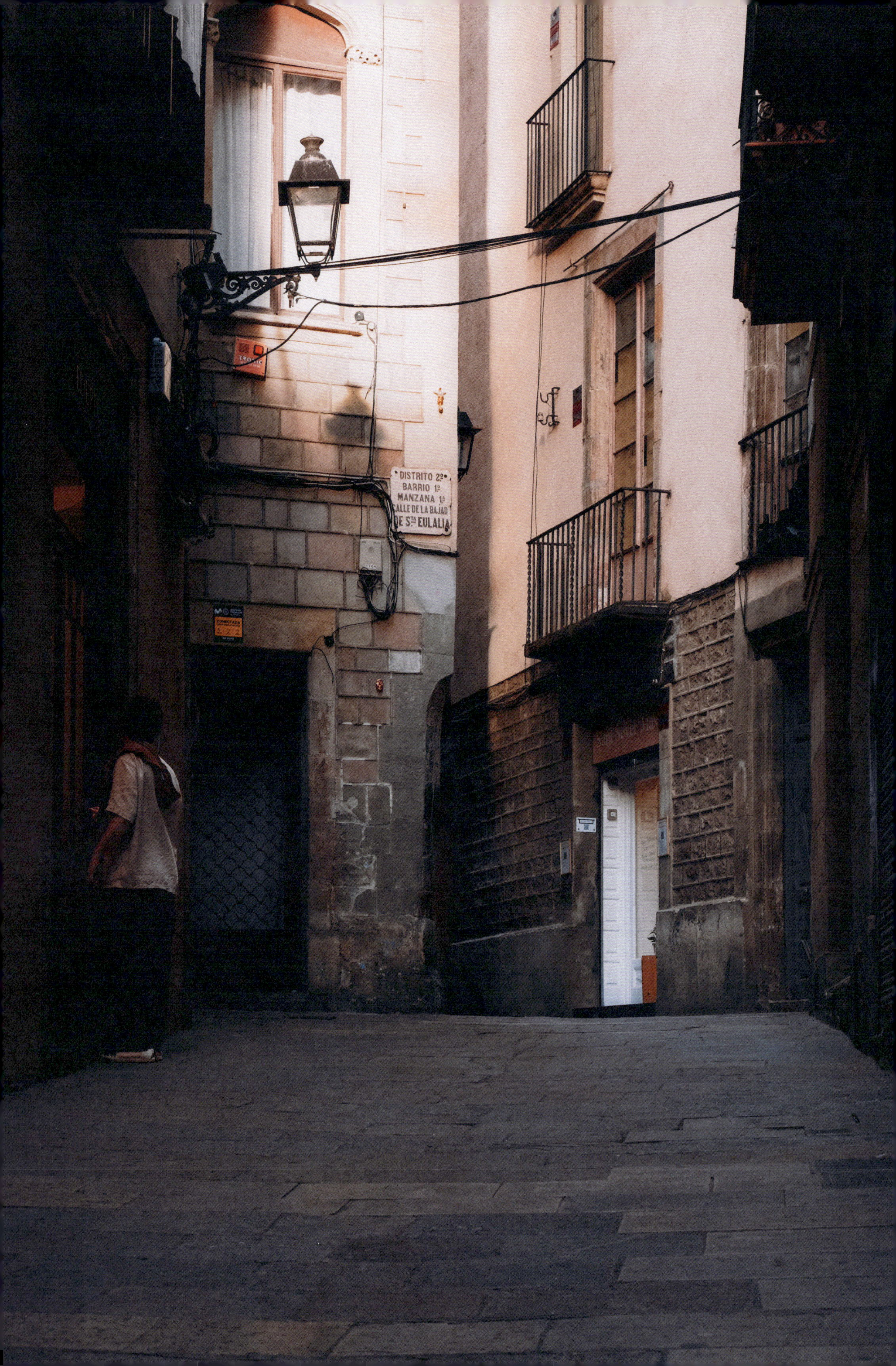
DISTRITO 2º
BARRIO 1º
MANZANA 1ª
CALLE DE LA BAJAD
DE Sta EULALIA

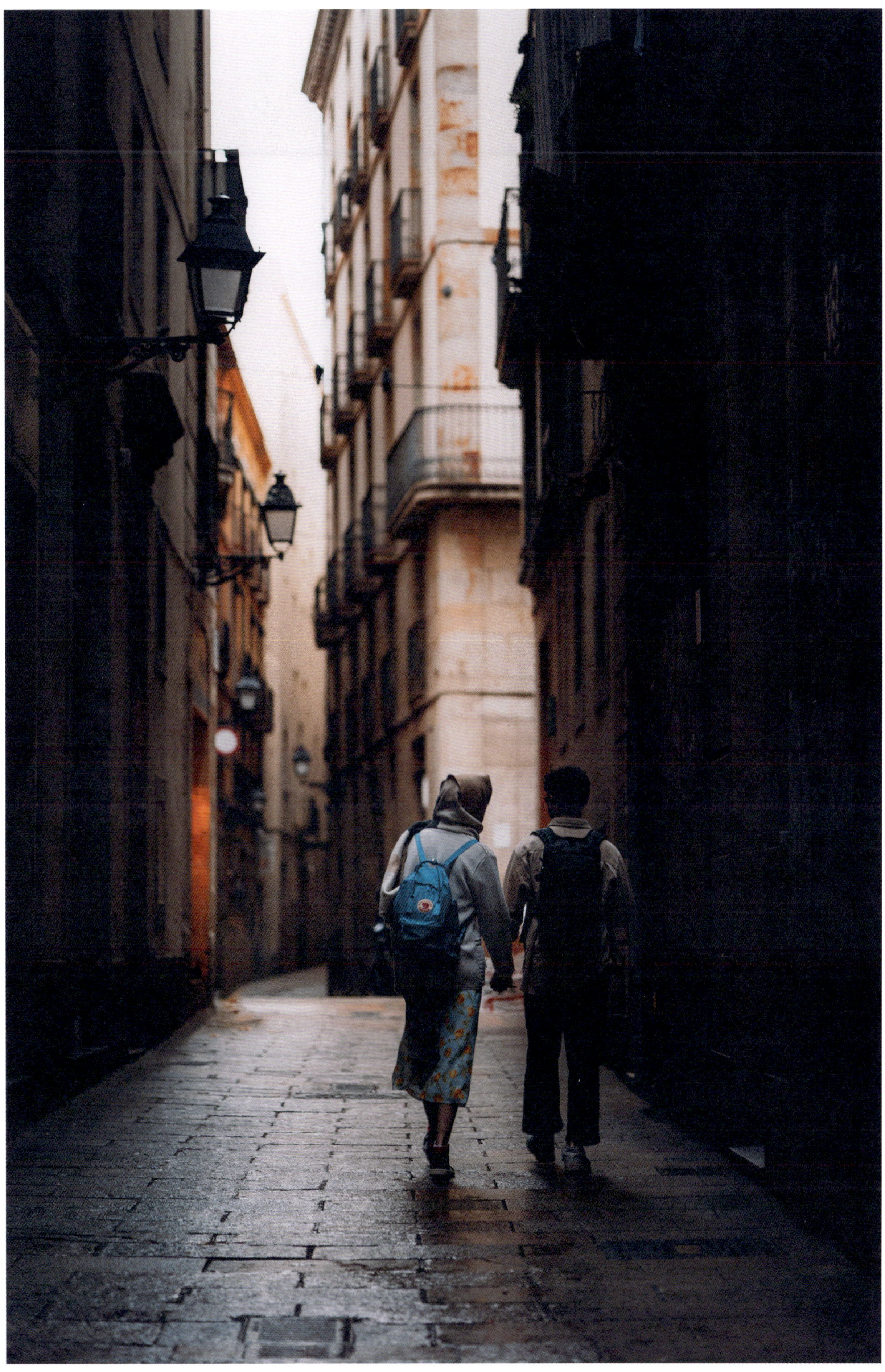

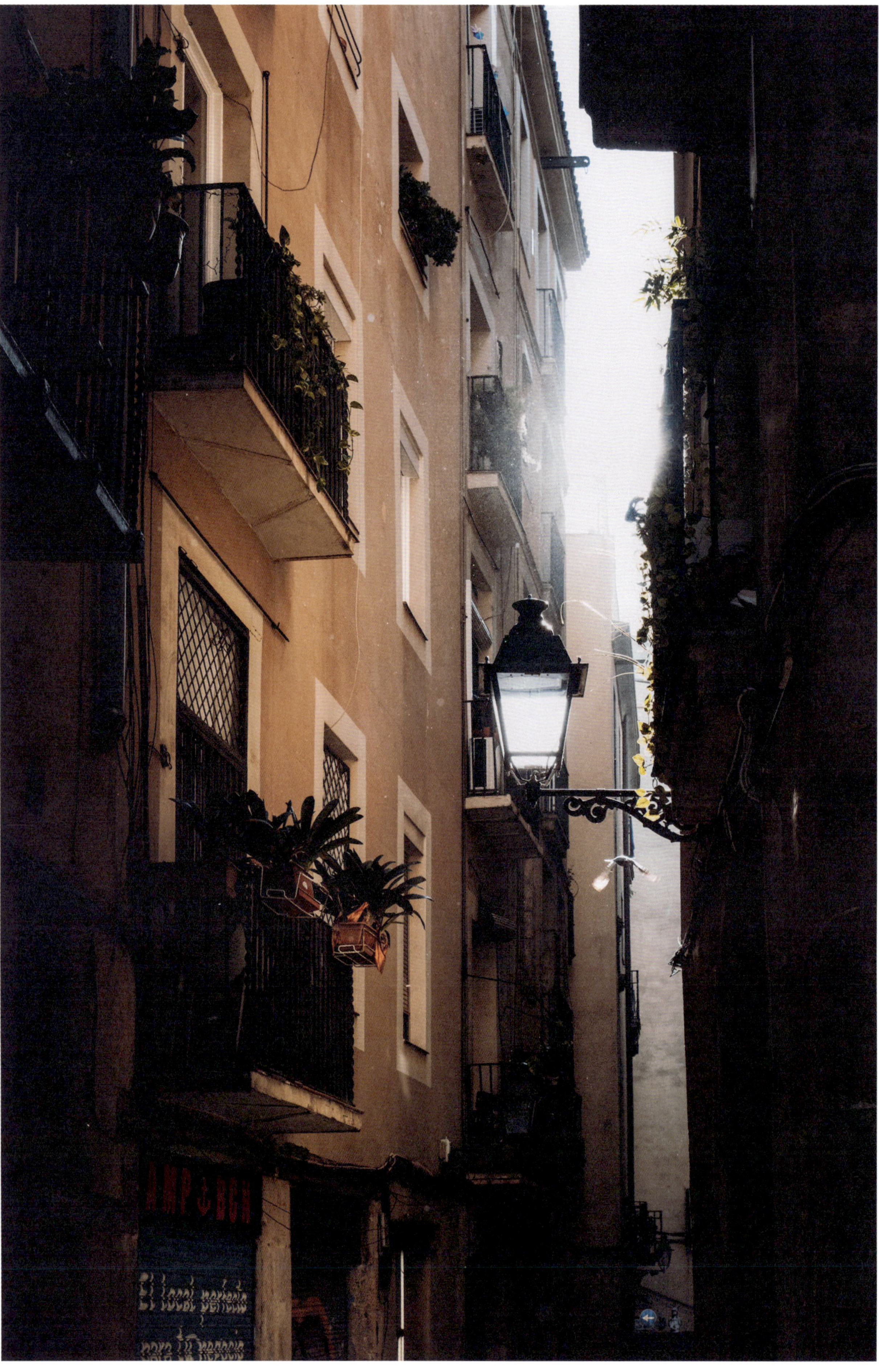

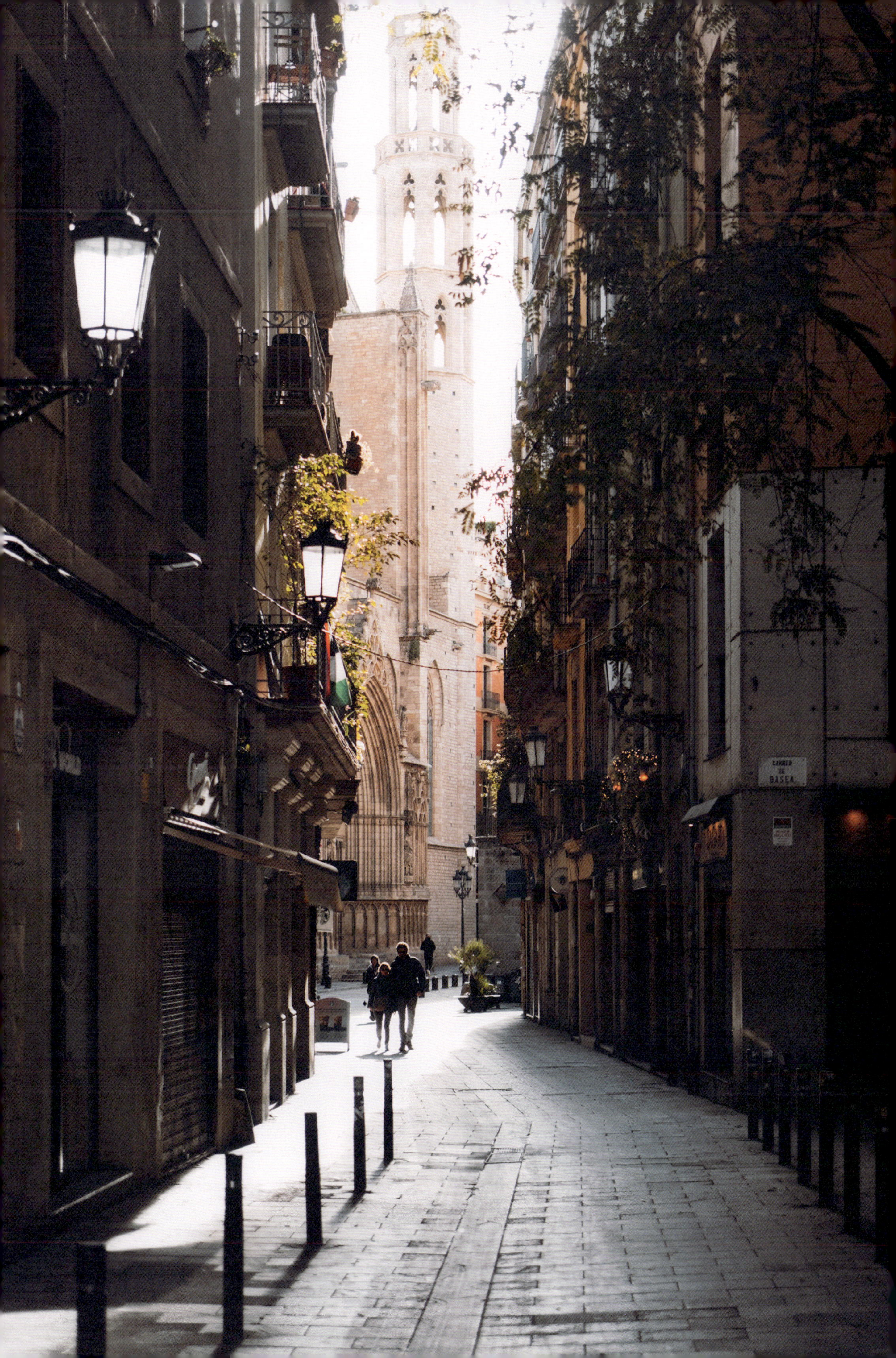
BASEA

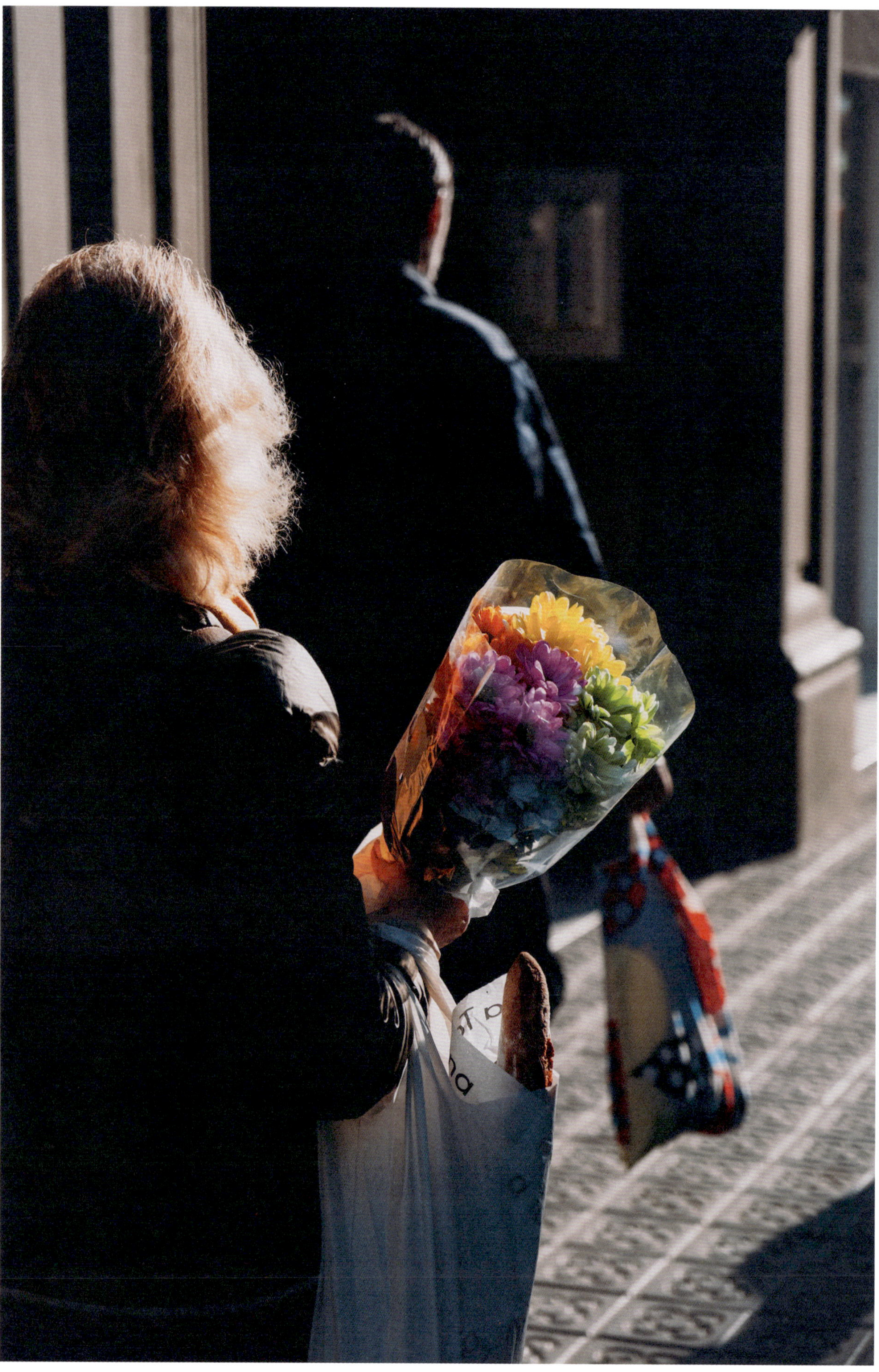

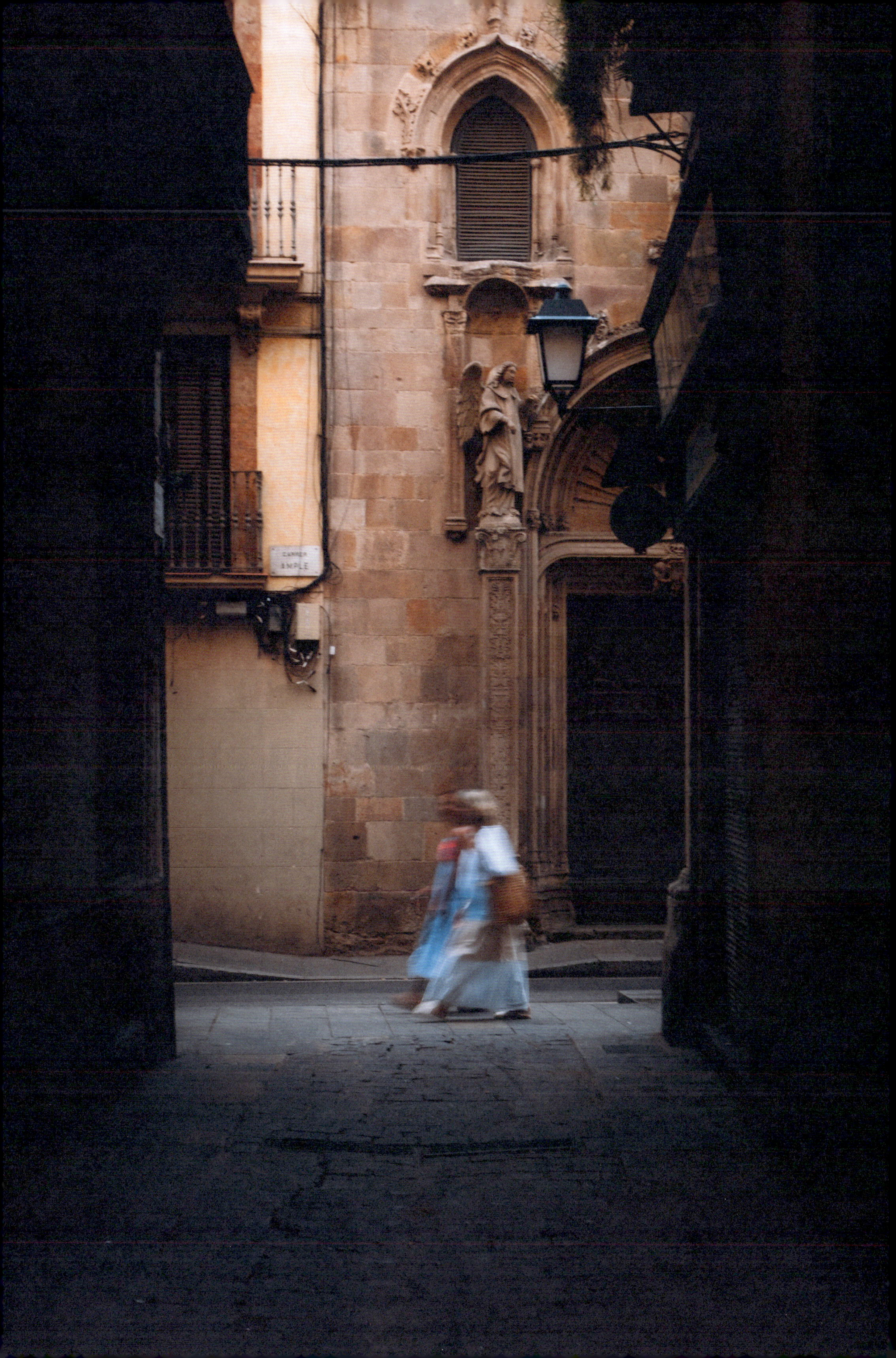

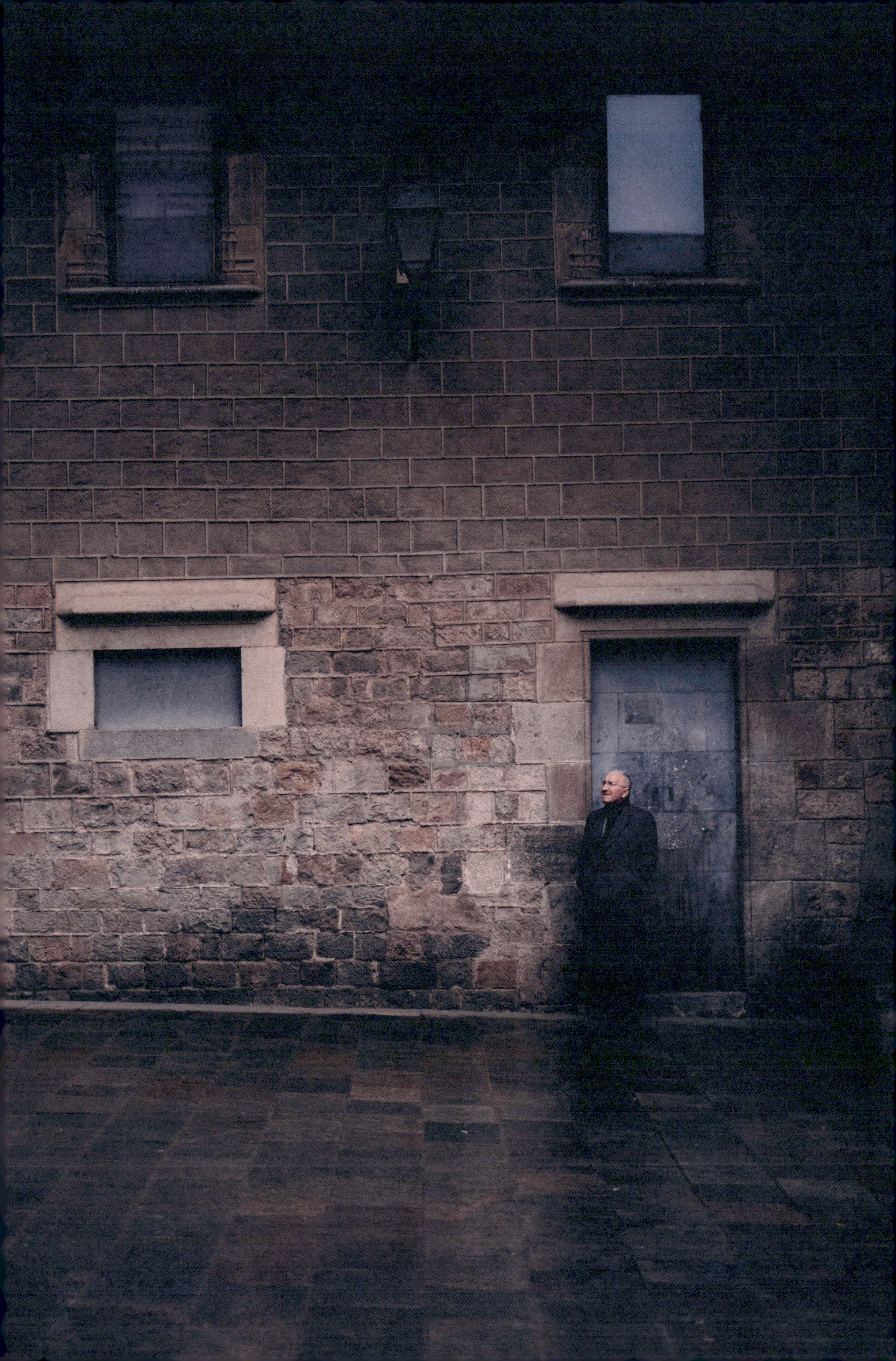

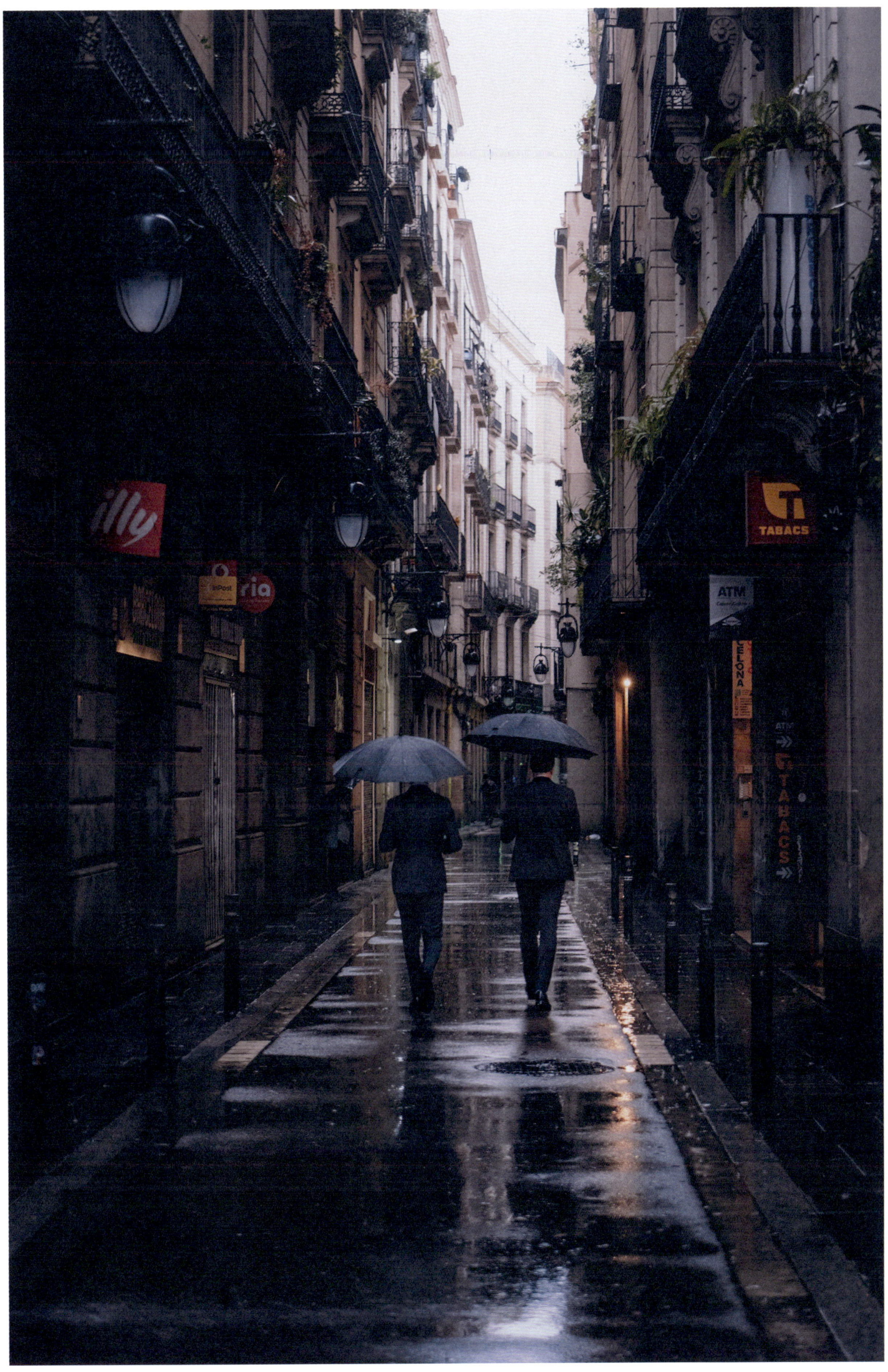
illy
InPost
ria
TABACS
ATM
TABACS

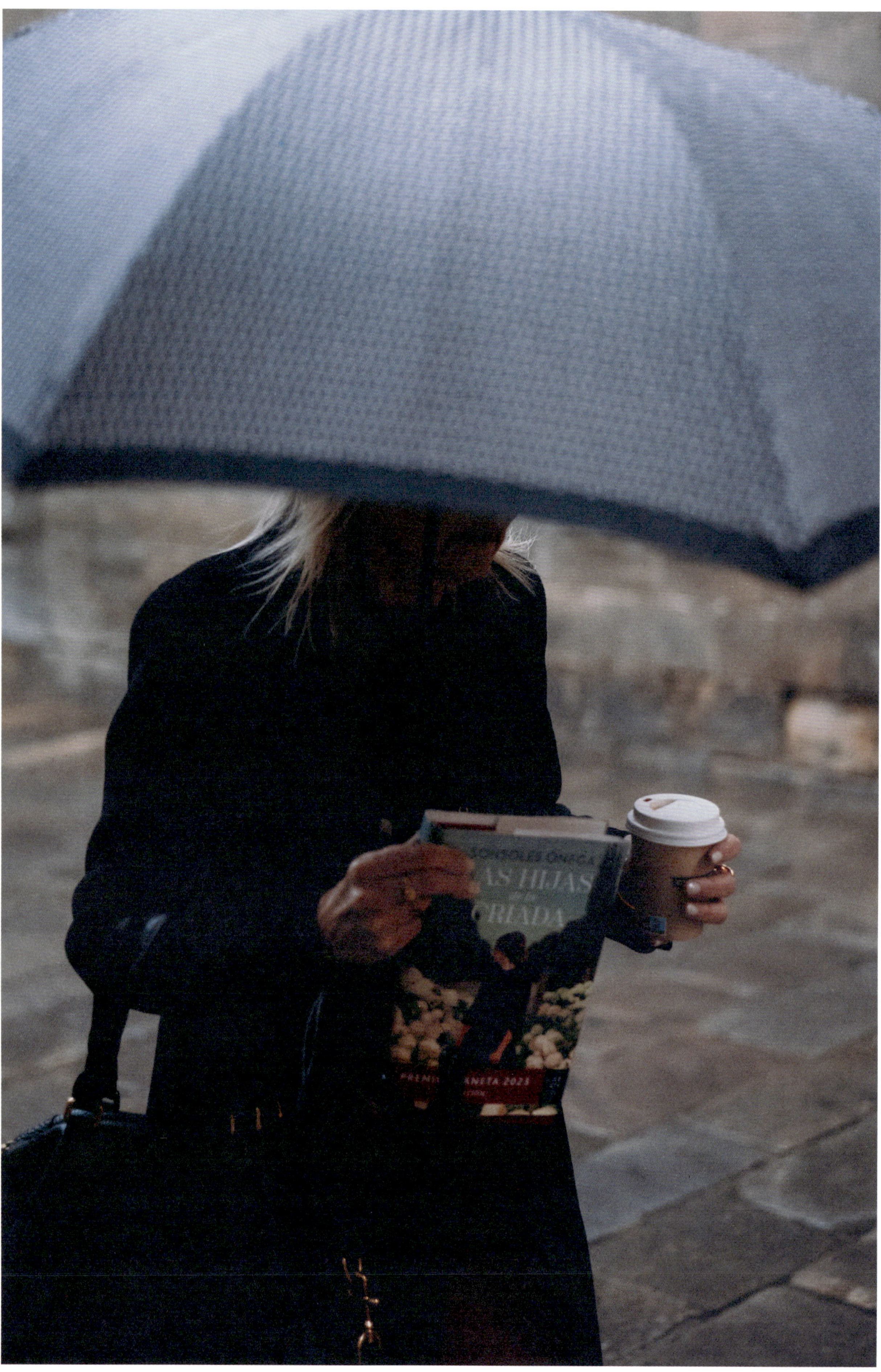
AS HIJAS

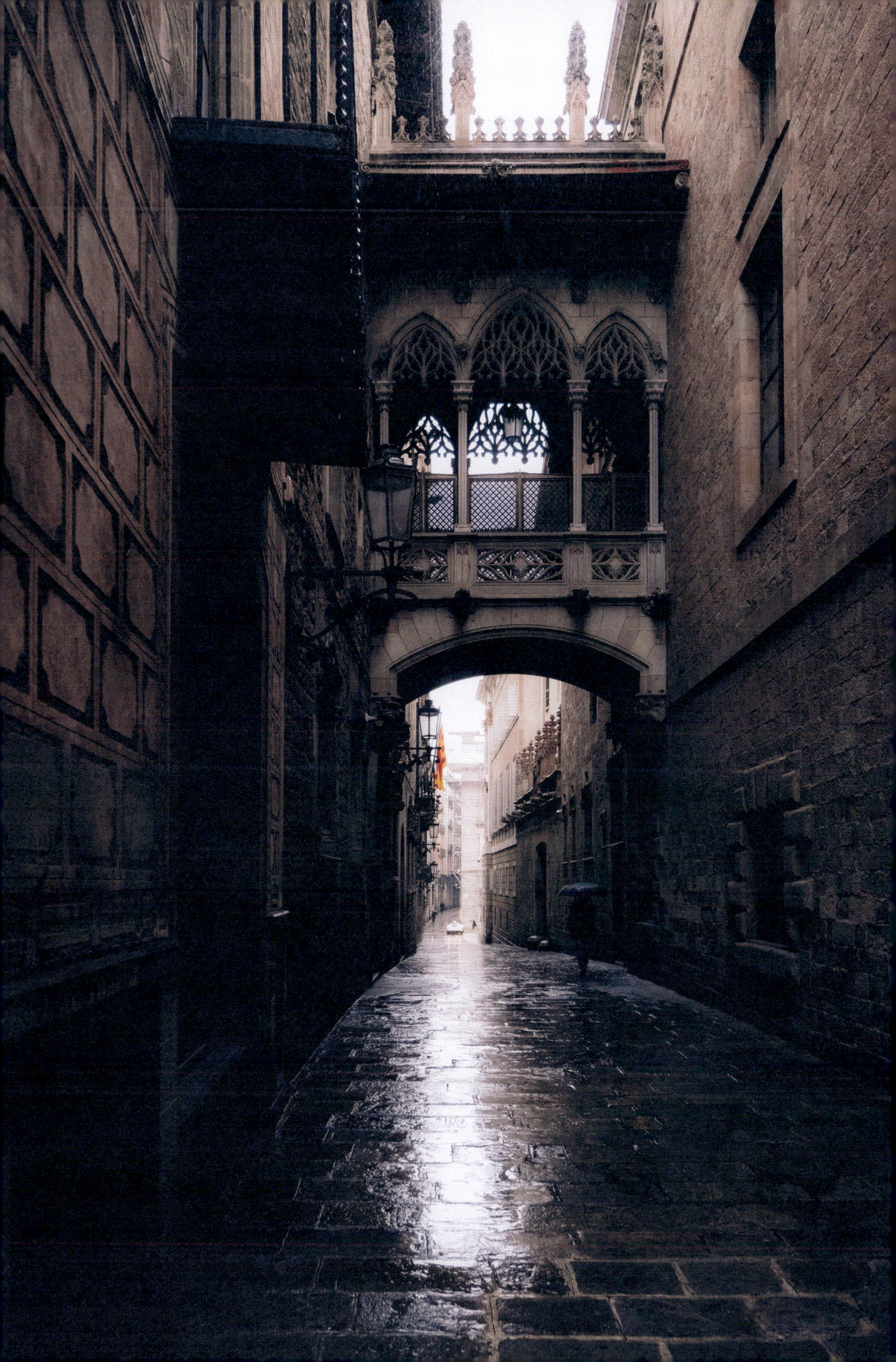

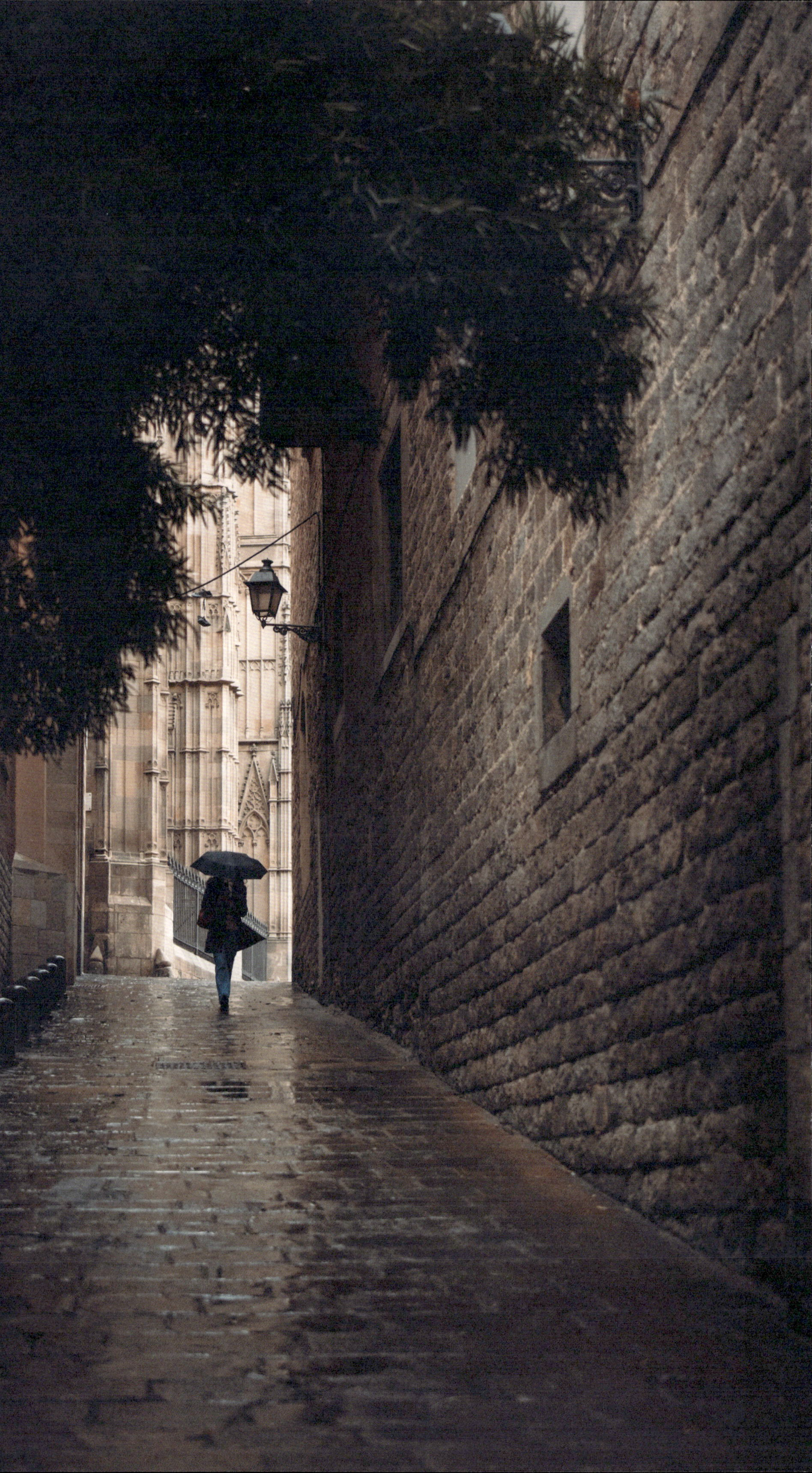

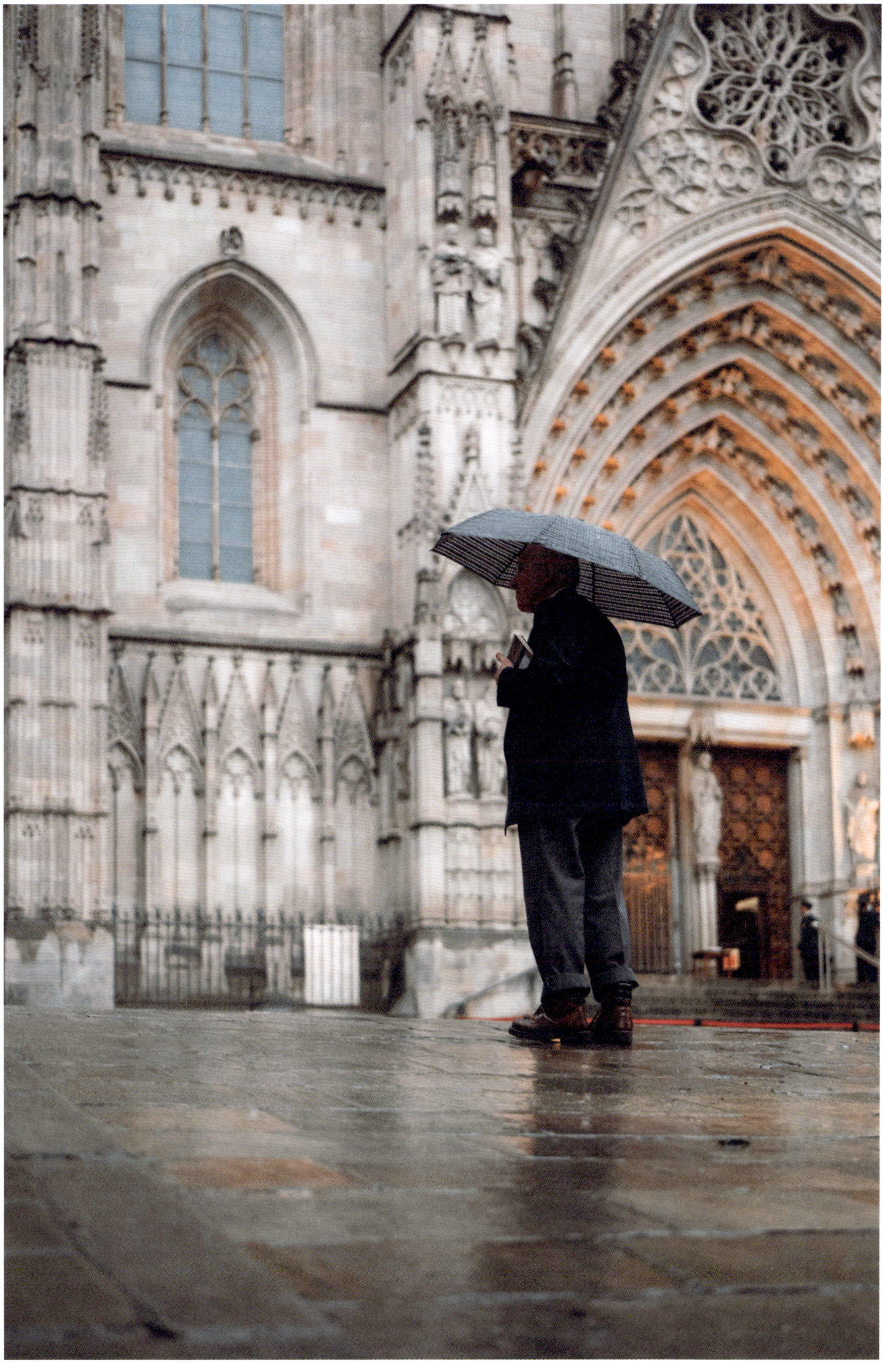

Barcelona—a city that is eternally youthful, vibrant, and modern in spirit, no matter how ancient its stones.

ROBERT HUGHES

Australian Art Critic

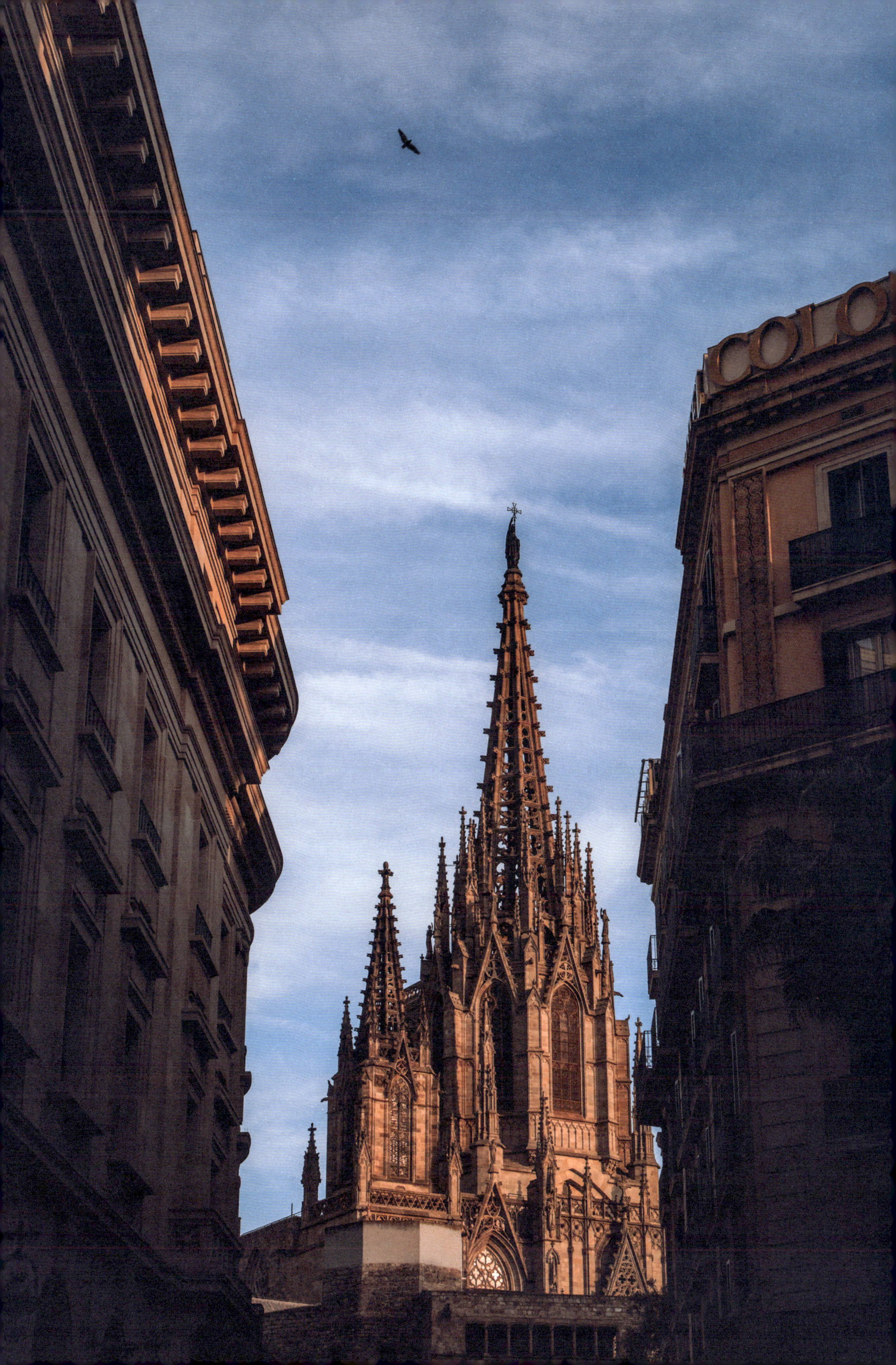

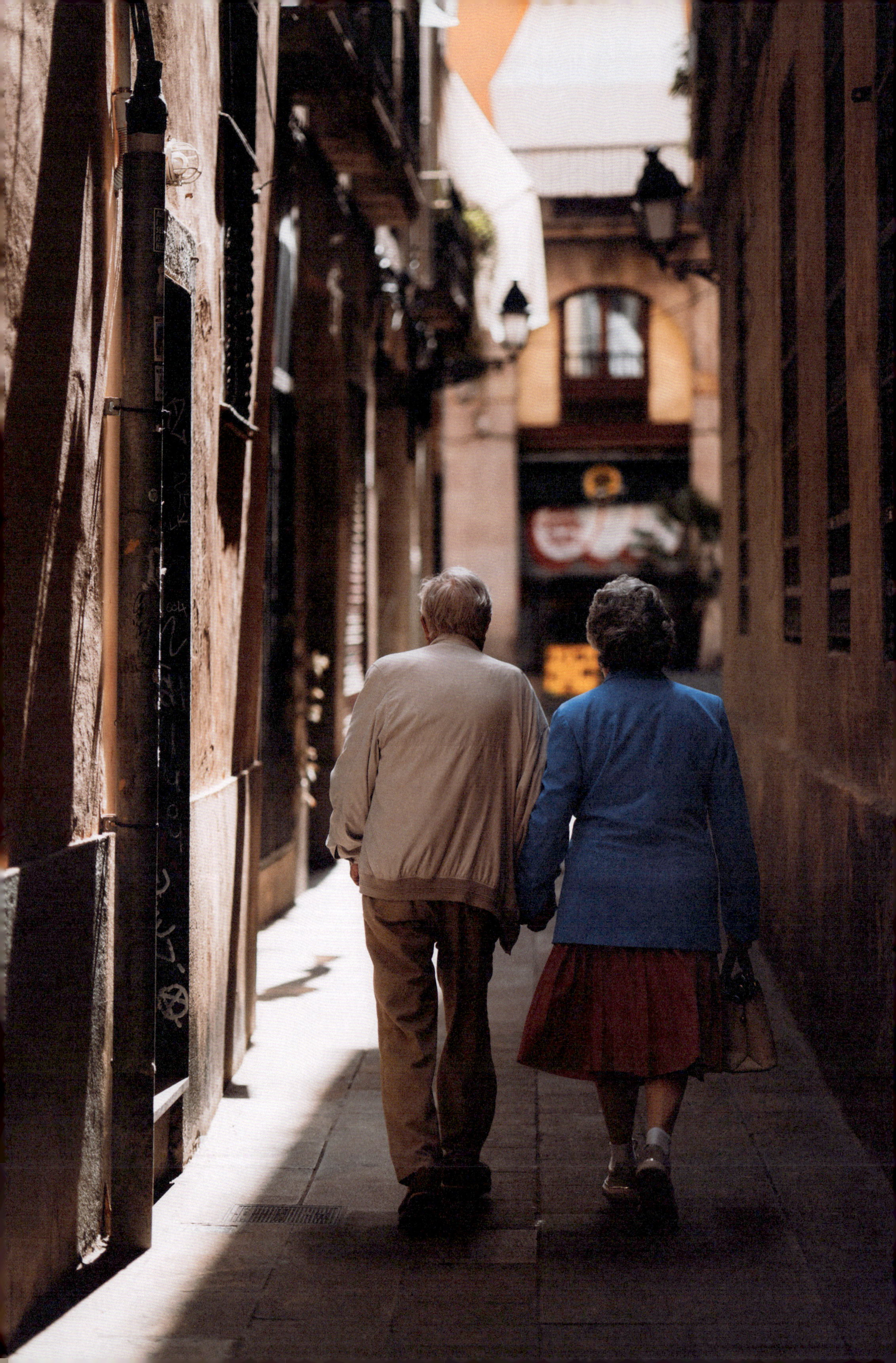

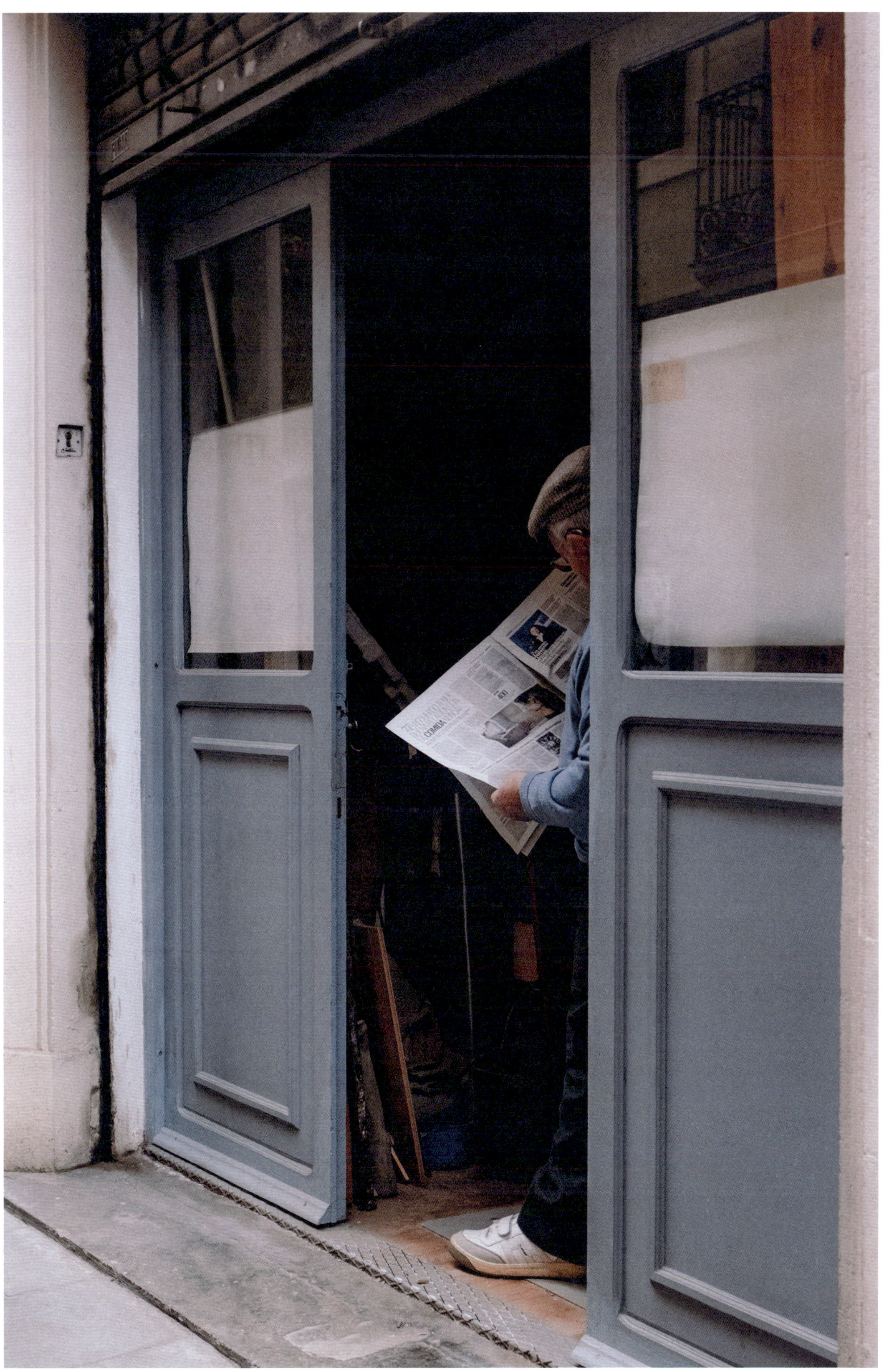

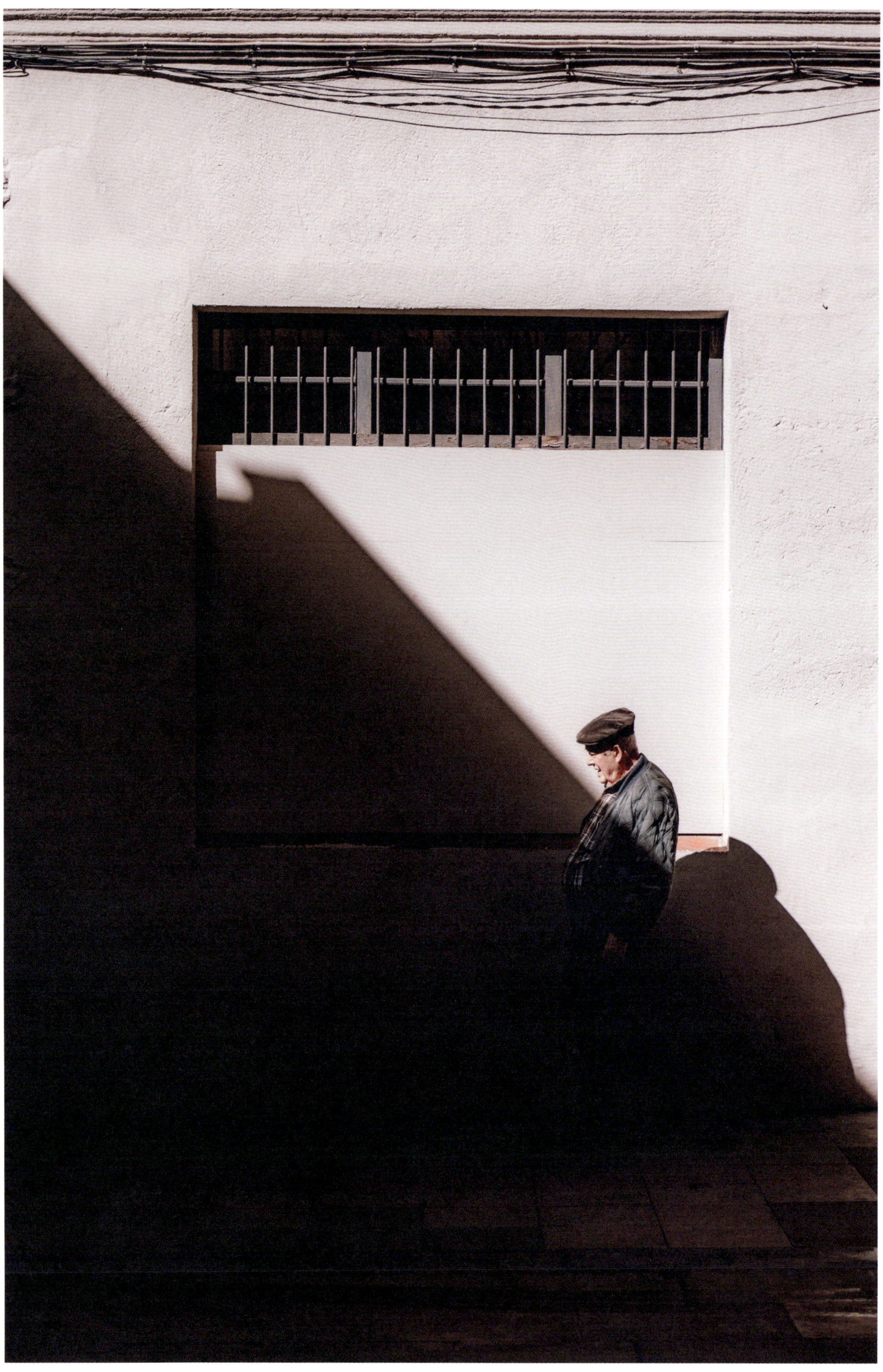

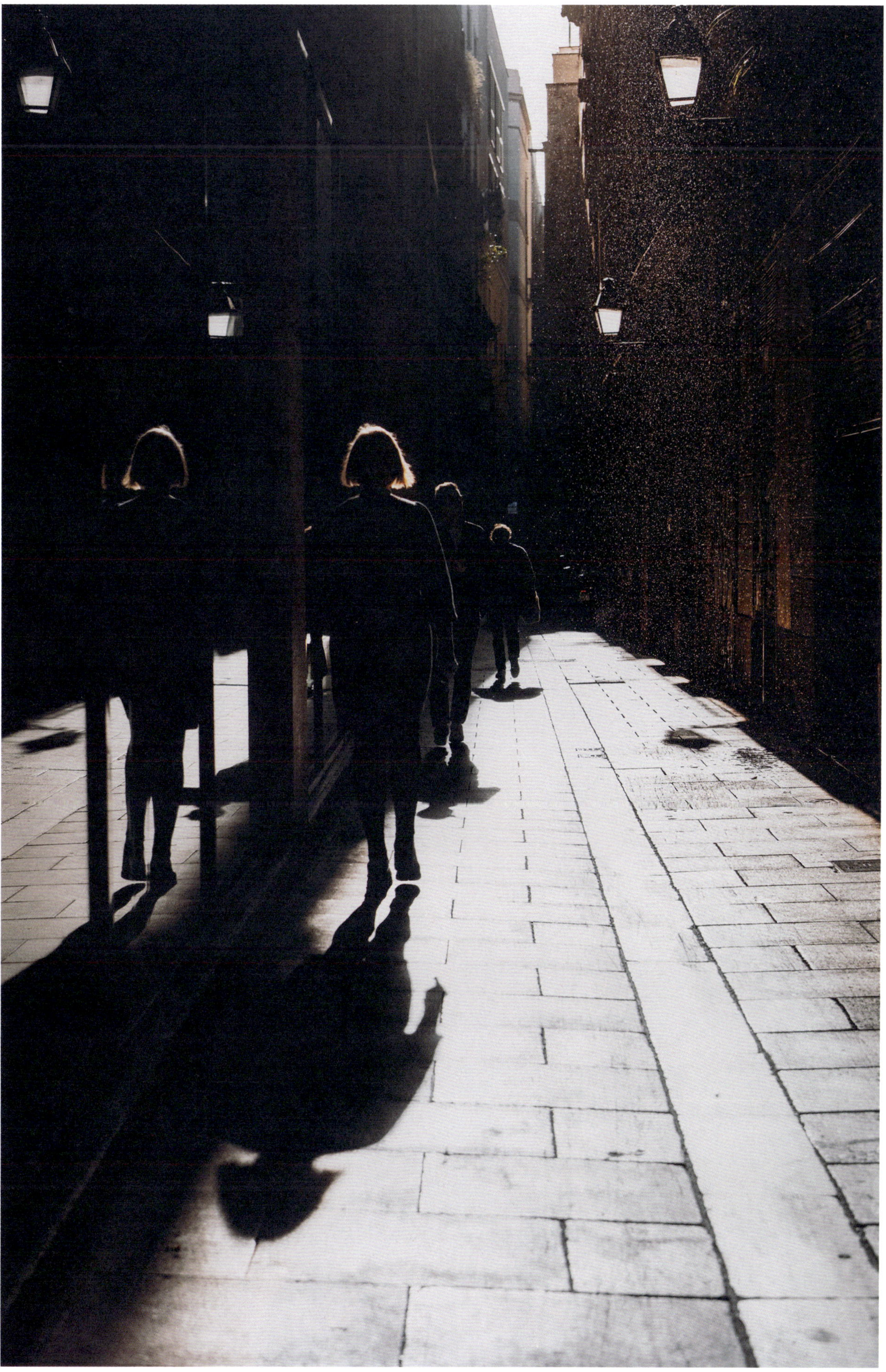

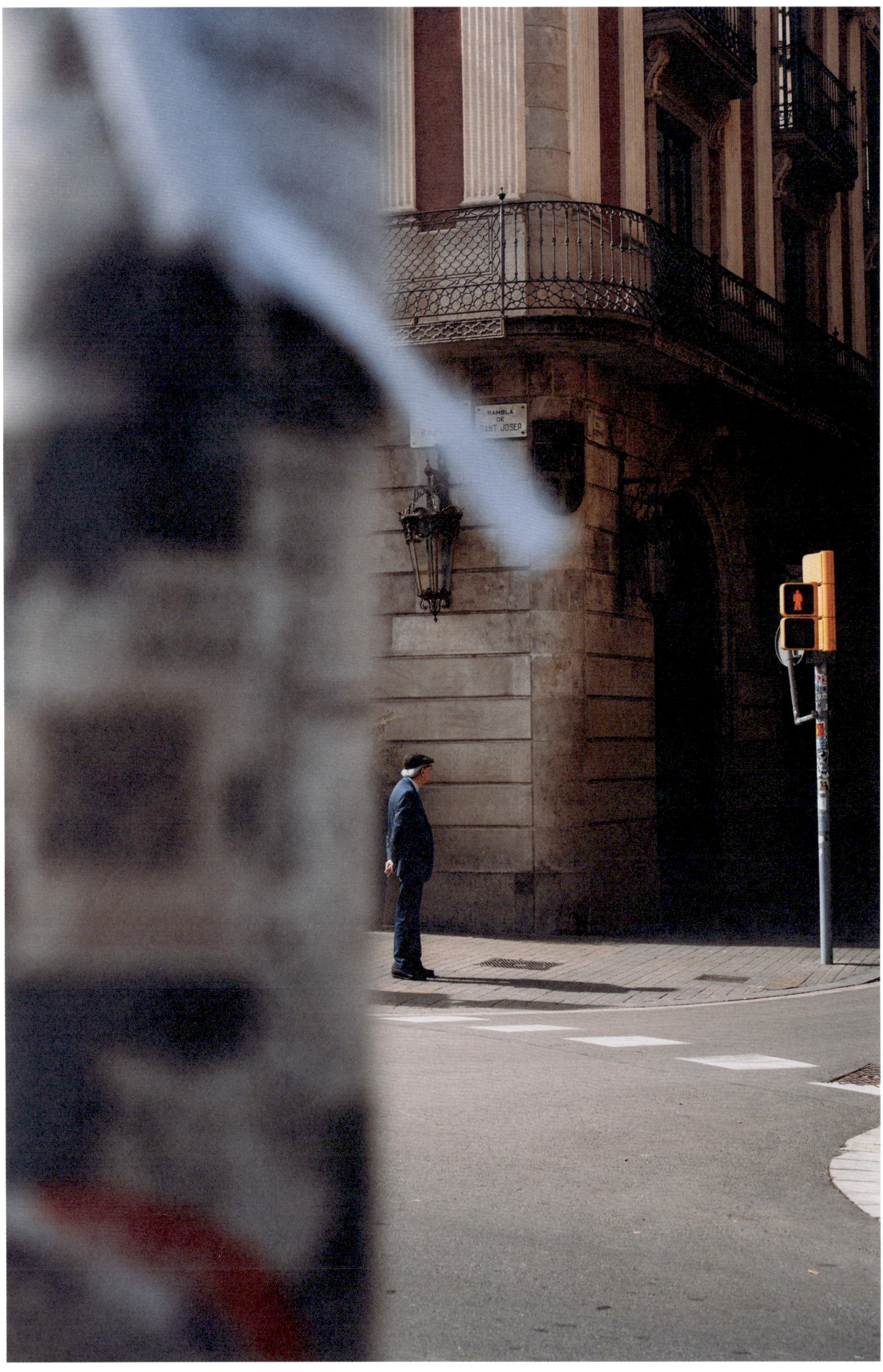
RAMBLA
DE
SANT JOSEP

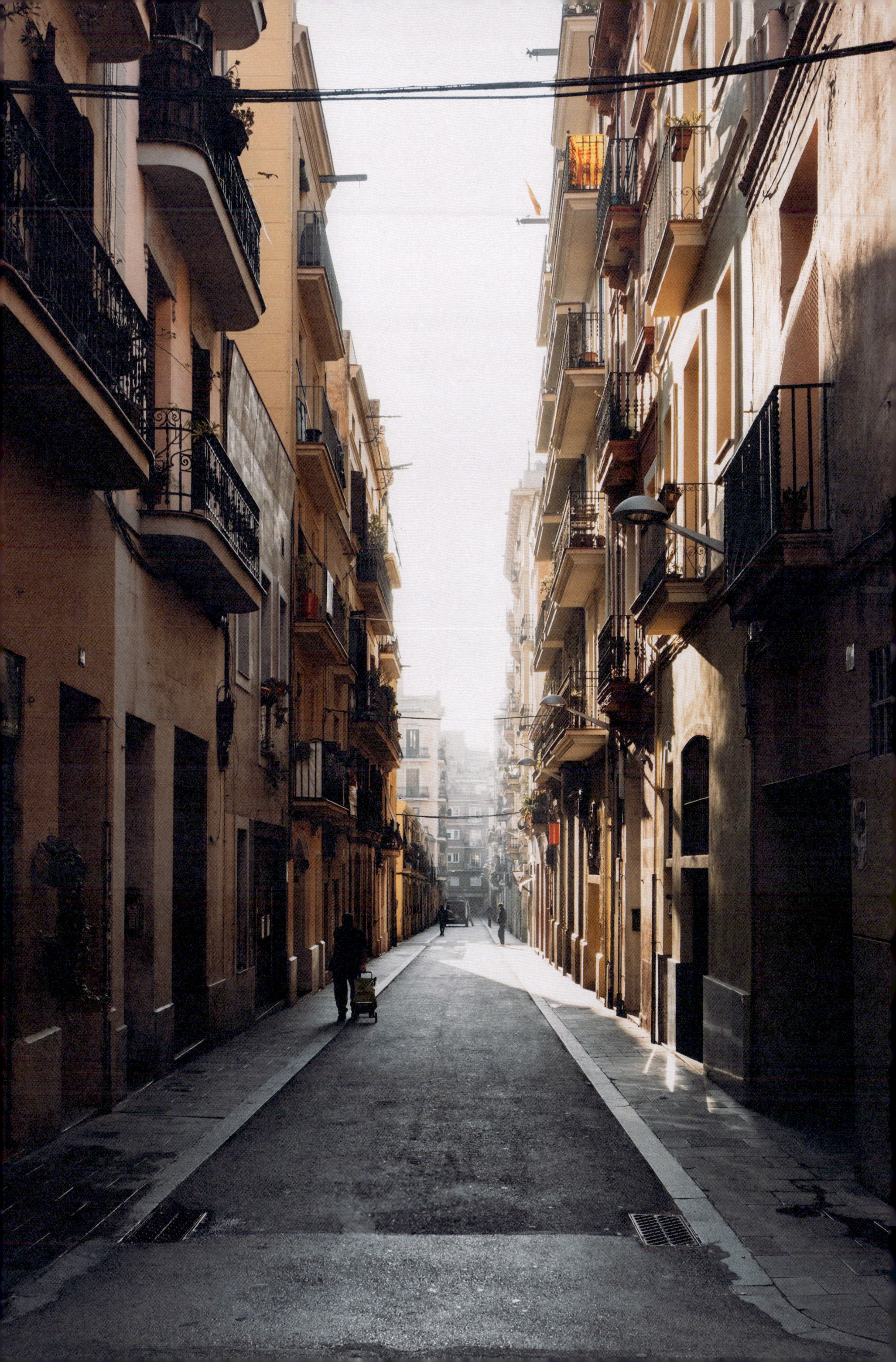

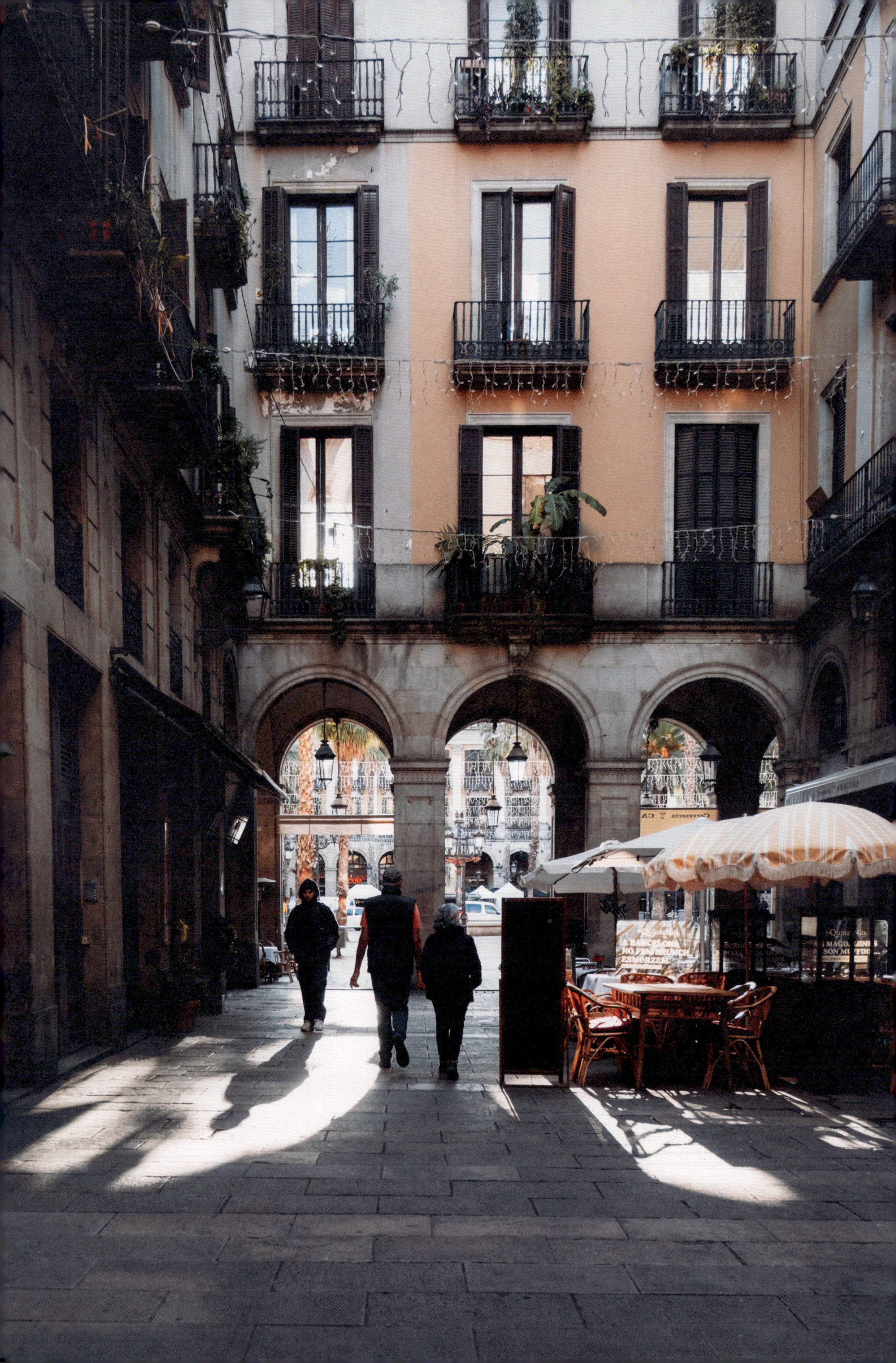
Cerveseria
A BARCELONA
NO FEM BRUNCH
ESMORZEM

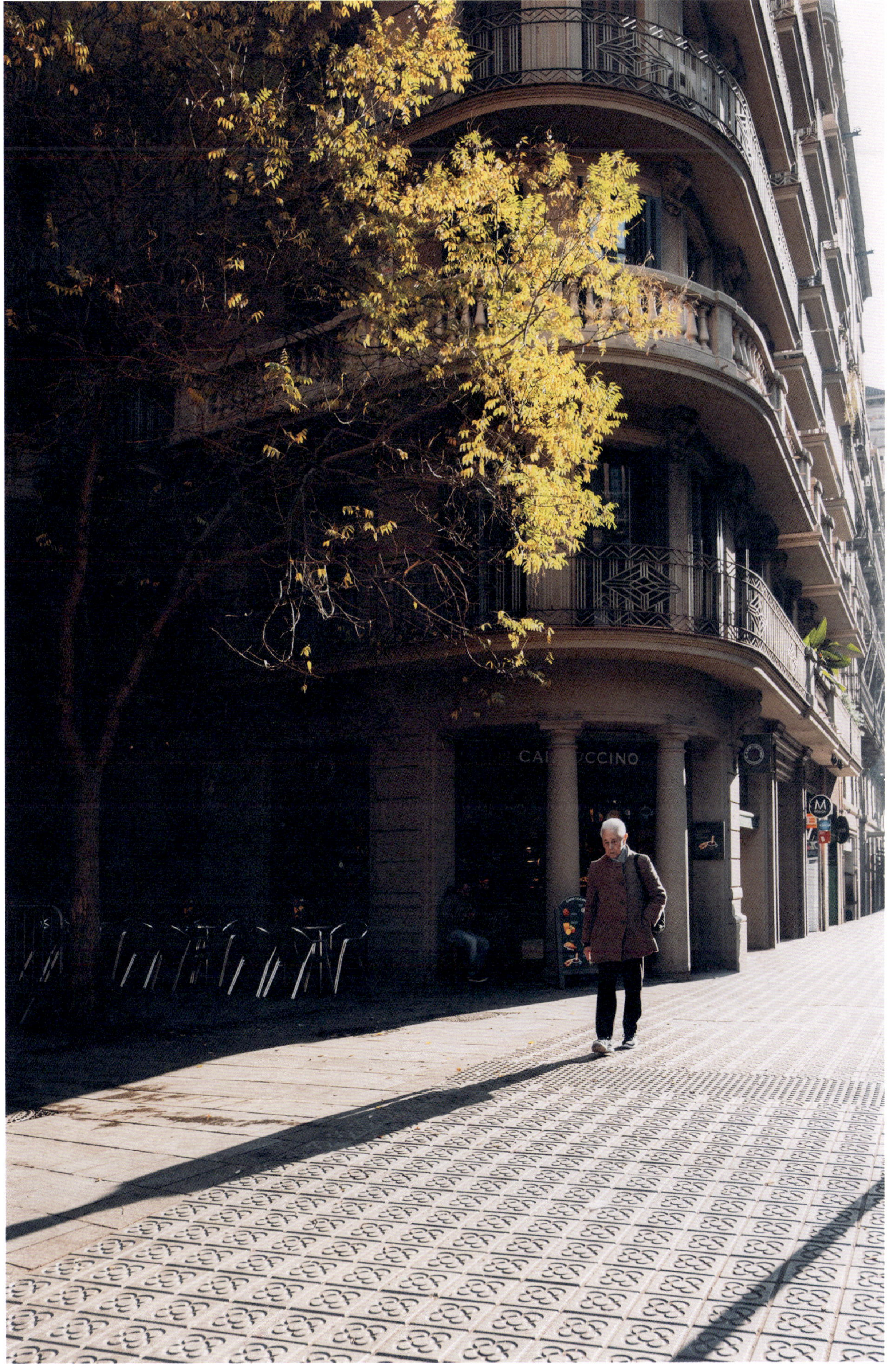

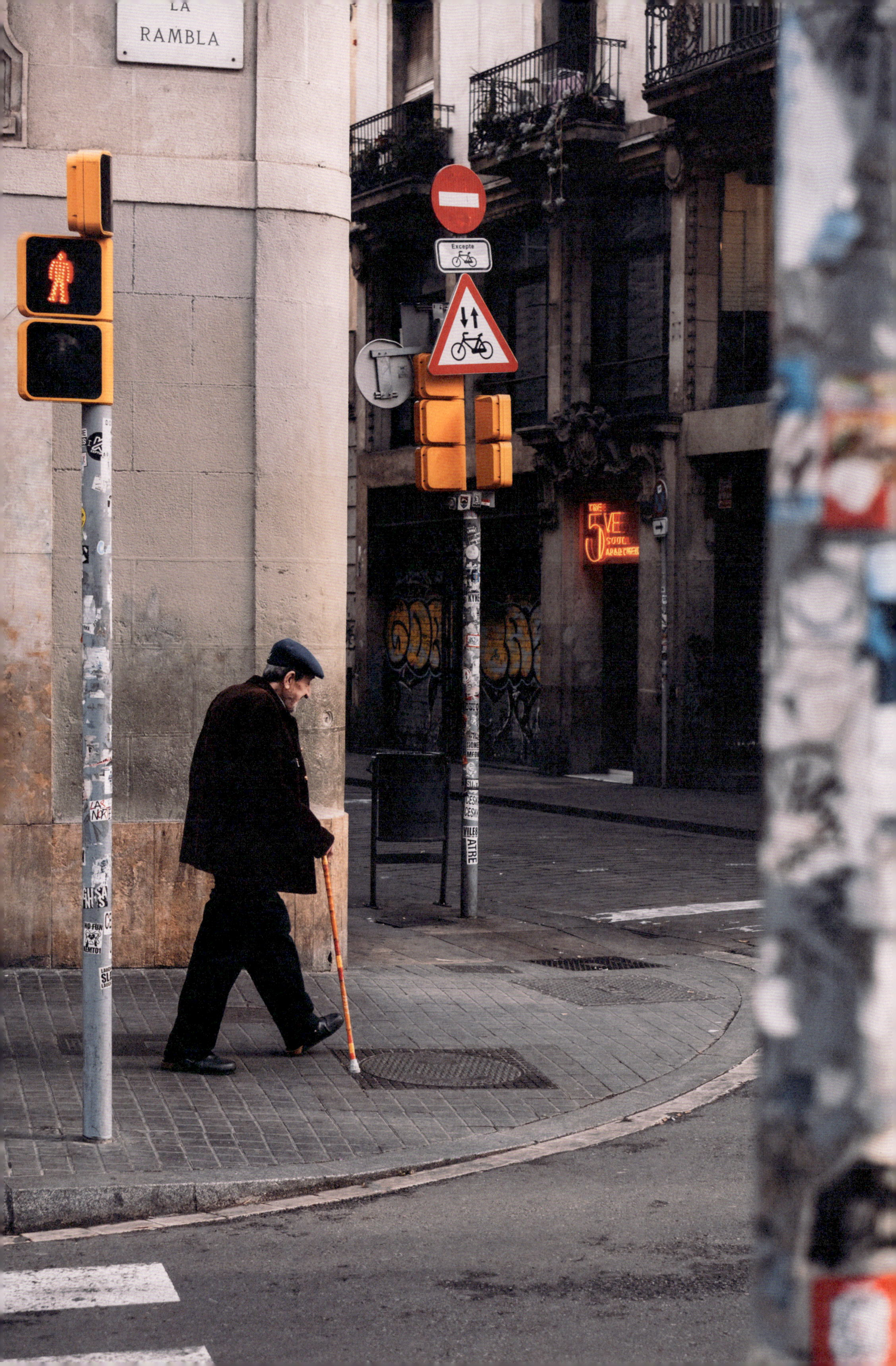
LA
RAMBLA
Excepte

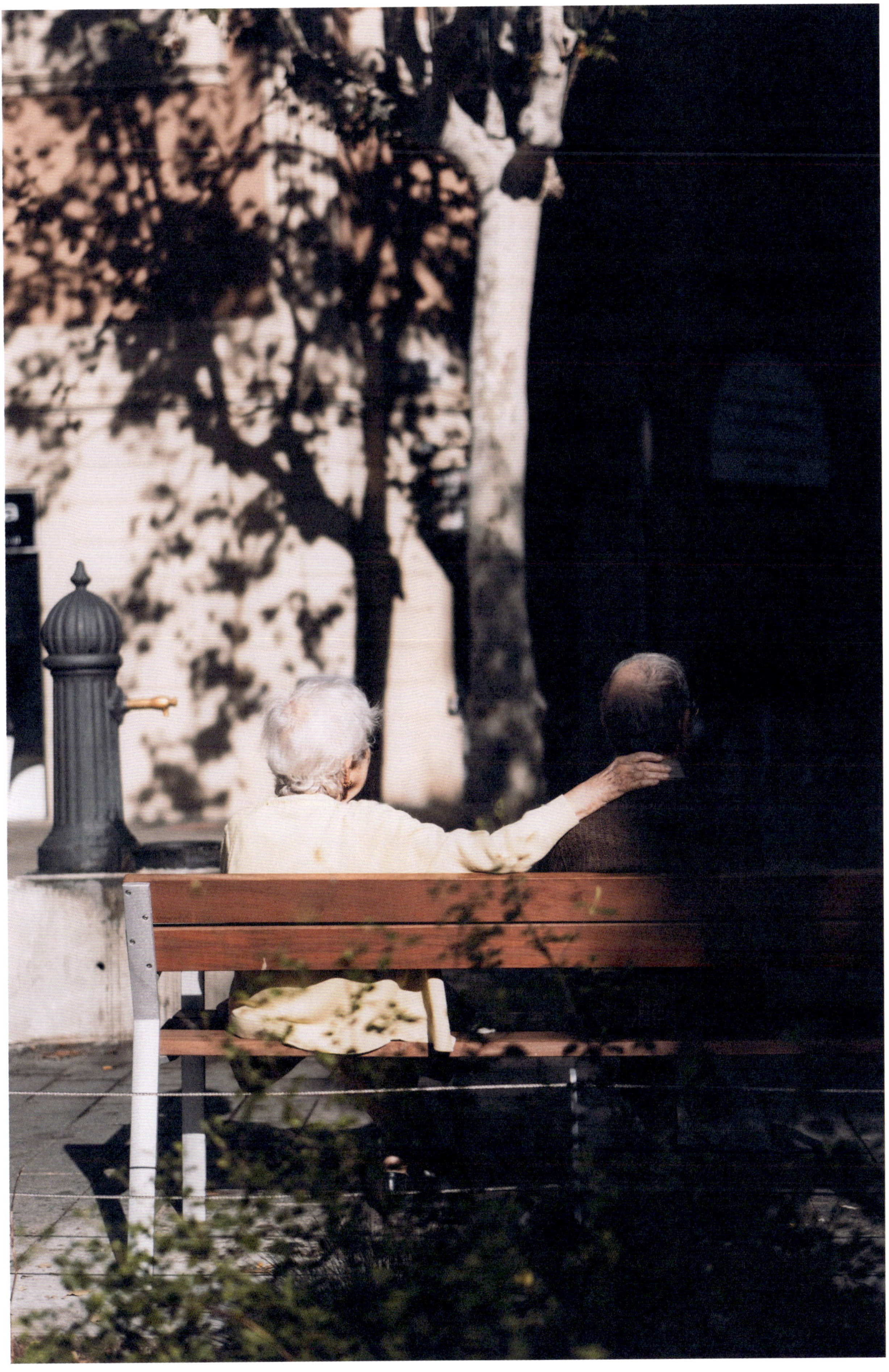

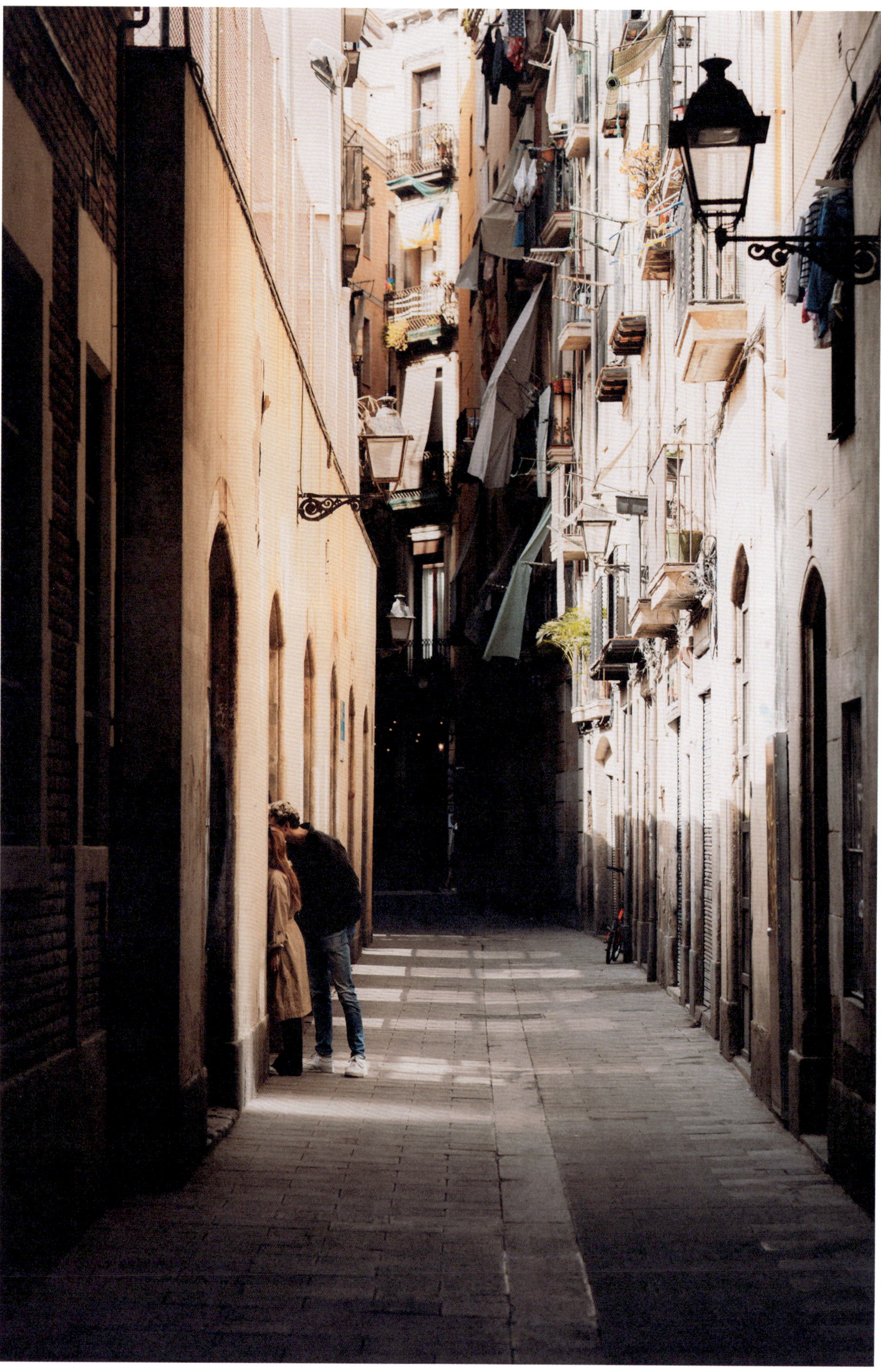

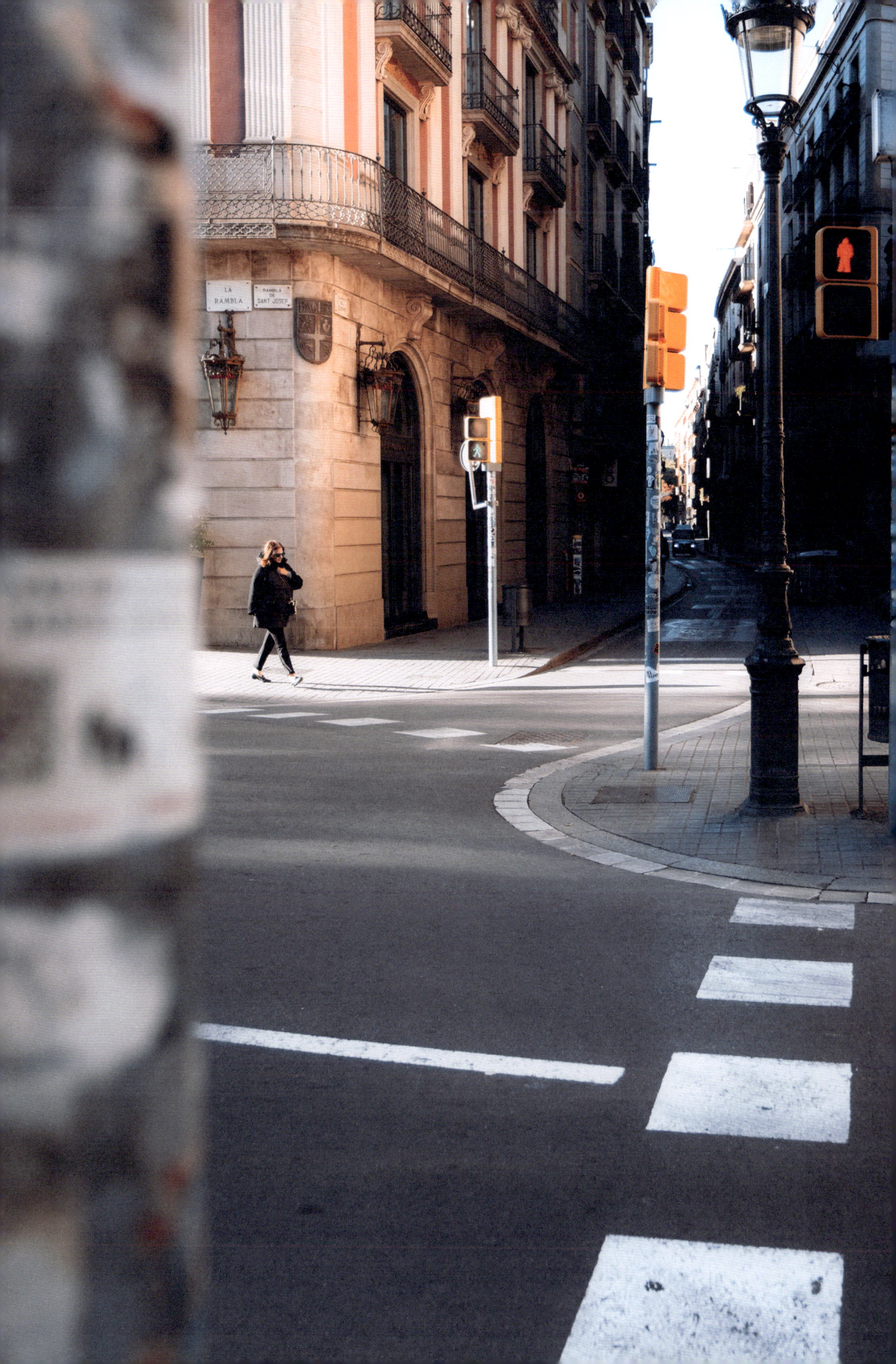
LA RAMBLA
RAMBLA DE SANT JOSEP

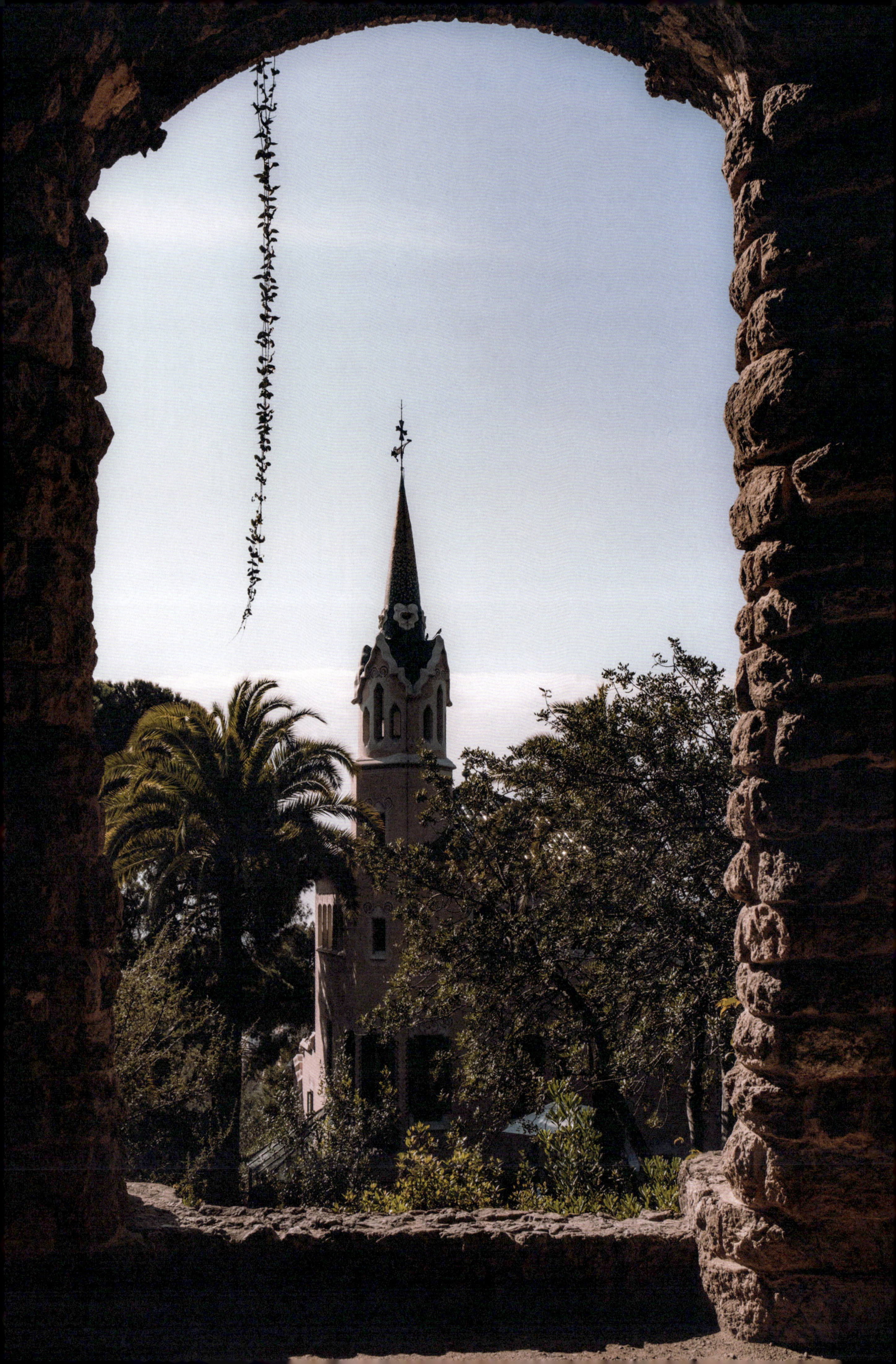

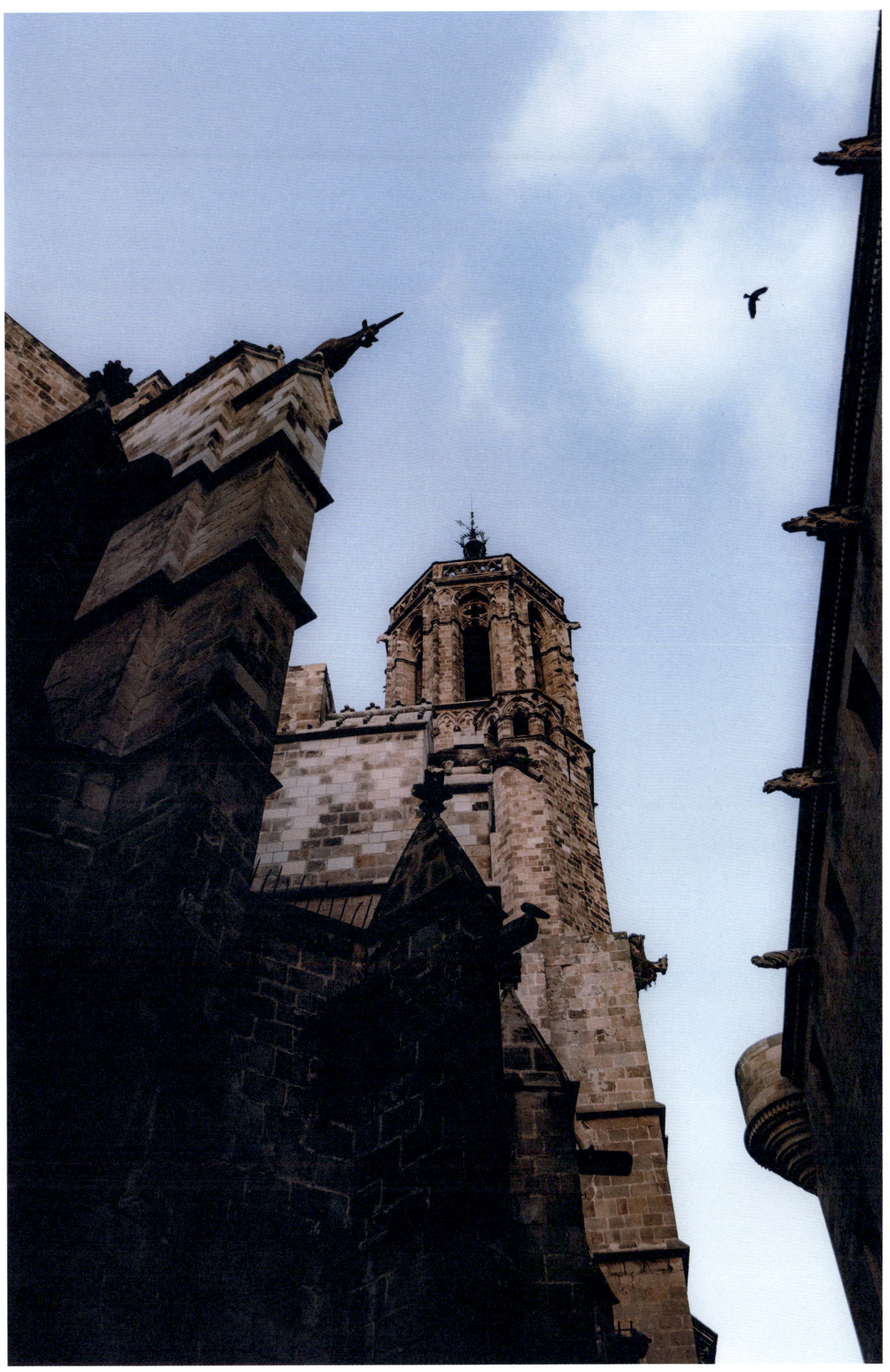

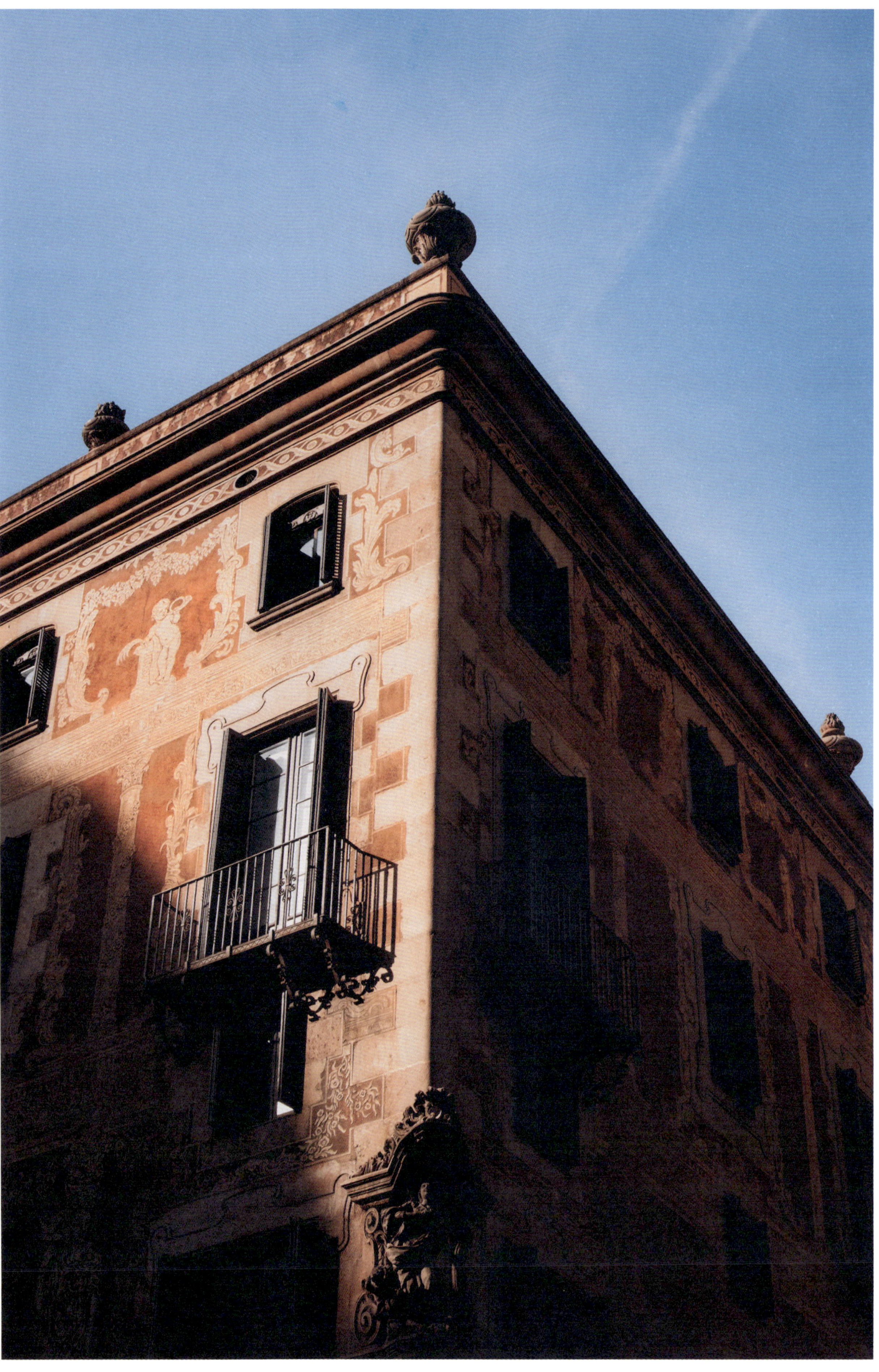

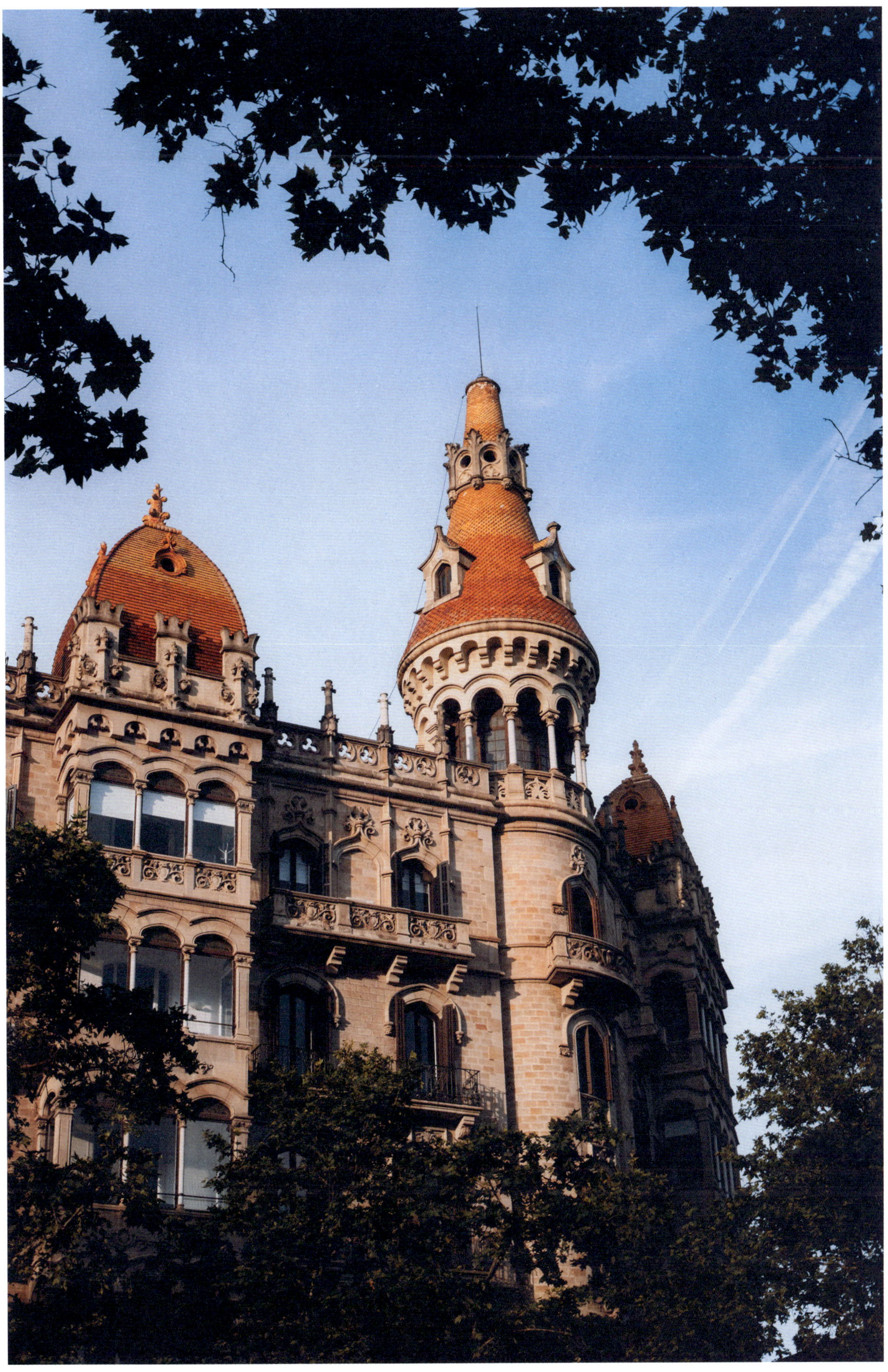

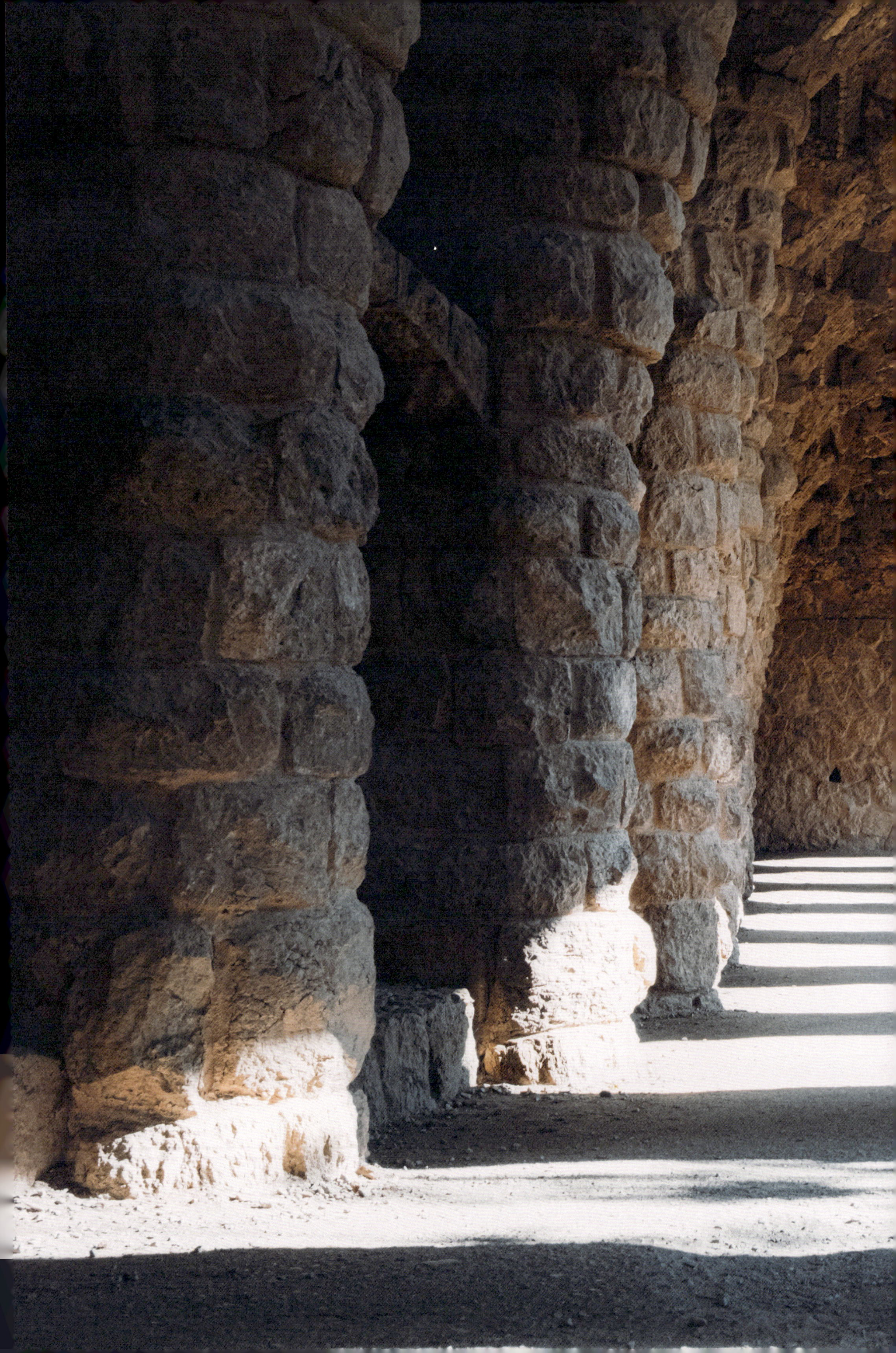

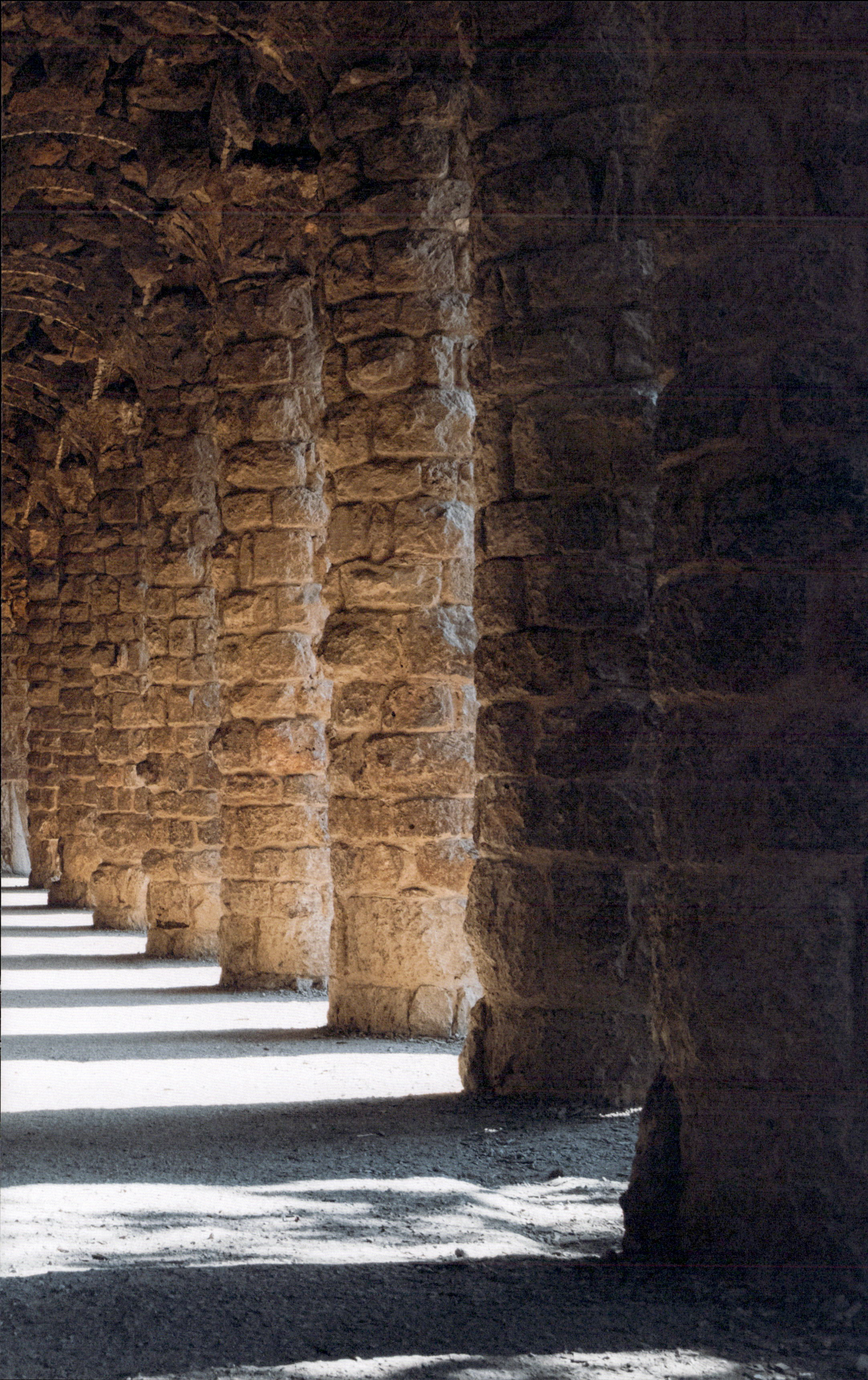

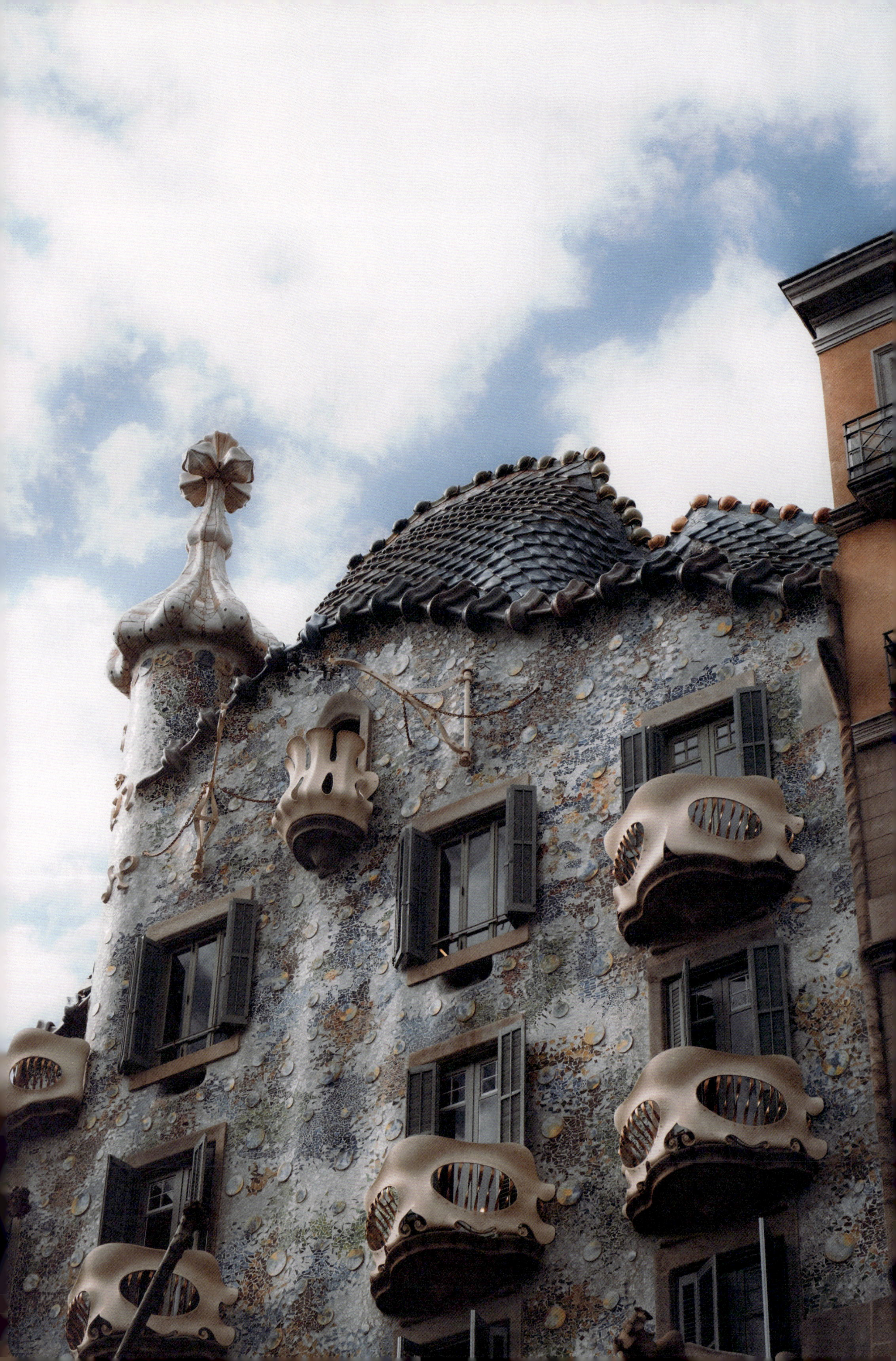

Gaudí was a genius. His work in Barcelona is a living lesson in organic architecture.

ZAHA HADID

Iraqi-British Architect

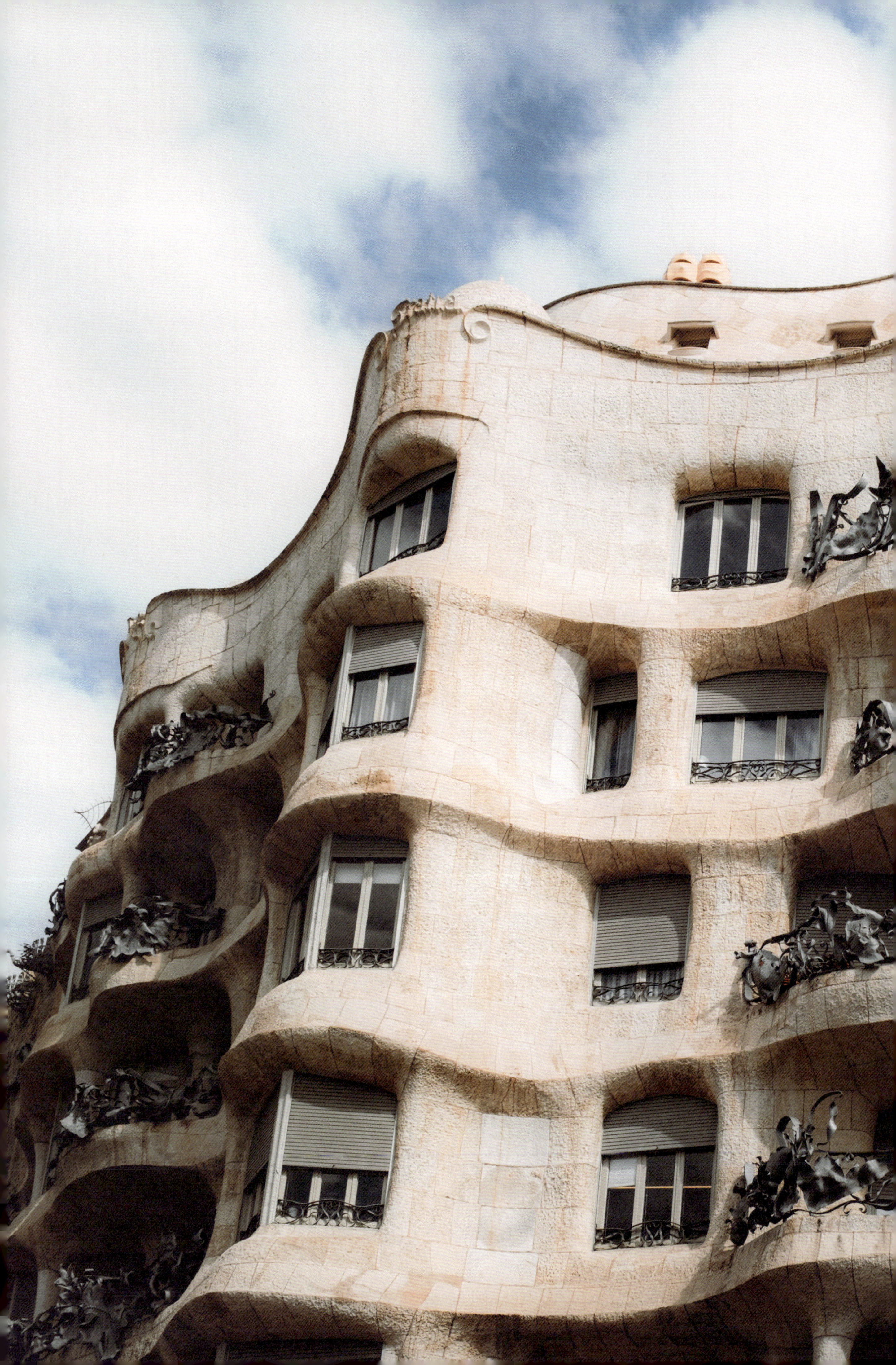

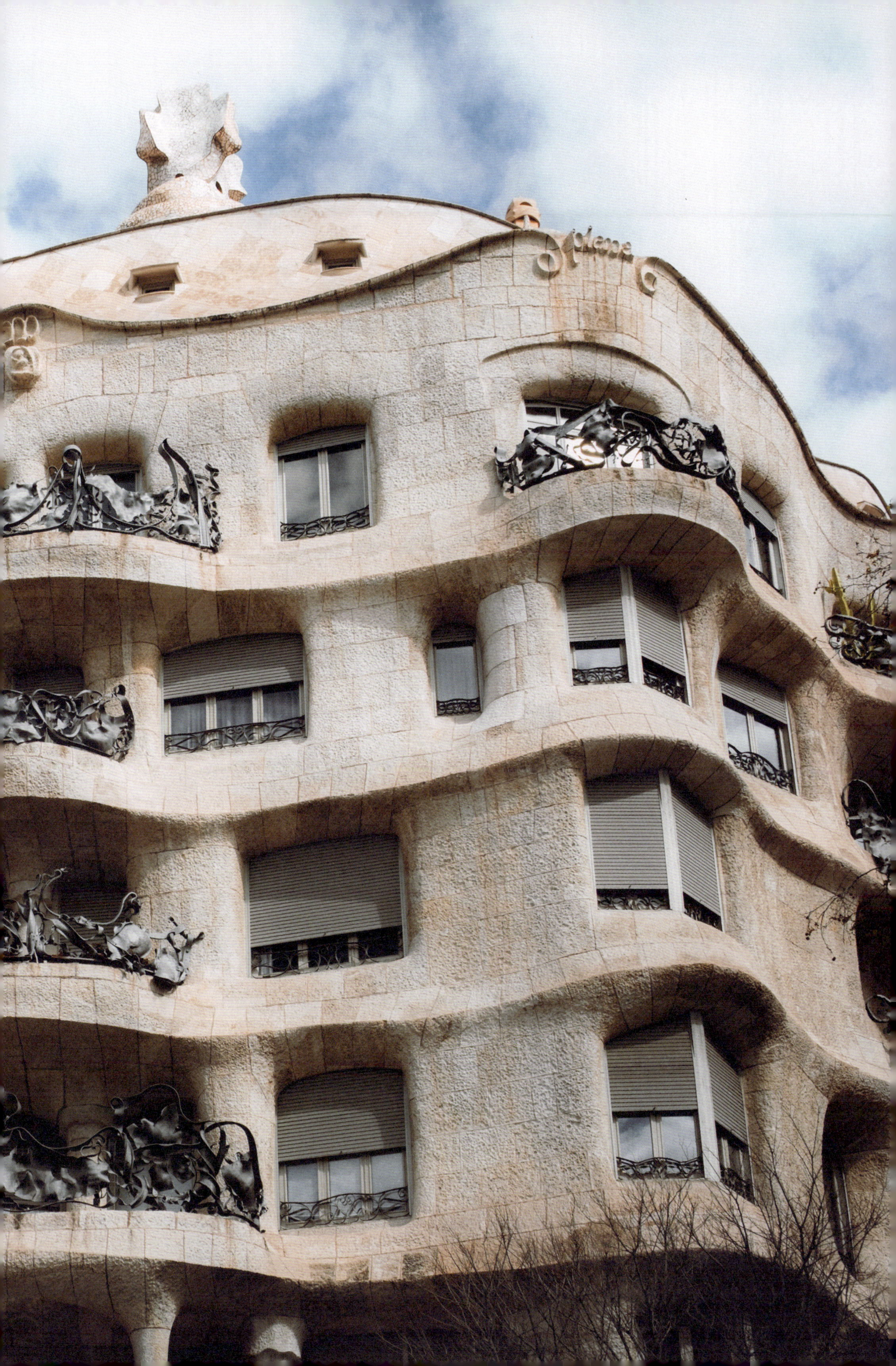
plena

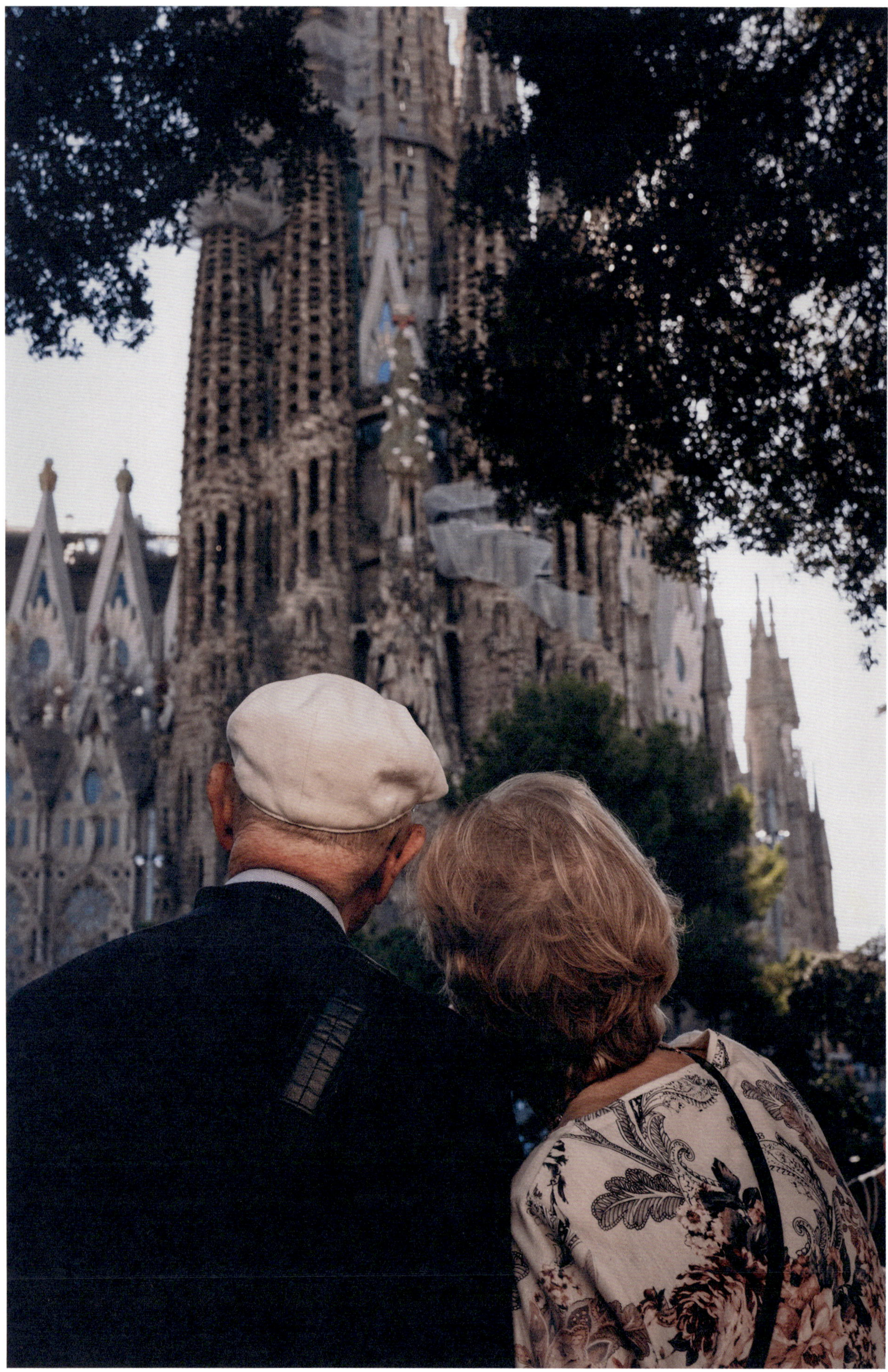

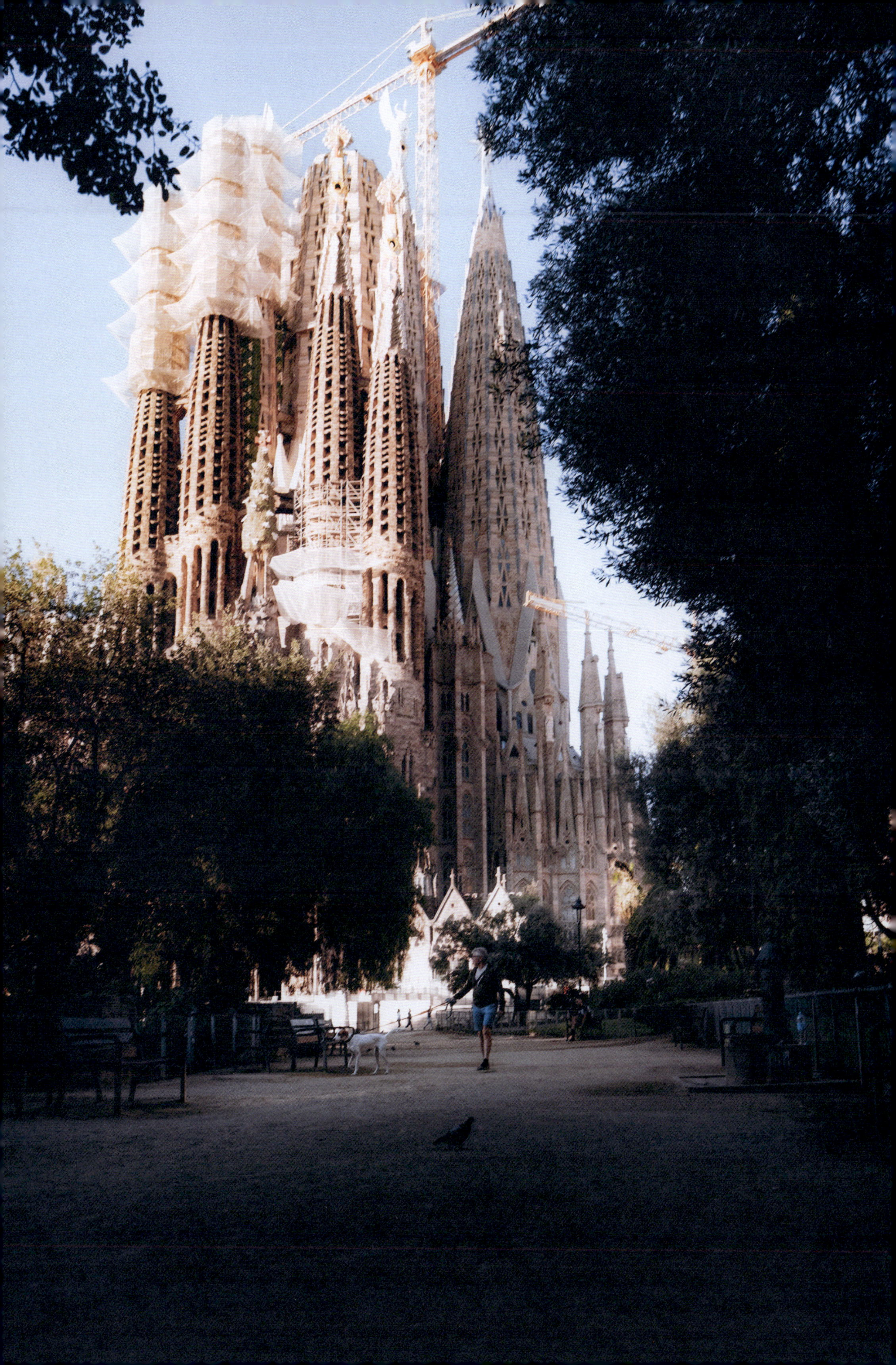

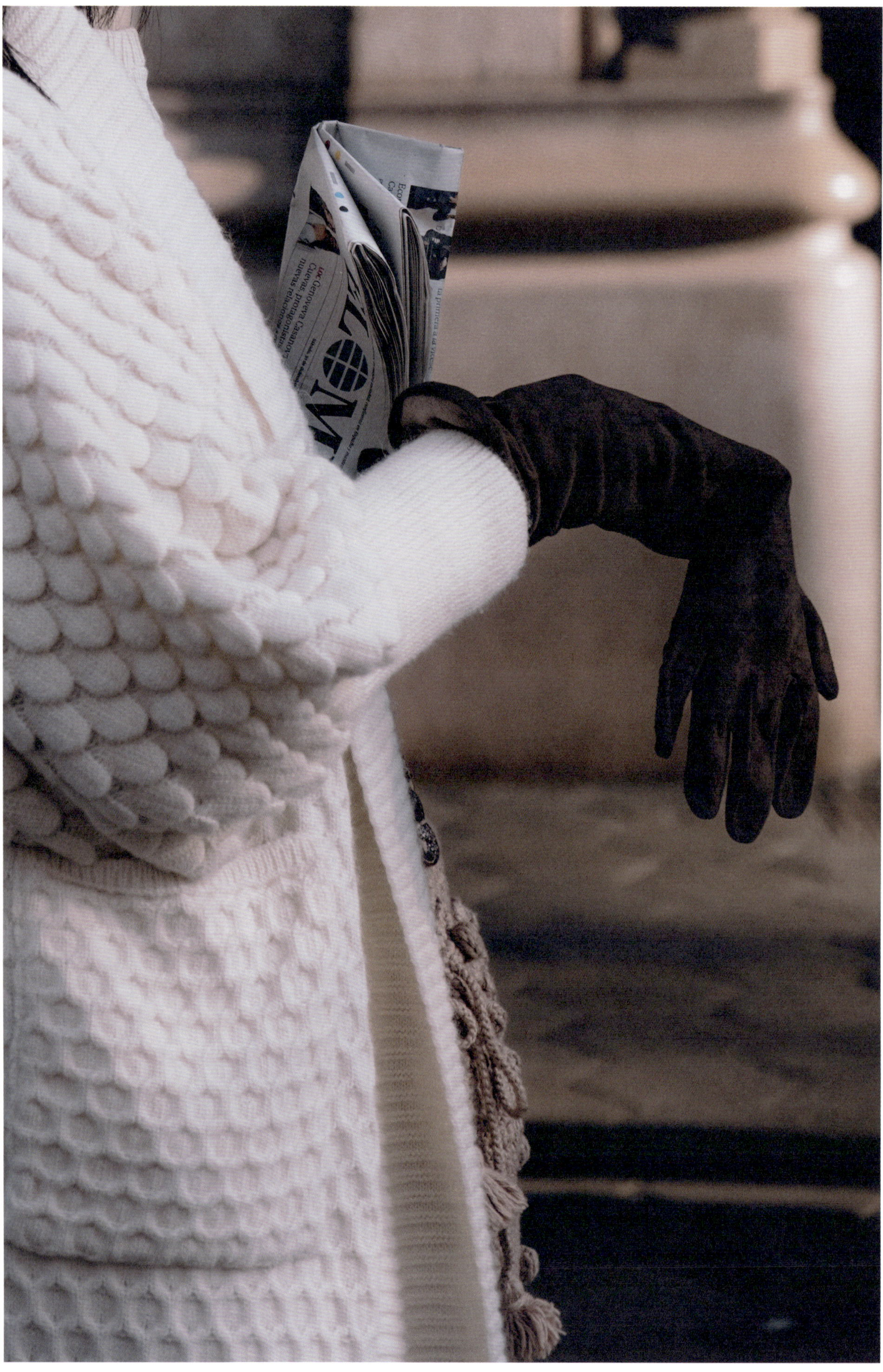

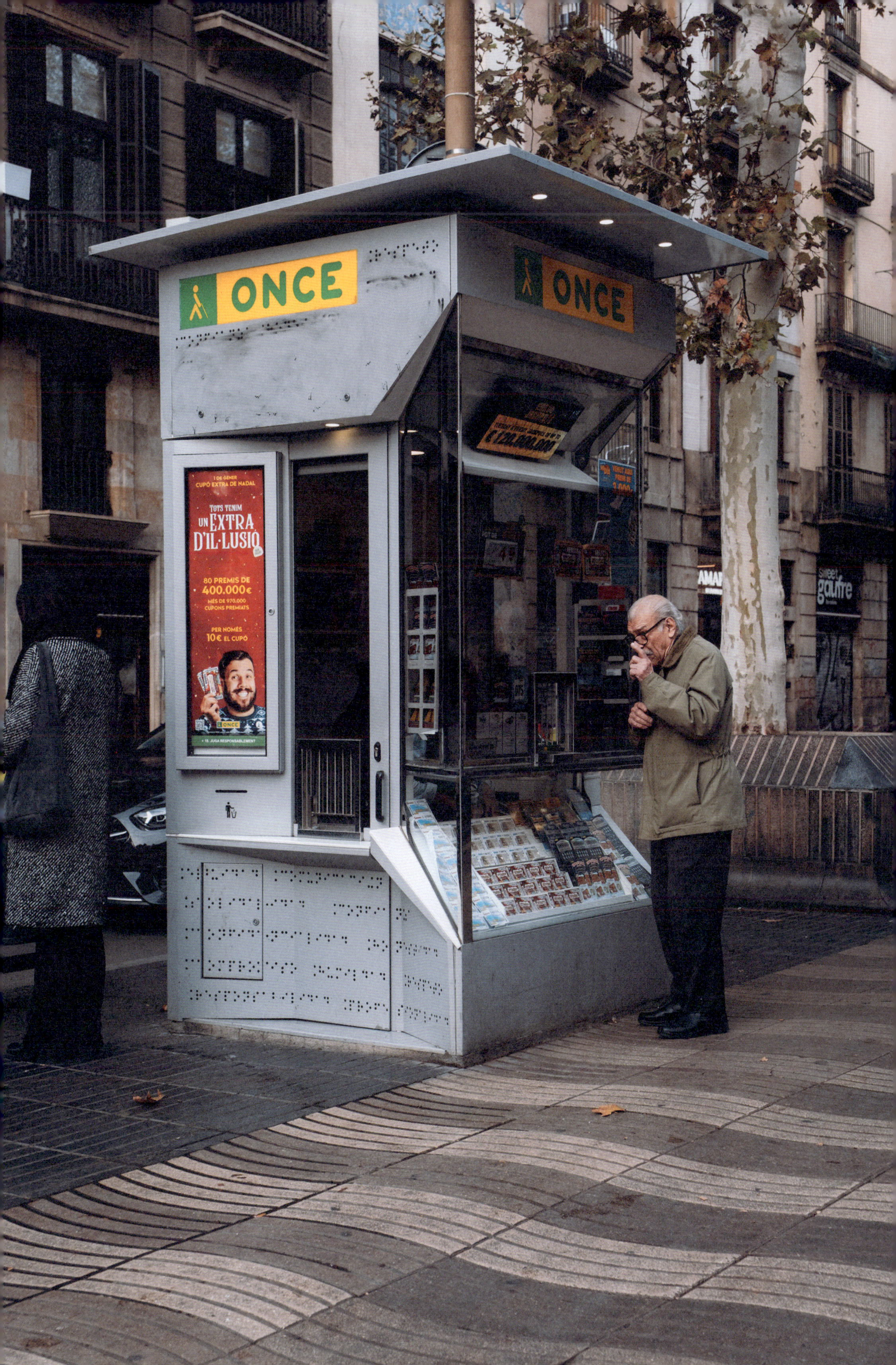
ONCE
ONCE
1 DE GENER
CUPÓ EXTRA DE NADAL
TOTS TENIM
UN EXTRA D'IL·LUSIÓ
80 PREMIS DE
400.000€
MÉS DE 970.000
CUPONS PREMIATS
PER NOMÉS
10€ EL CUPÓ
ONCE
+18. JUGA RESPONSABLEMENT
sweet gaufre

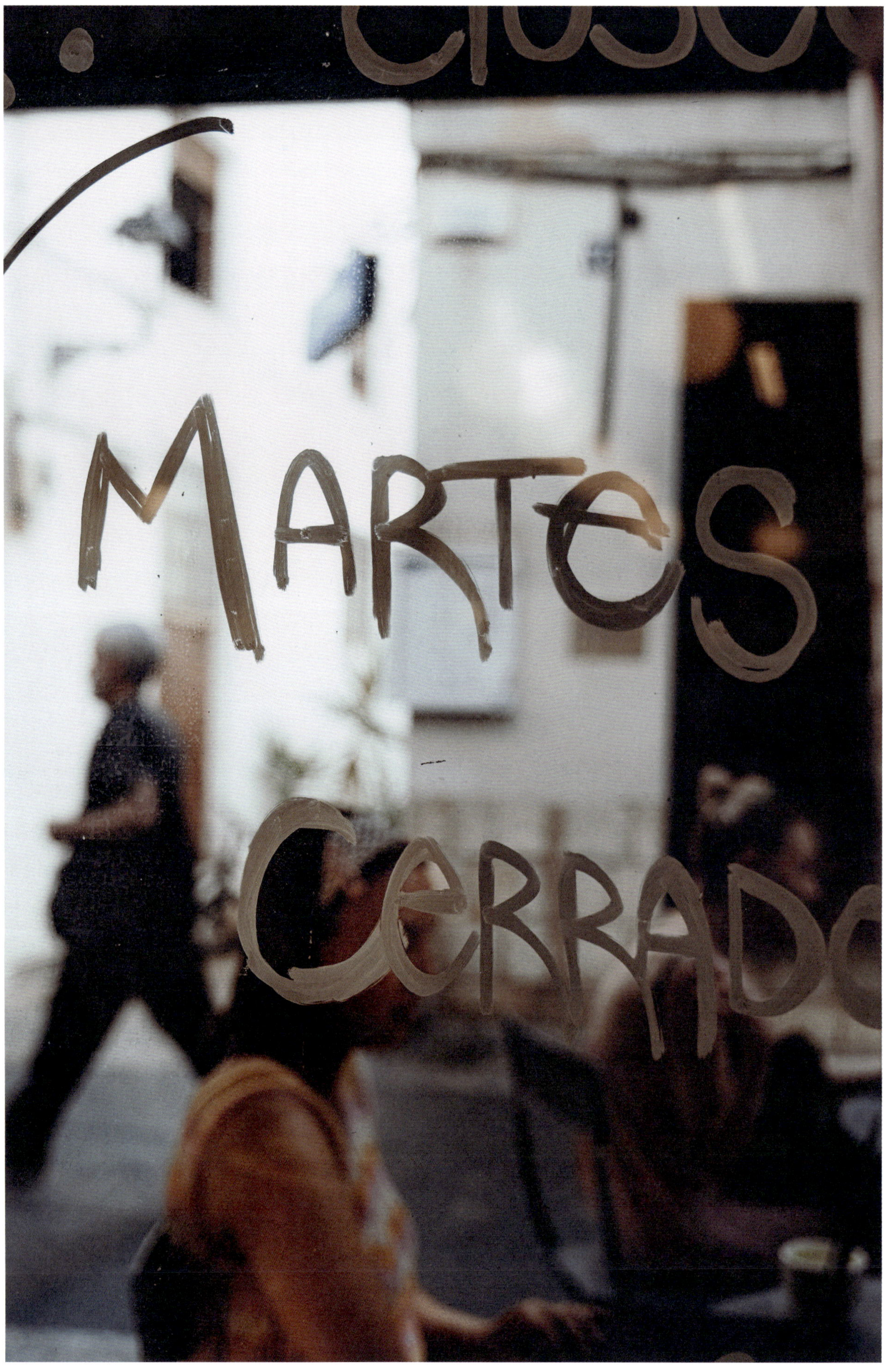
MARTES
CERRAD

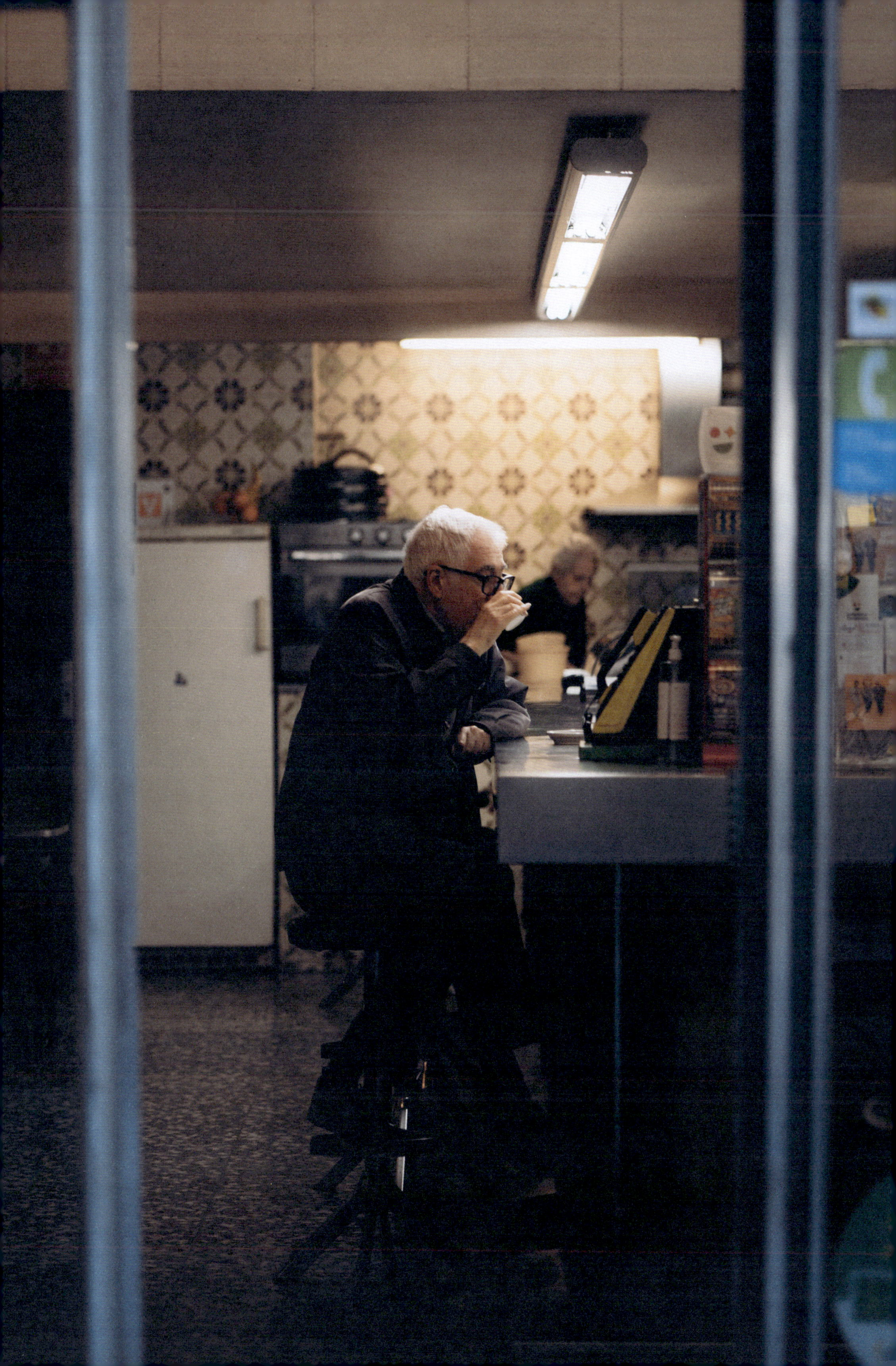

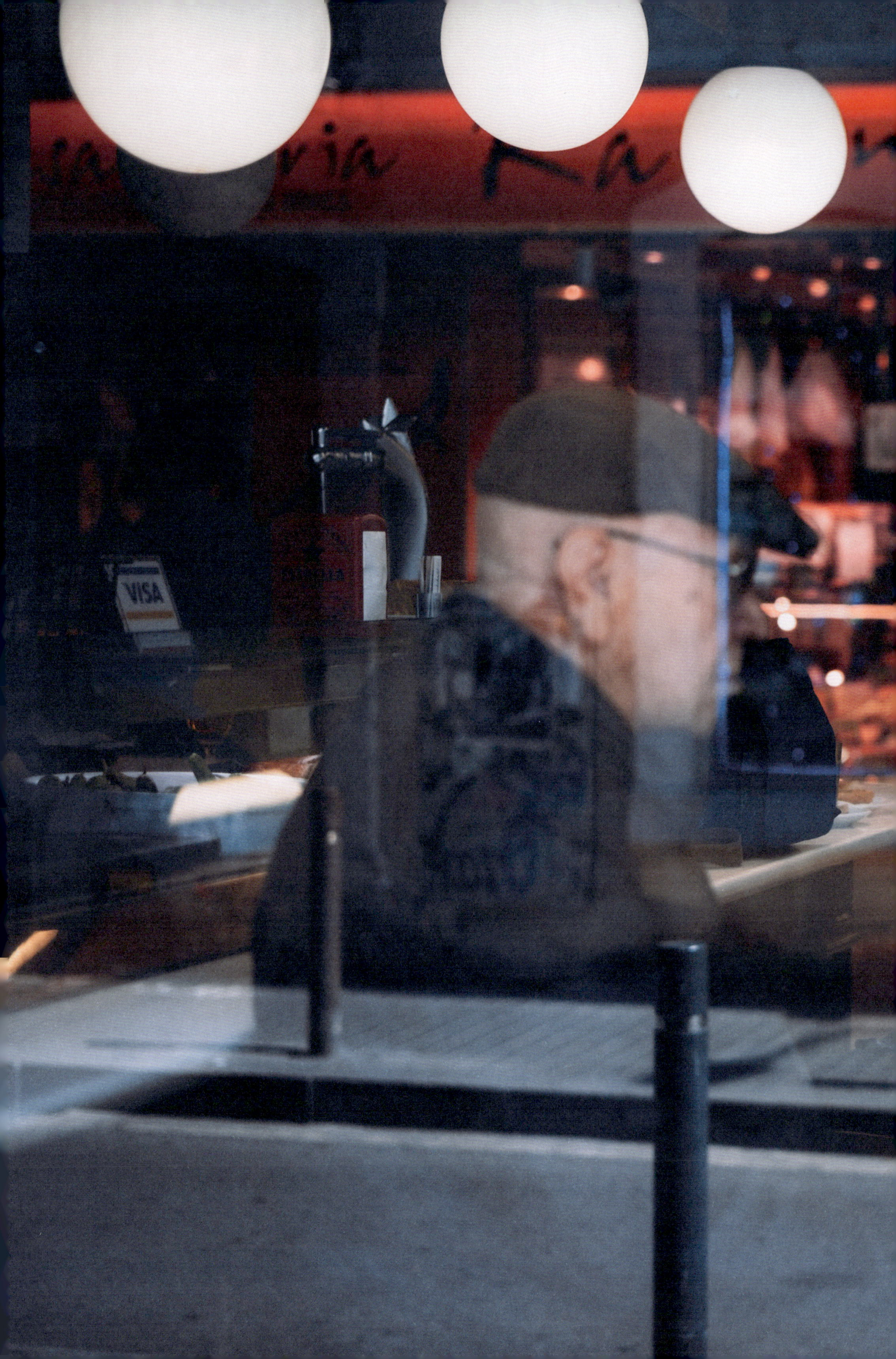
VISA

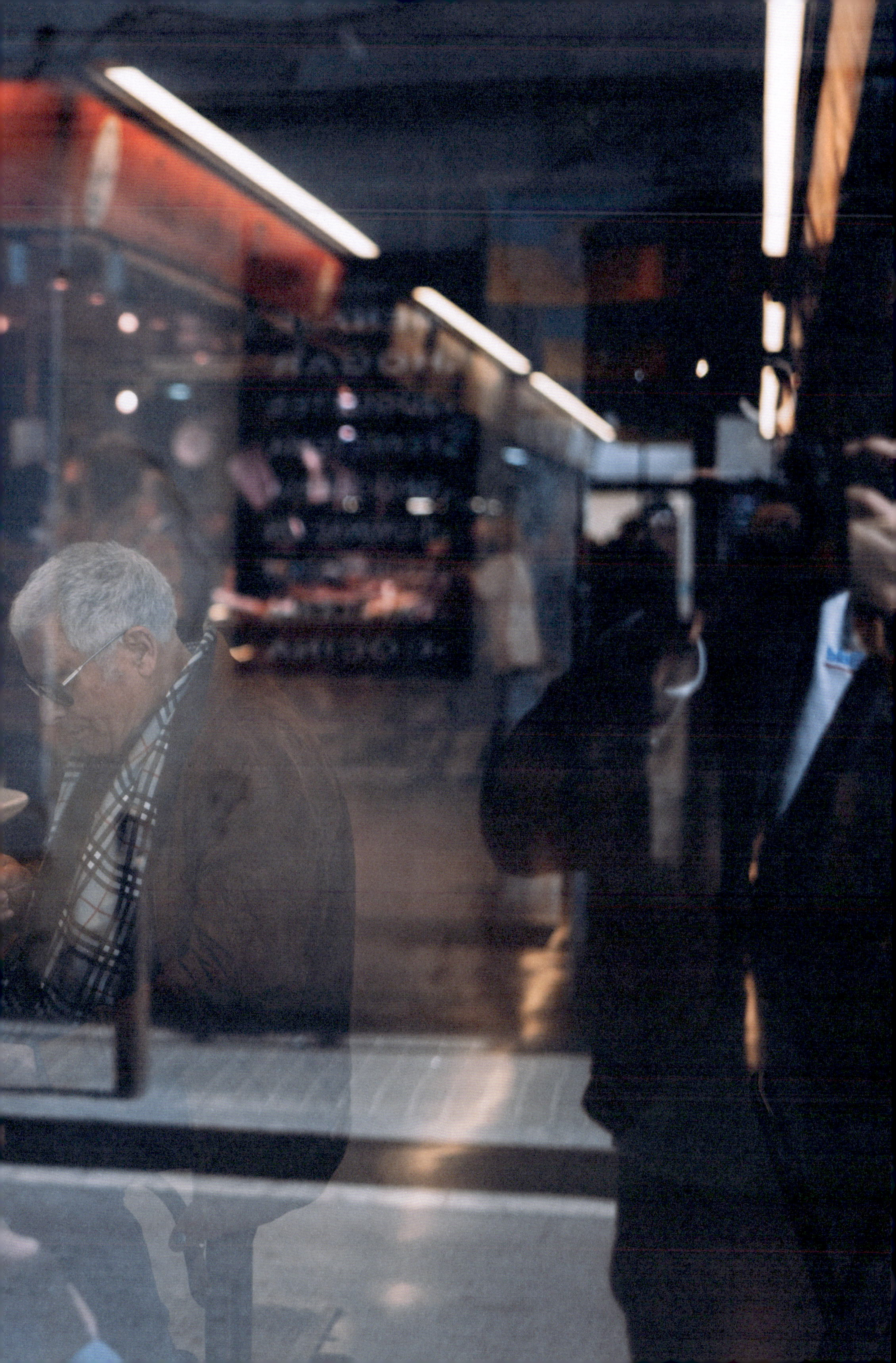

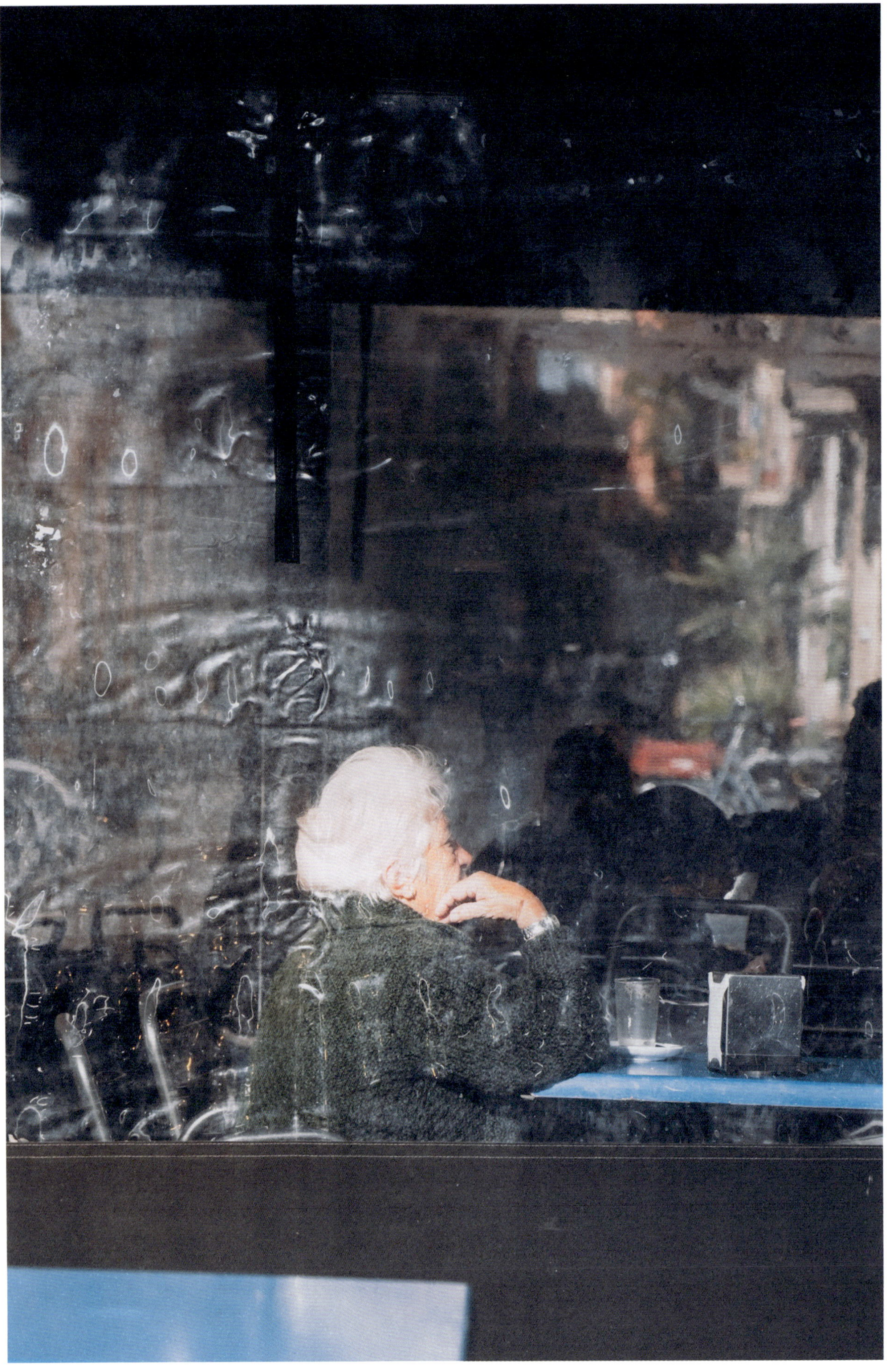

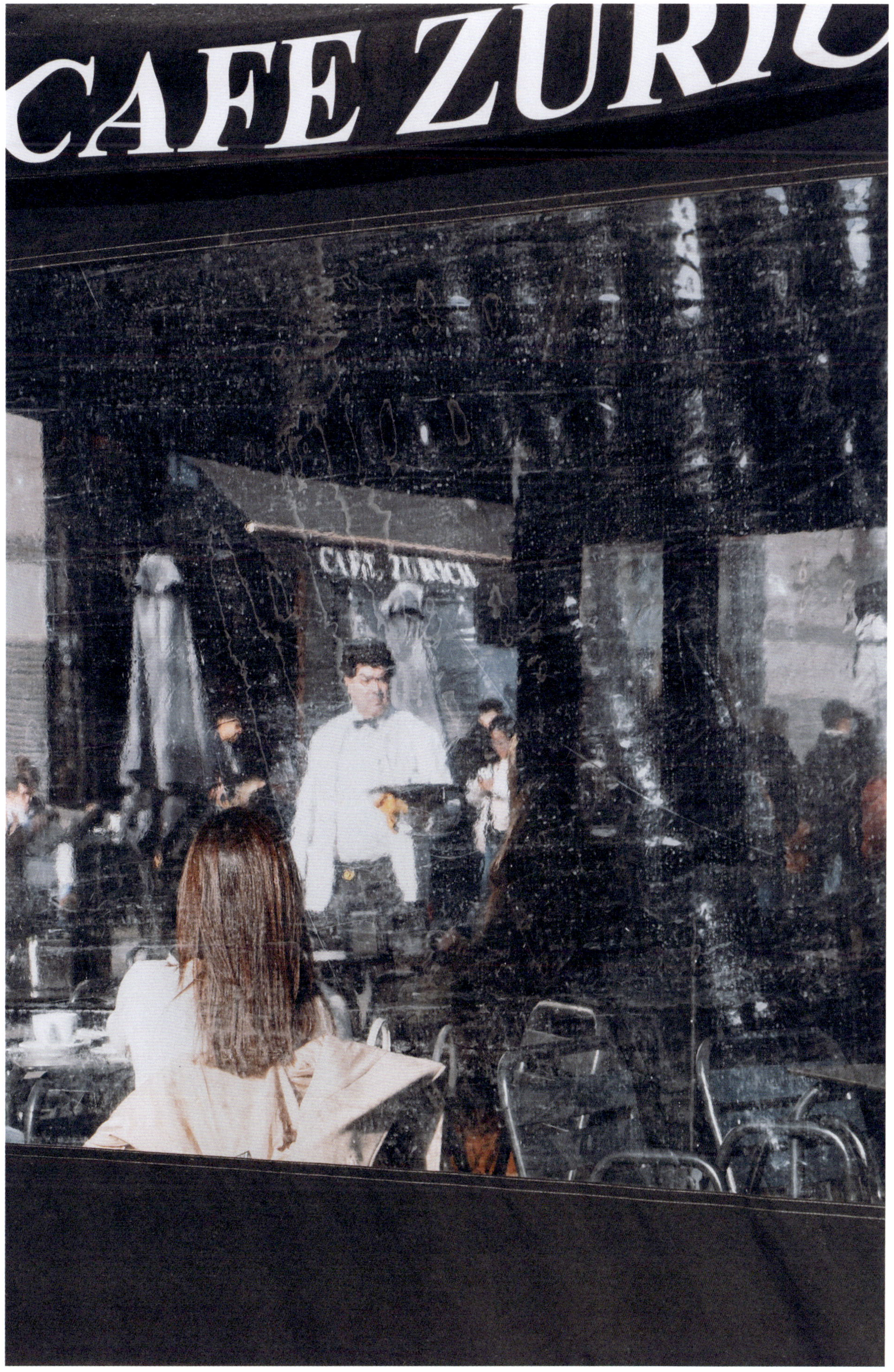
CAFE ZURIC
CAFE ZURICH

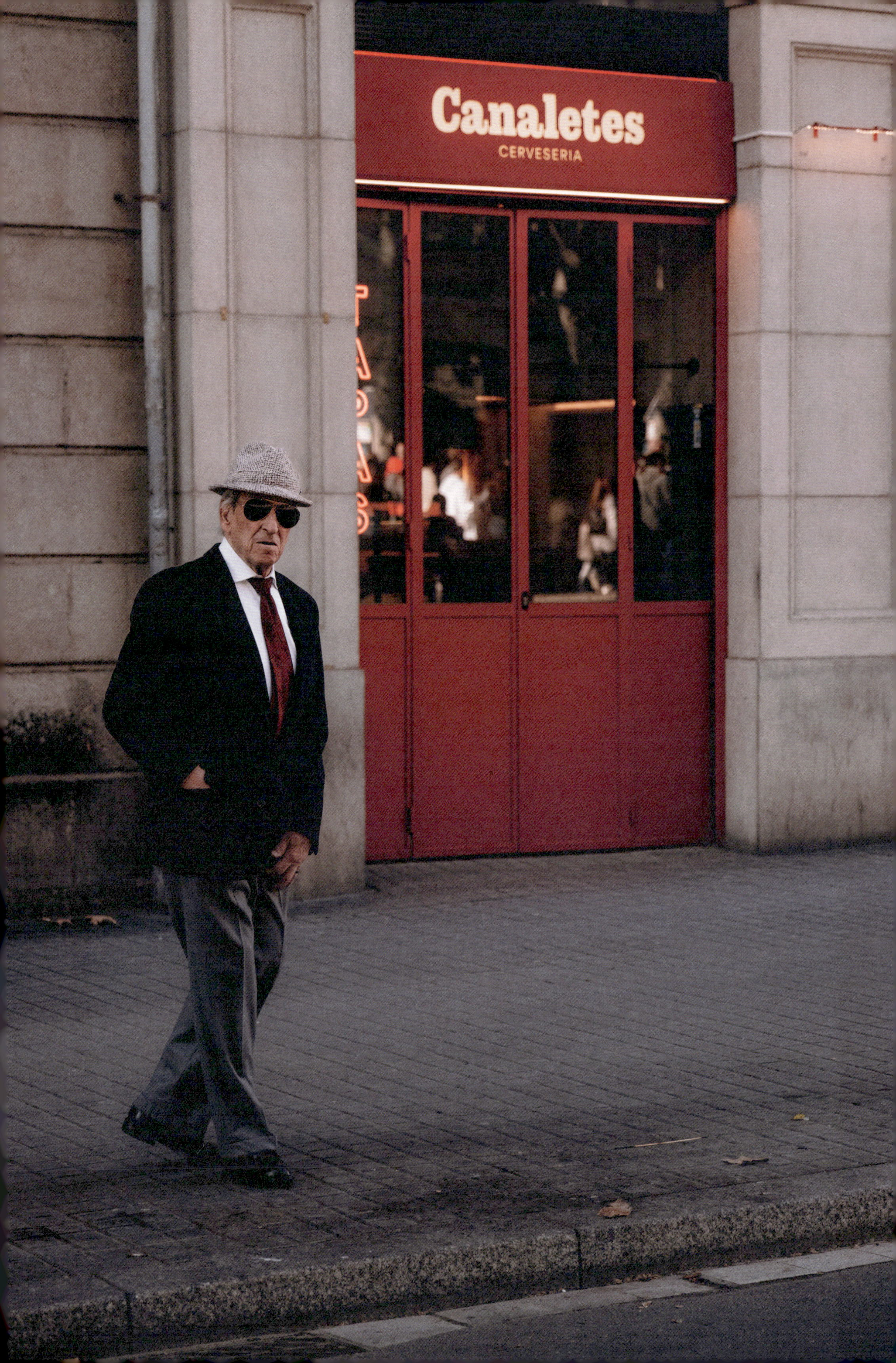
Canaletes
CERVESERIA

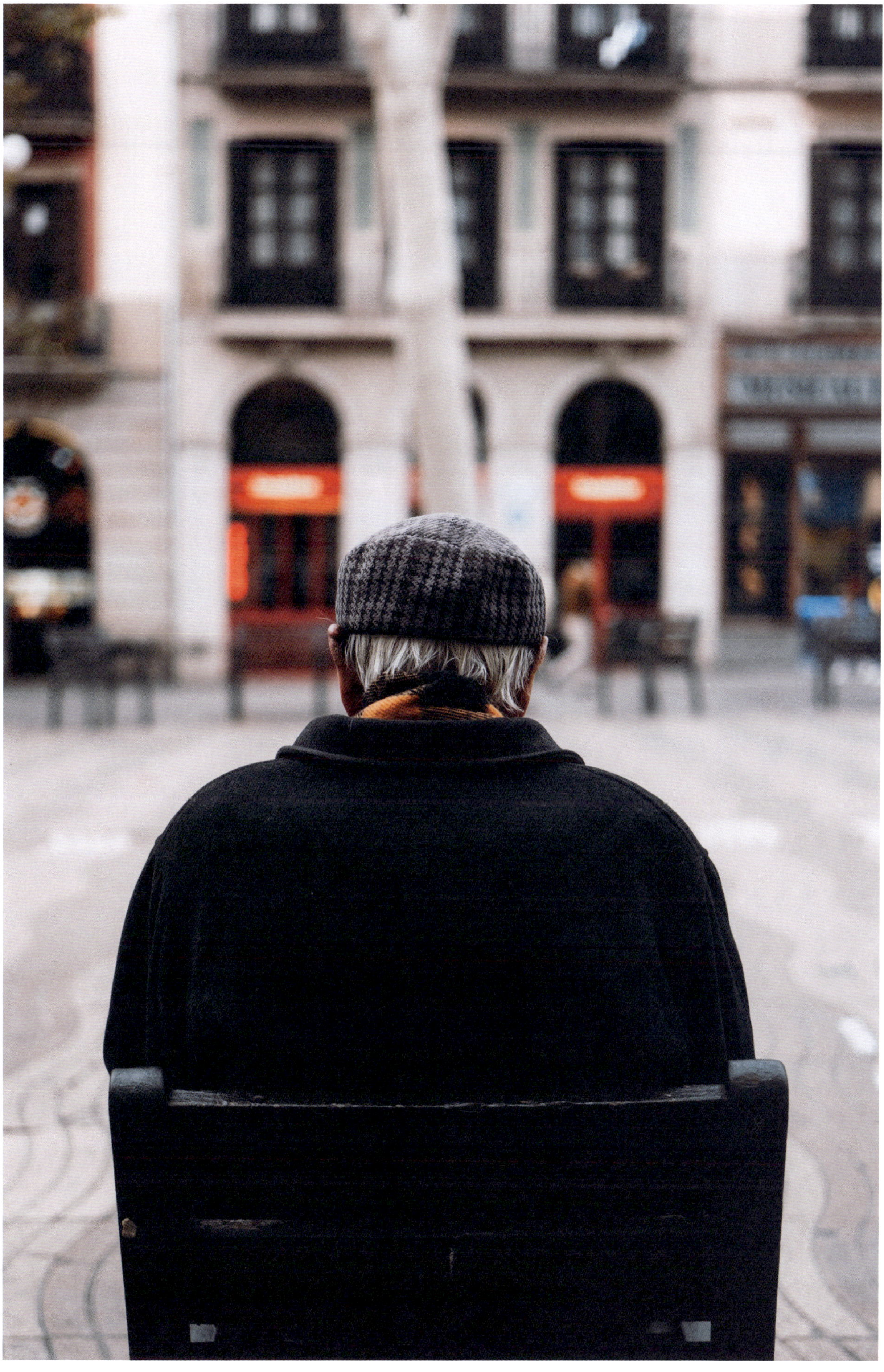

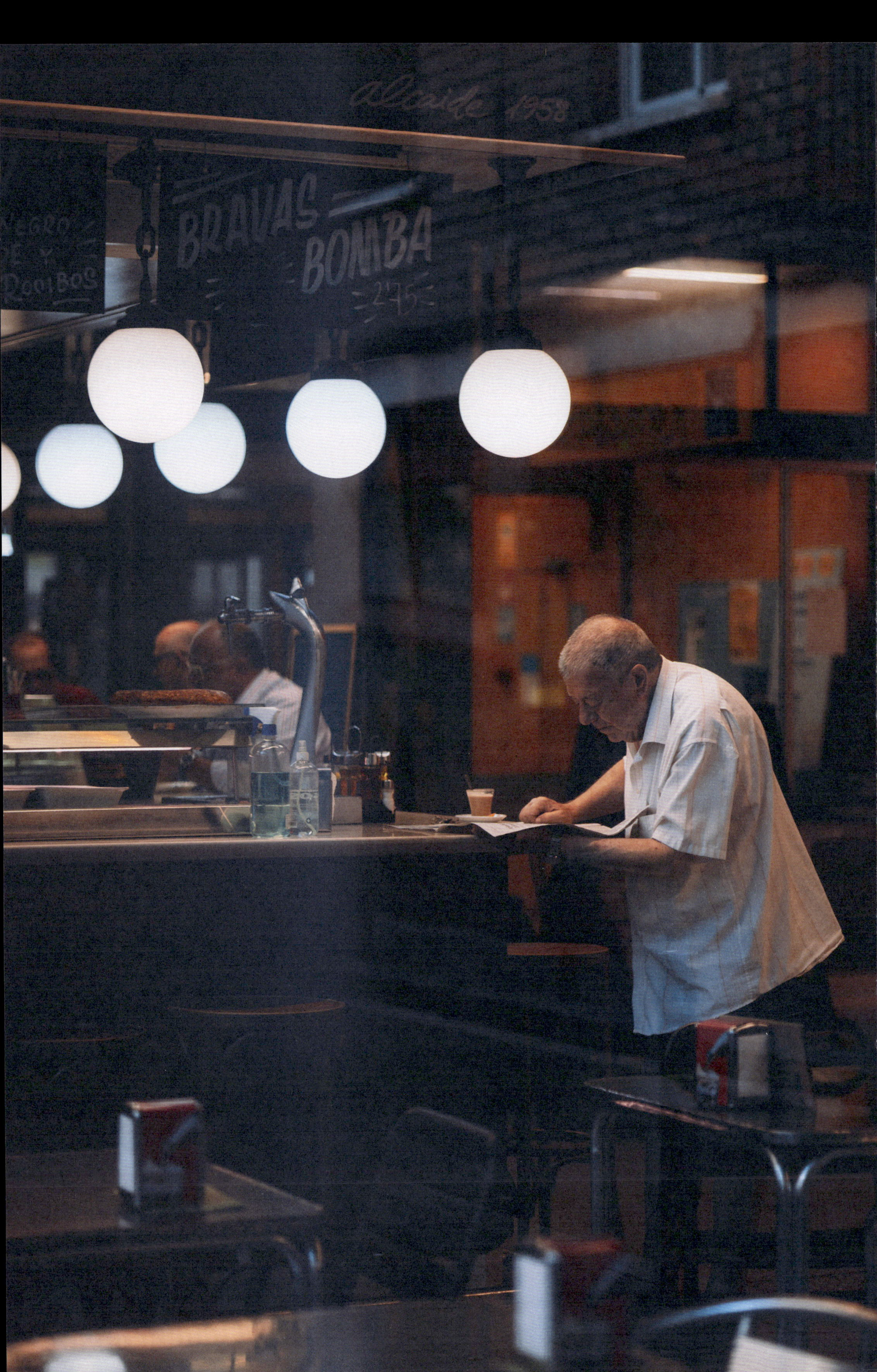
alcaide 1958
BRAVAS
BOMBA
2'75

Barcelona is the only city in the world where you can find a Picasso next to a sandwich shop.

ANTHONY BOURDAIN

Chef and Author

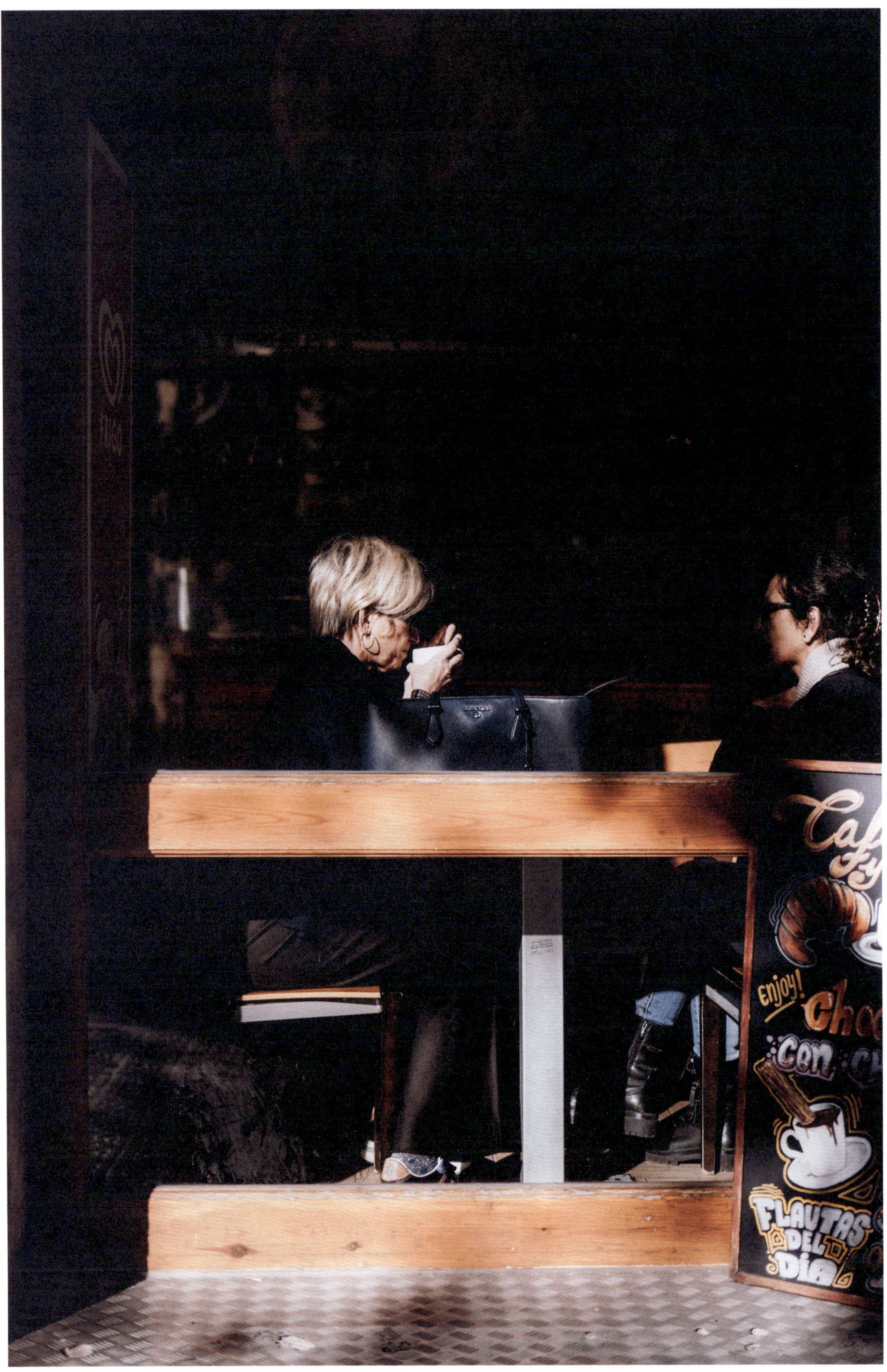
enjoy!
Con
FLAUTAS
DEL
DÍA

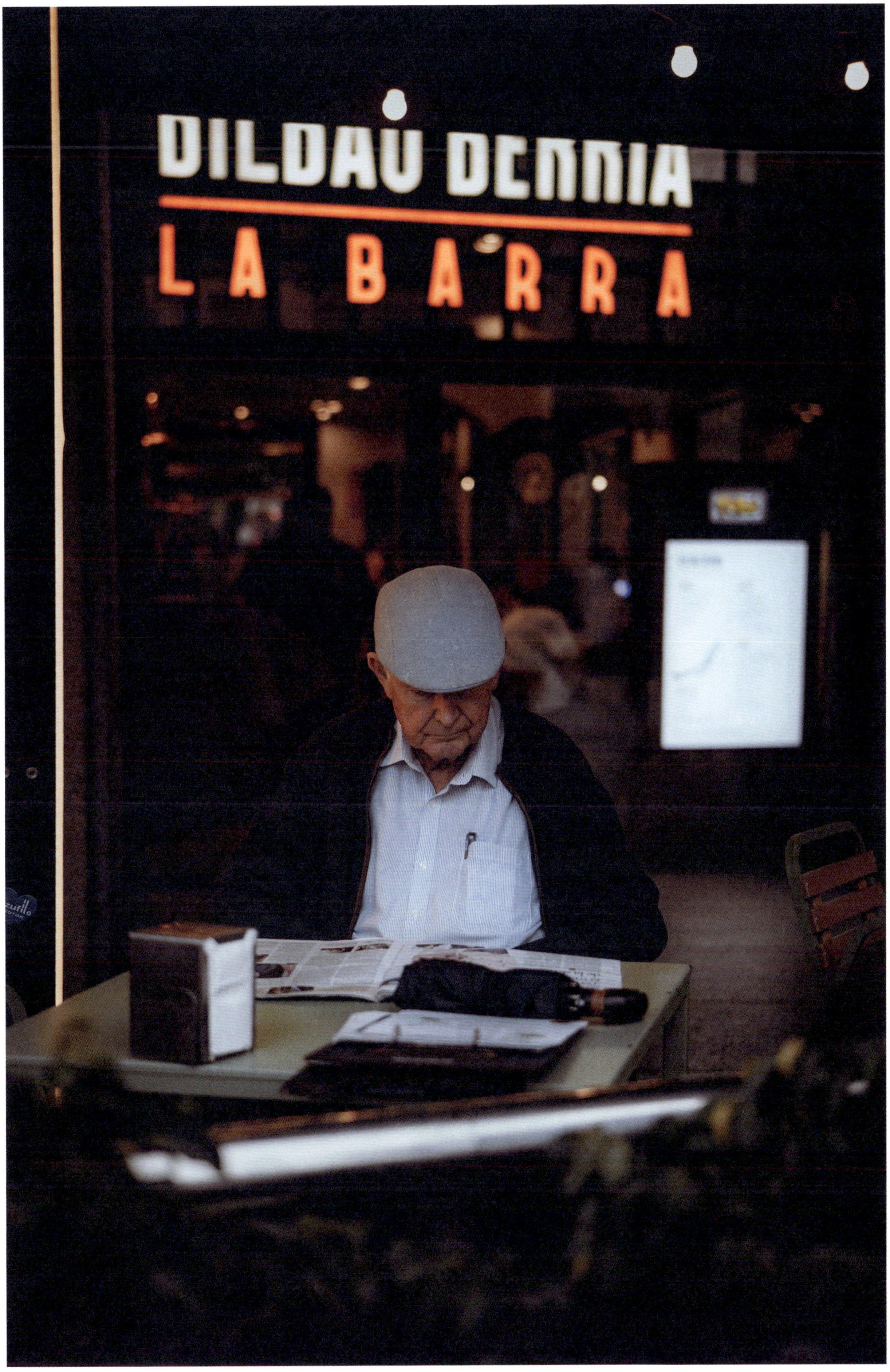
LA BARRA

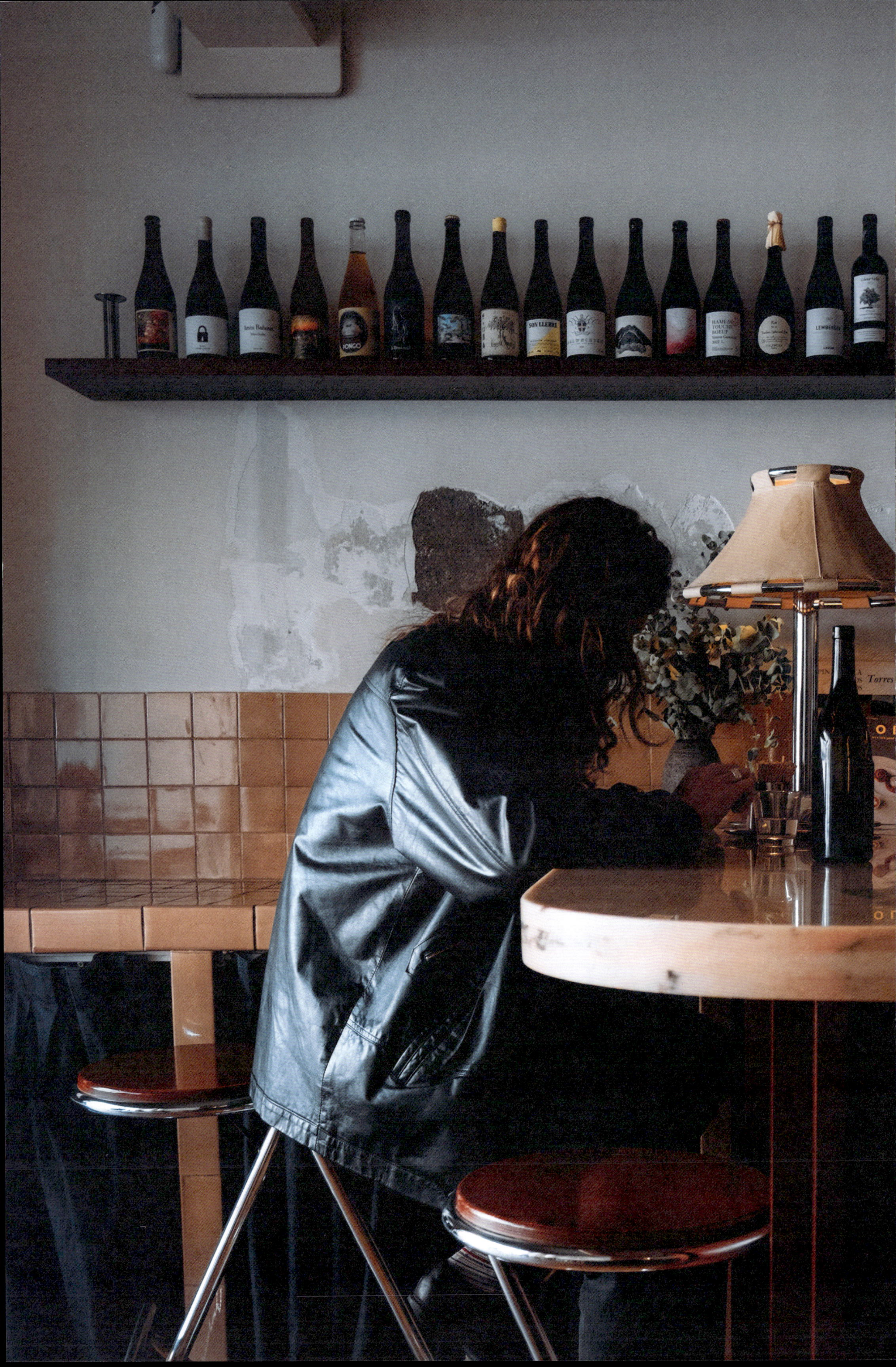
PONGO
SON LLEBRE
HAMEAU
TOUCHE
BOEUF
LEMBERGER

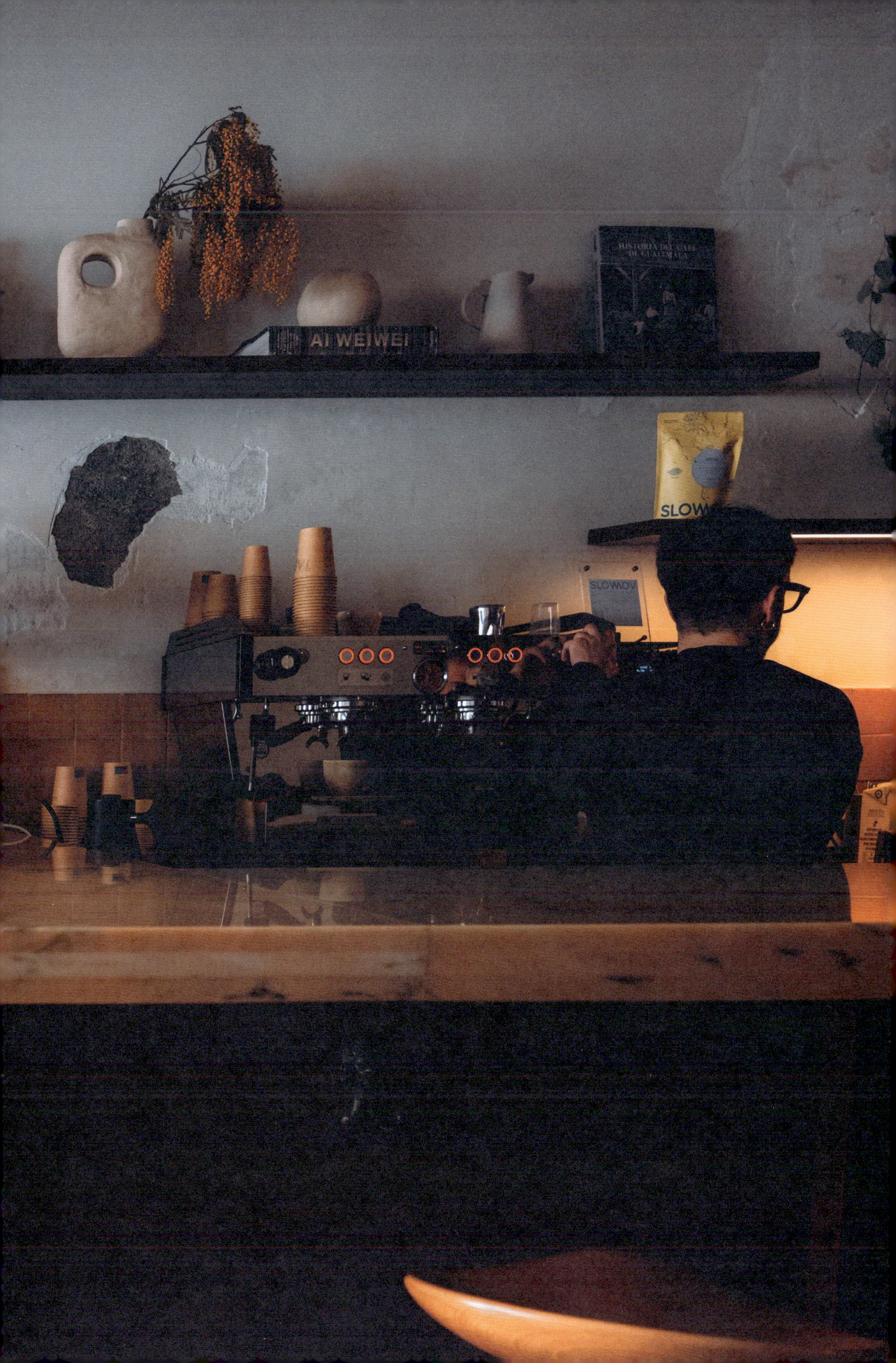
AI WEIWEI
SLOW

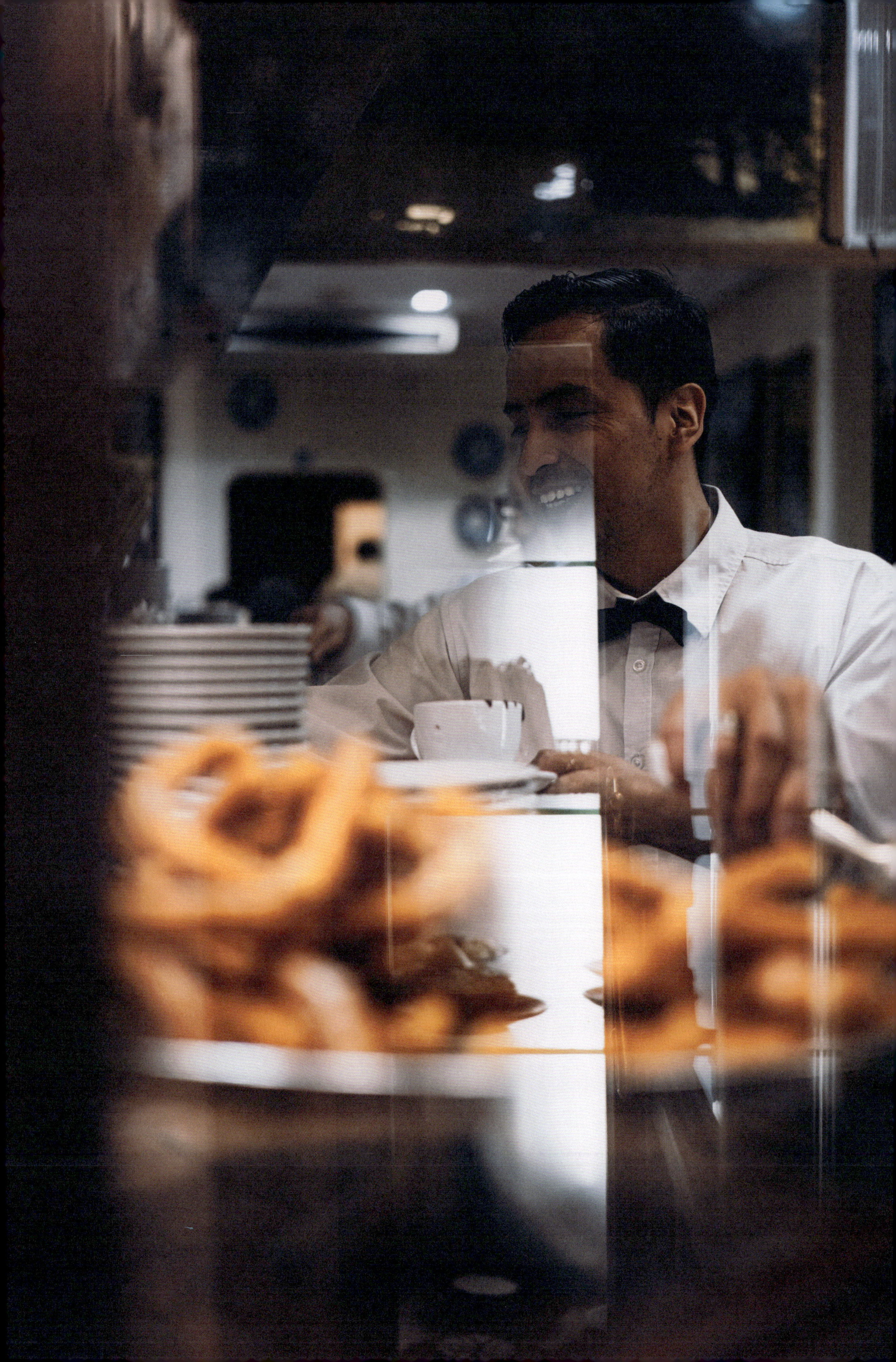

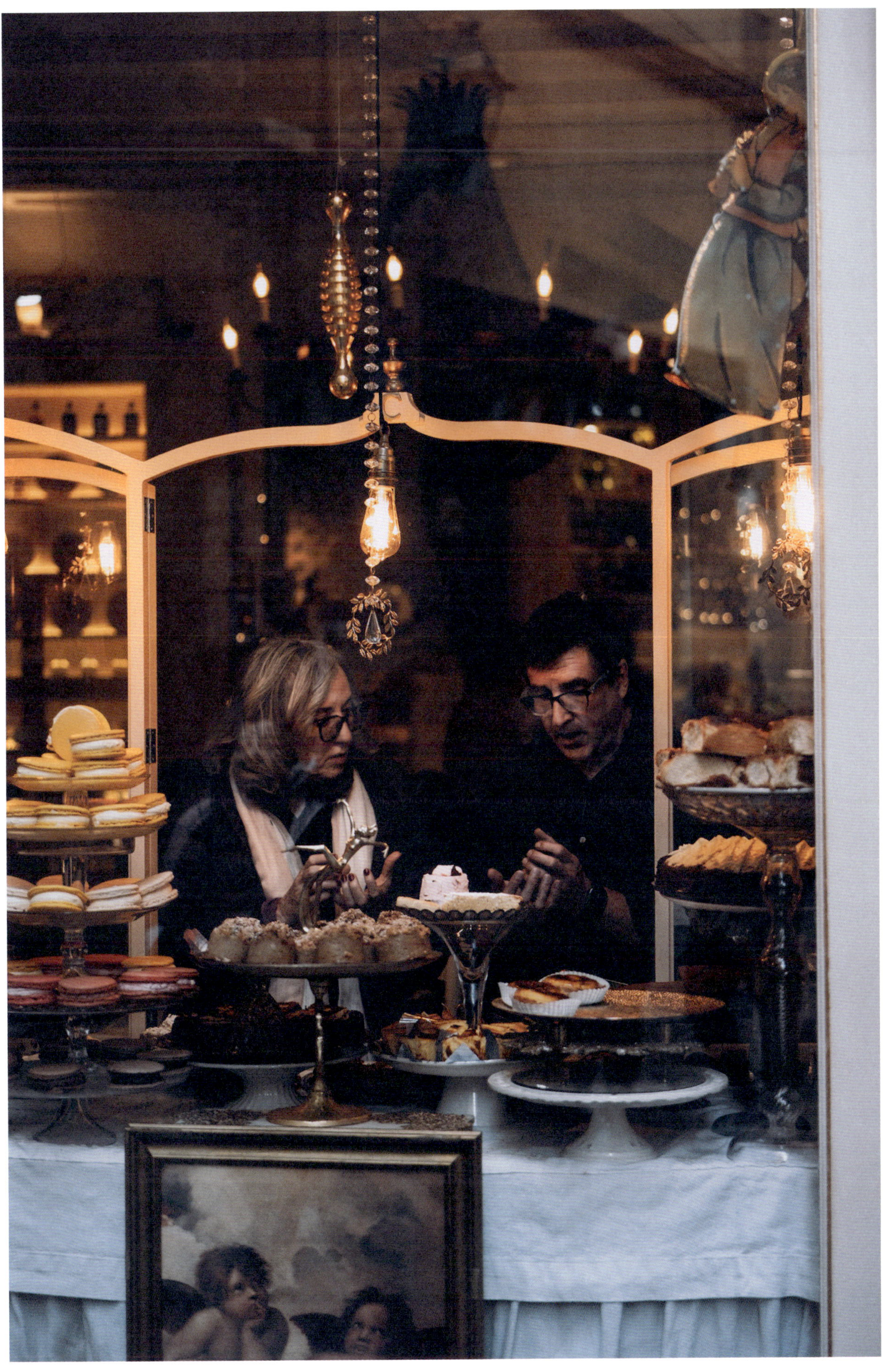

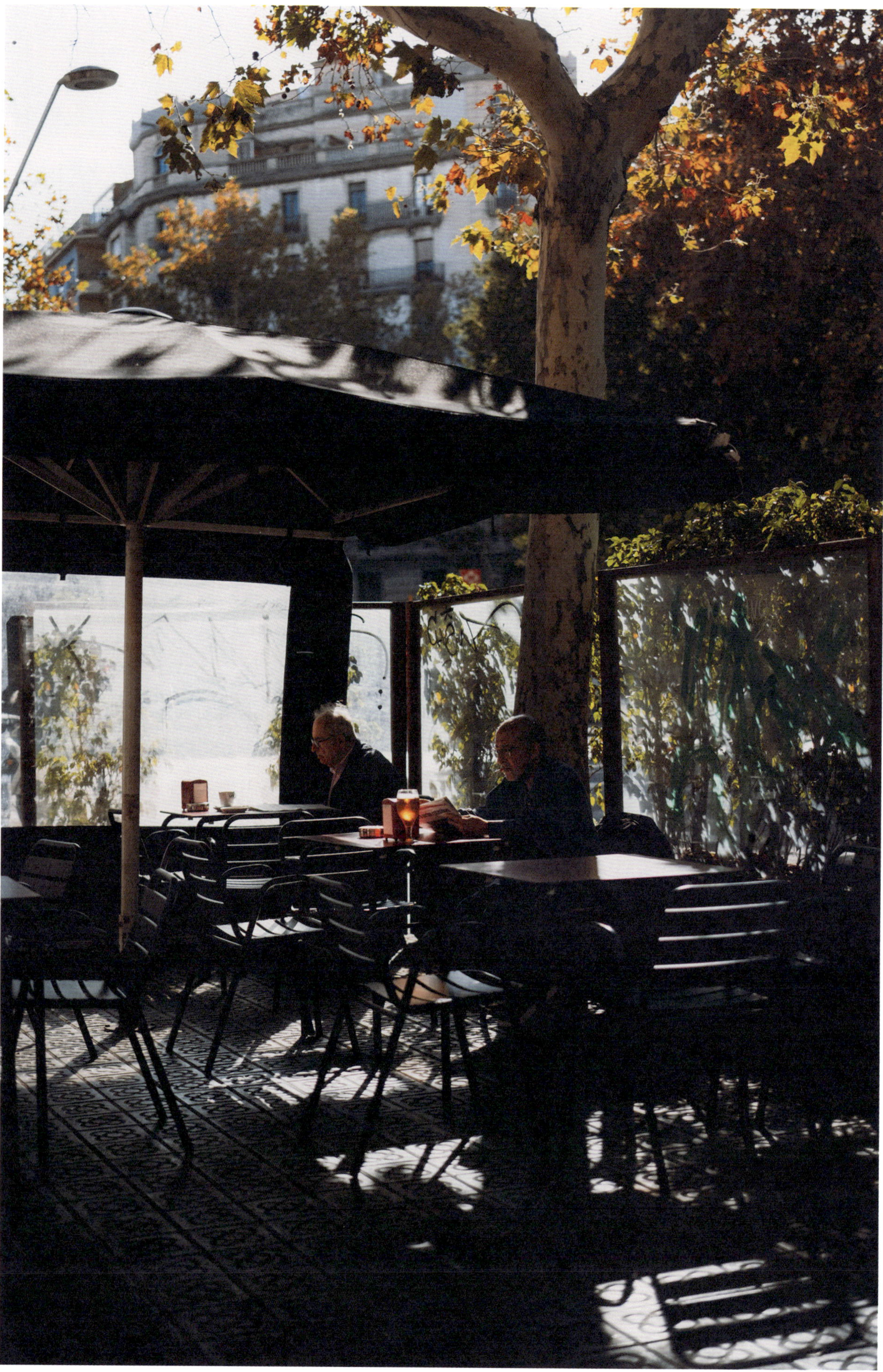

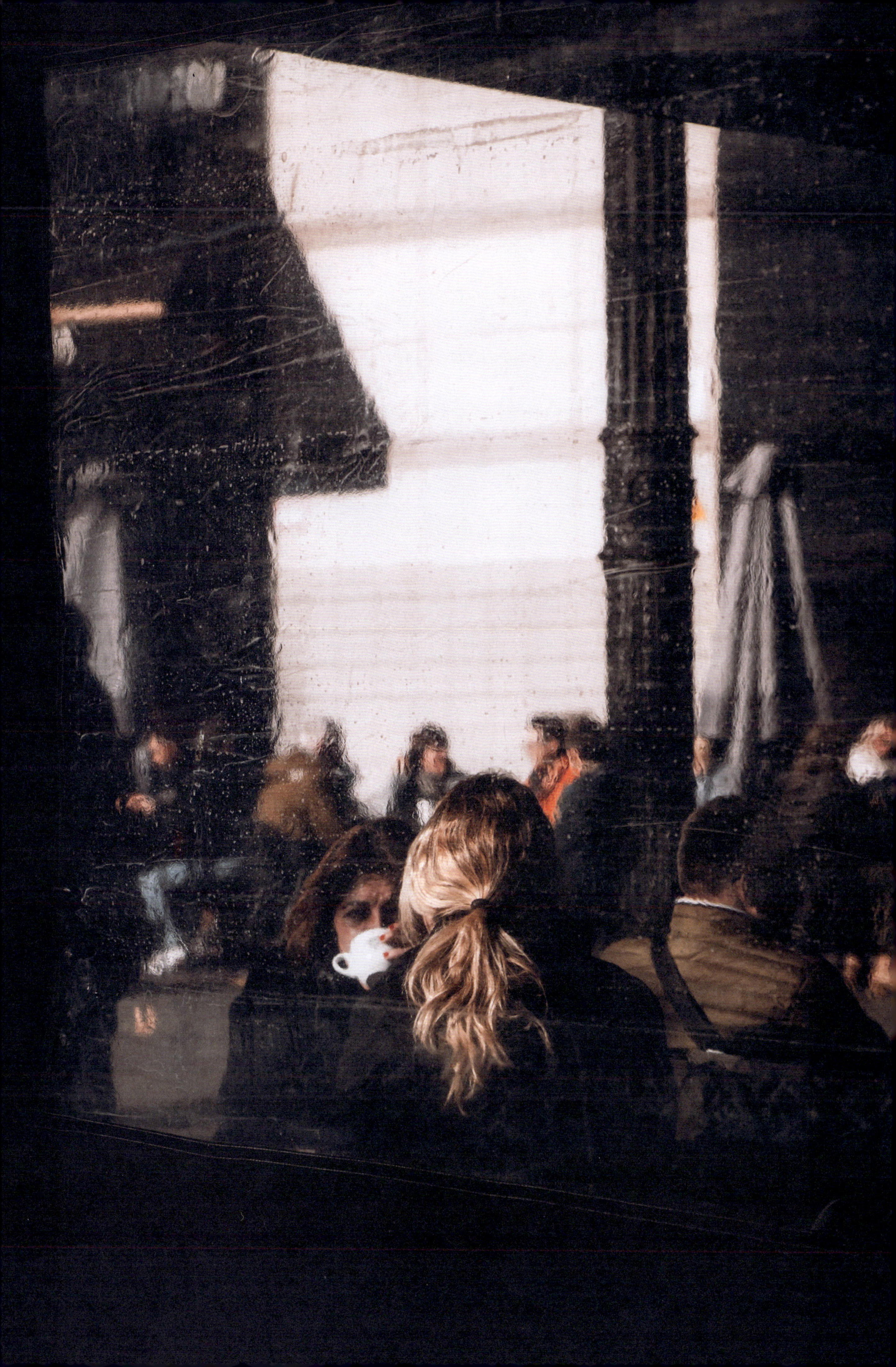

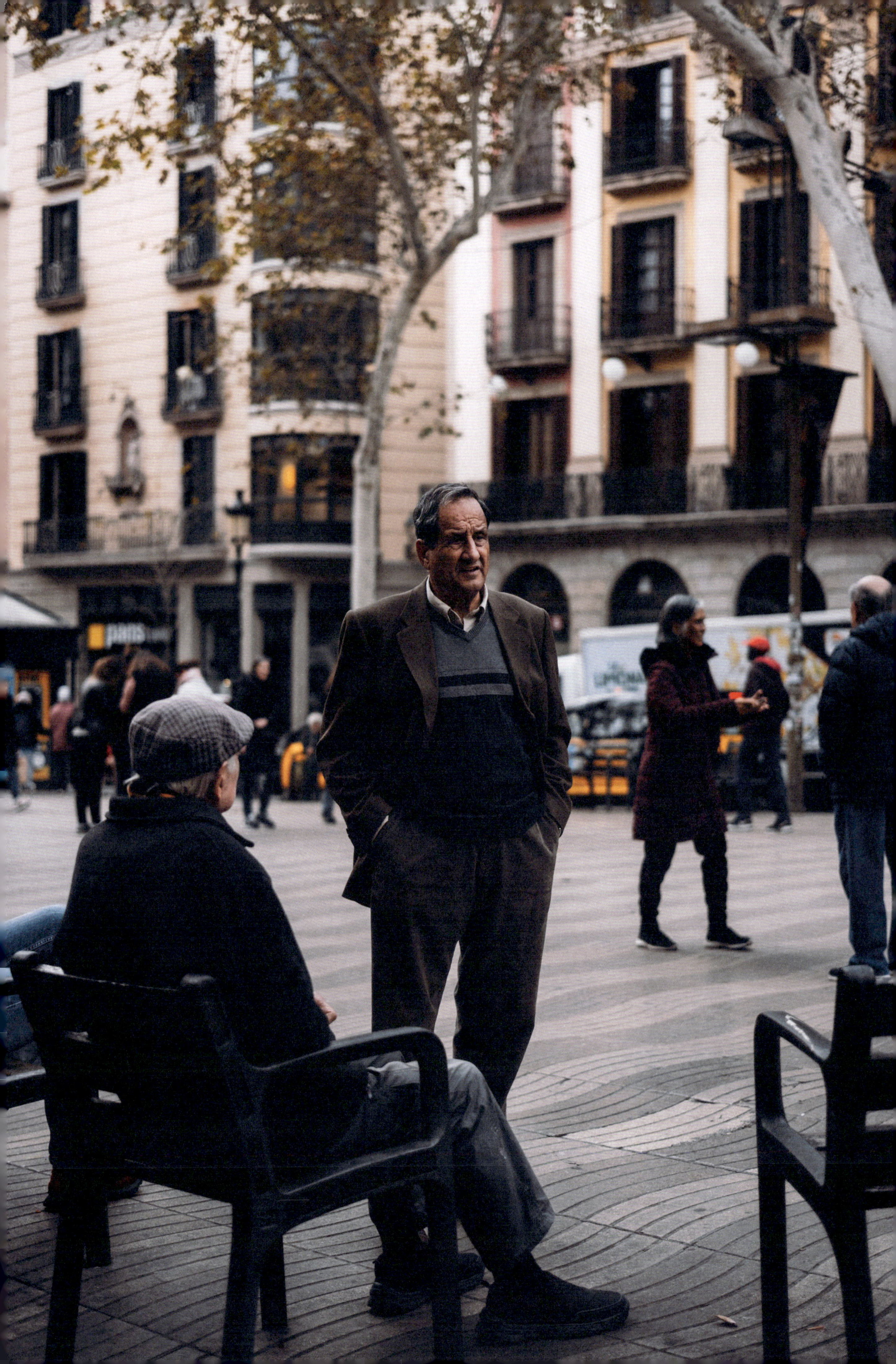

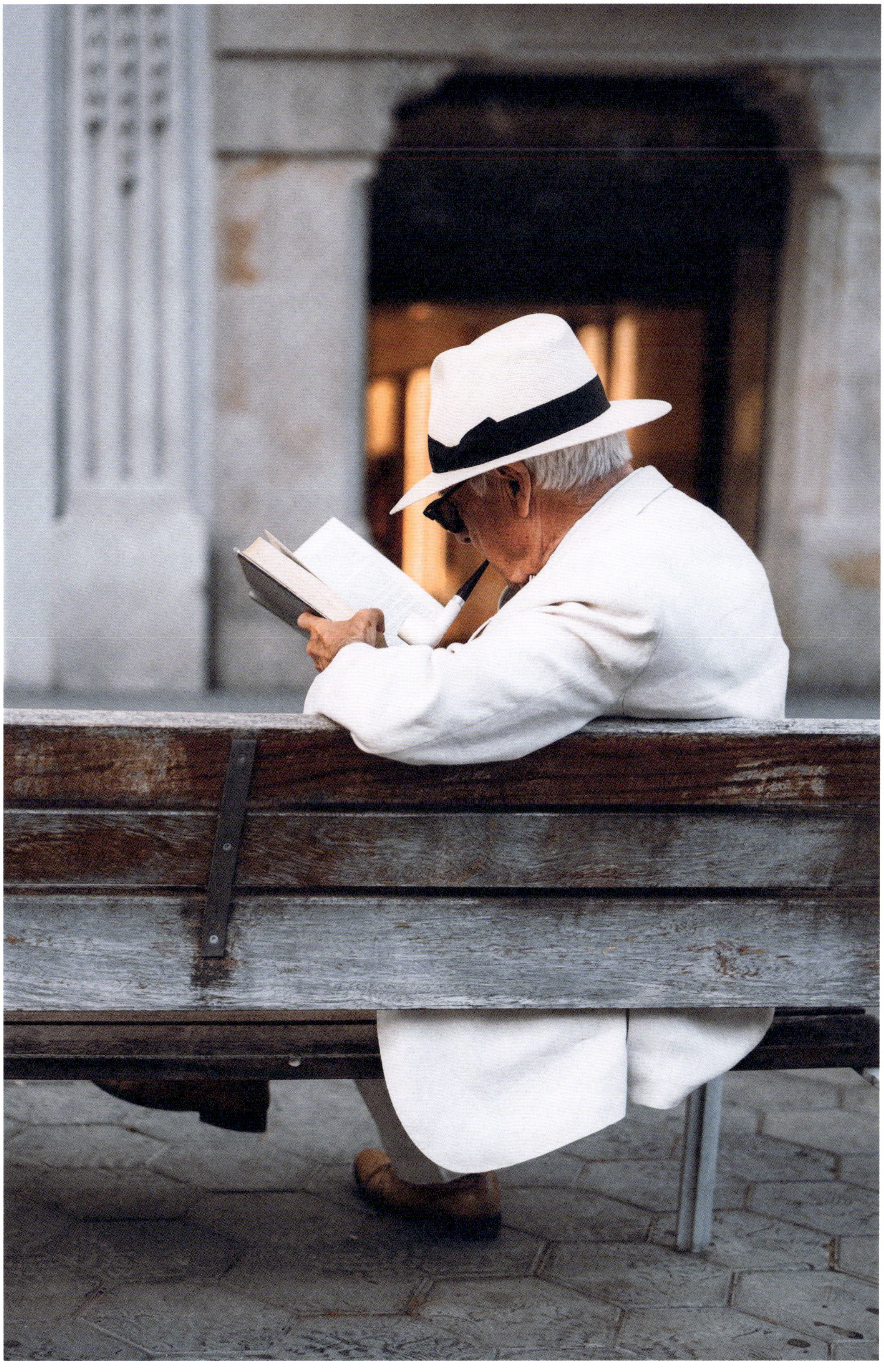

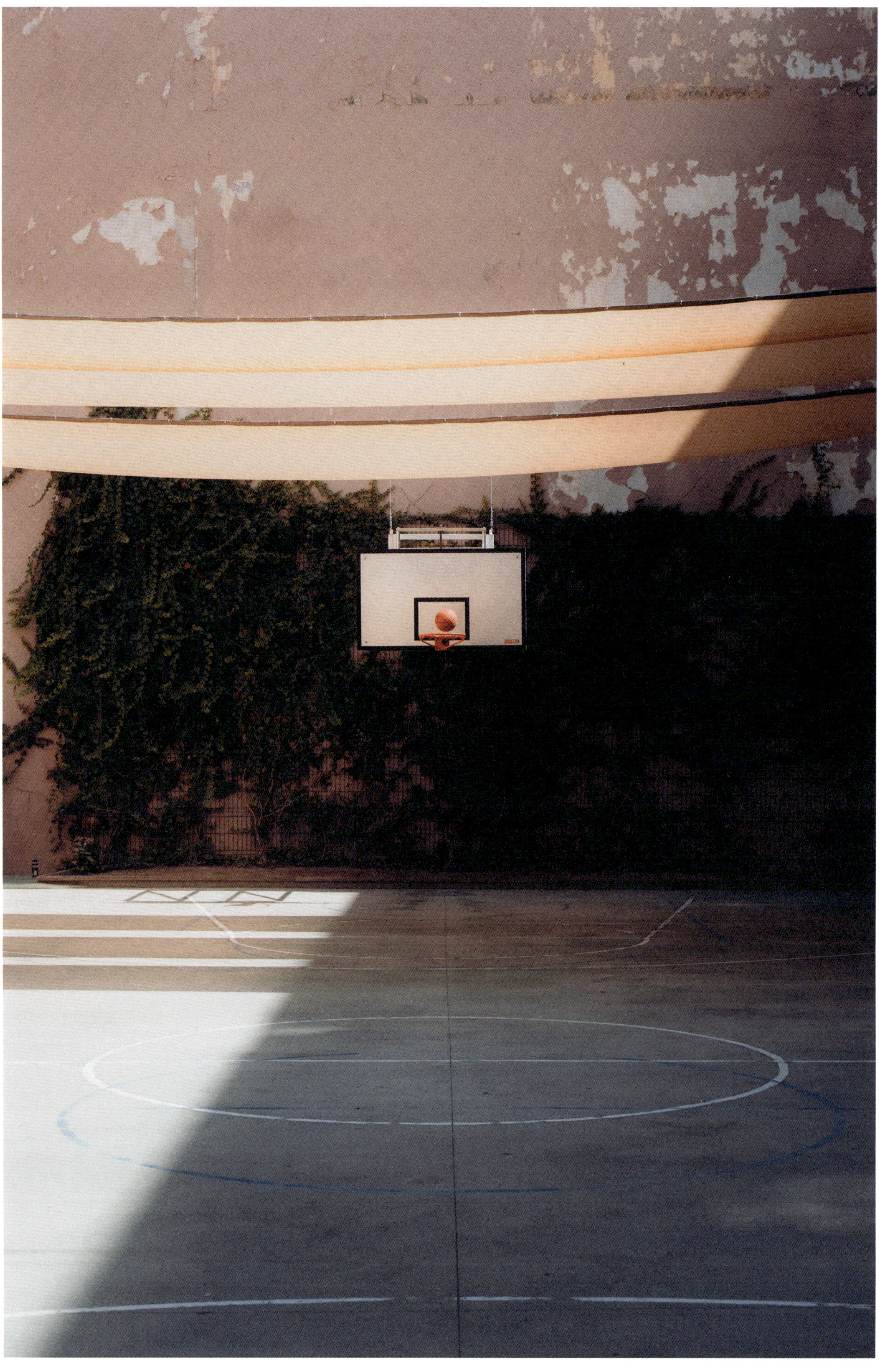

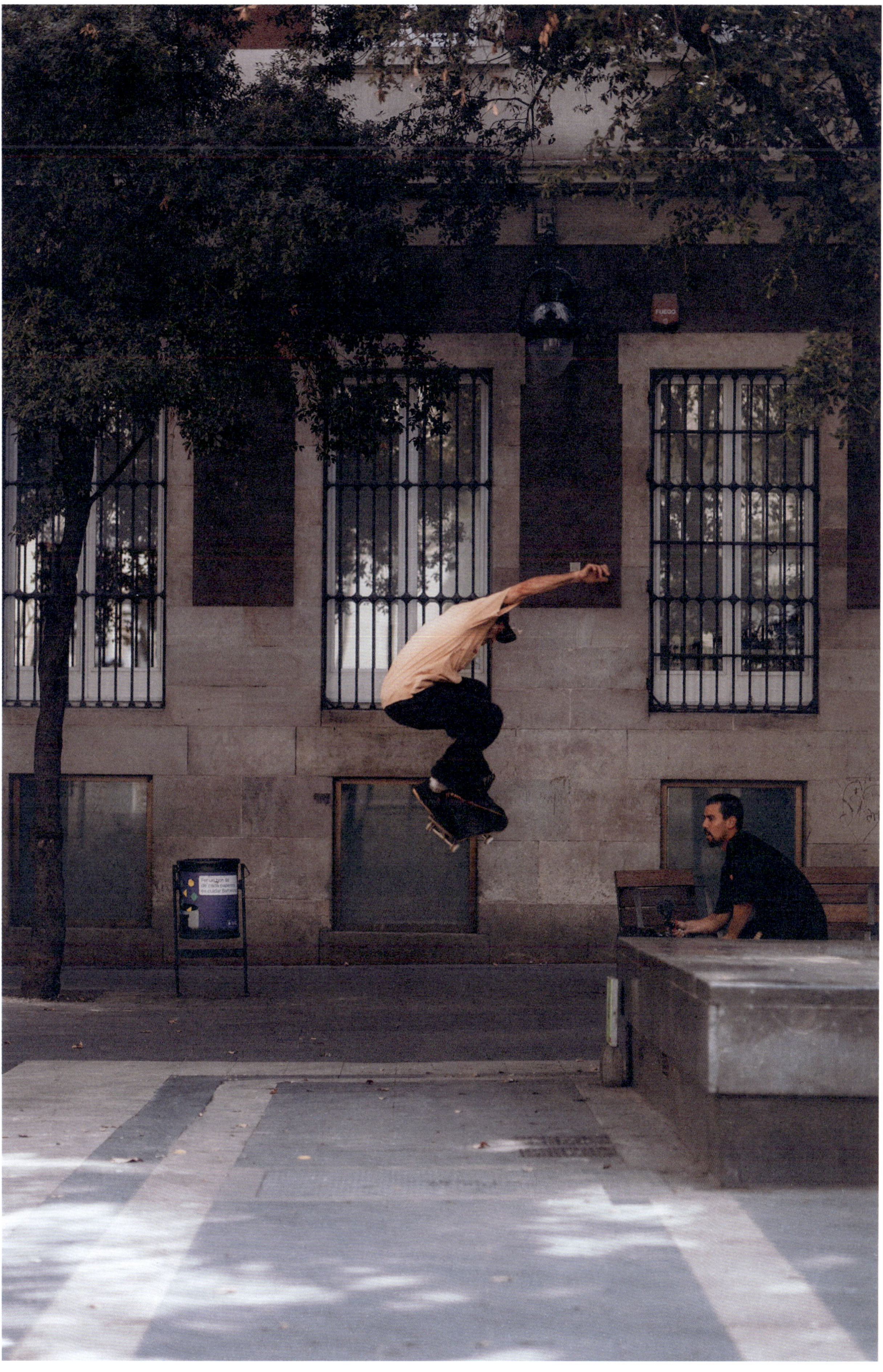

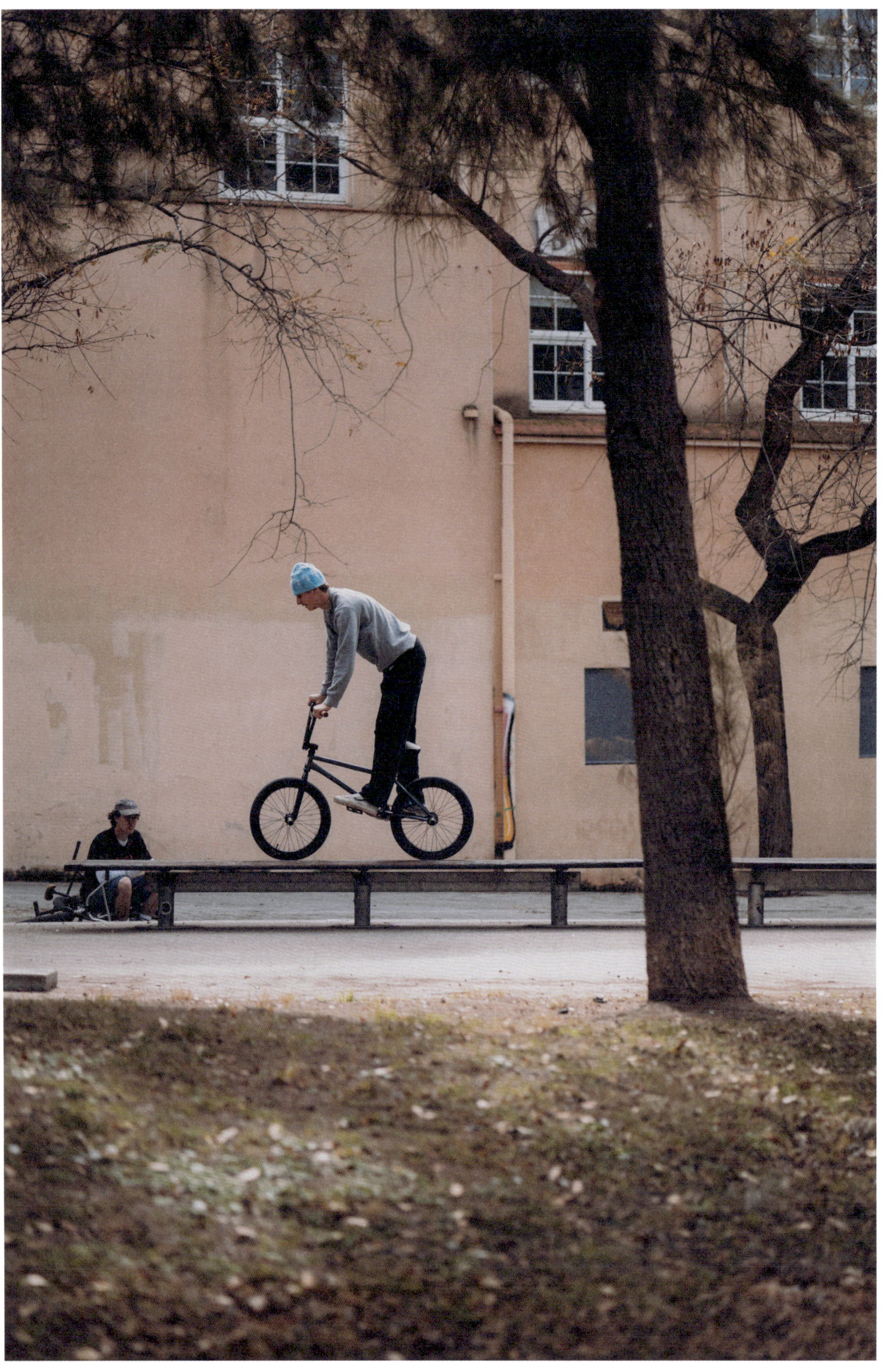

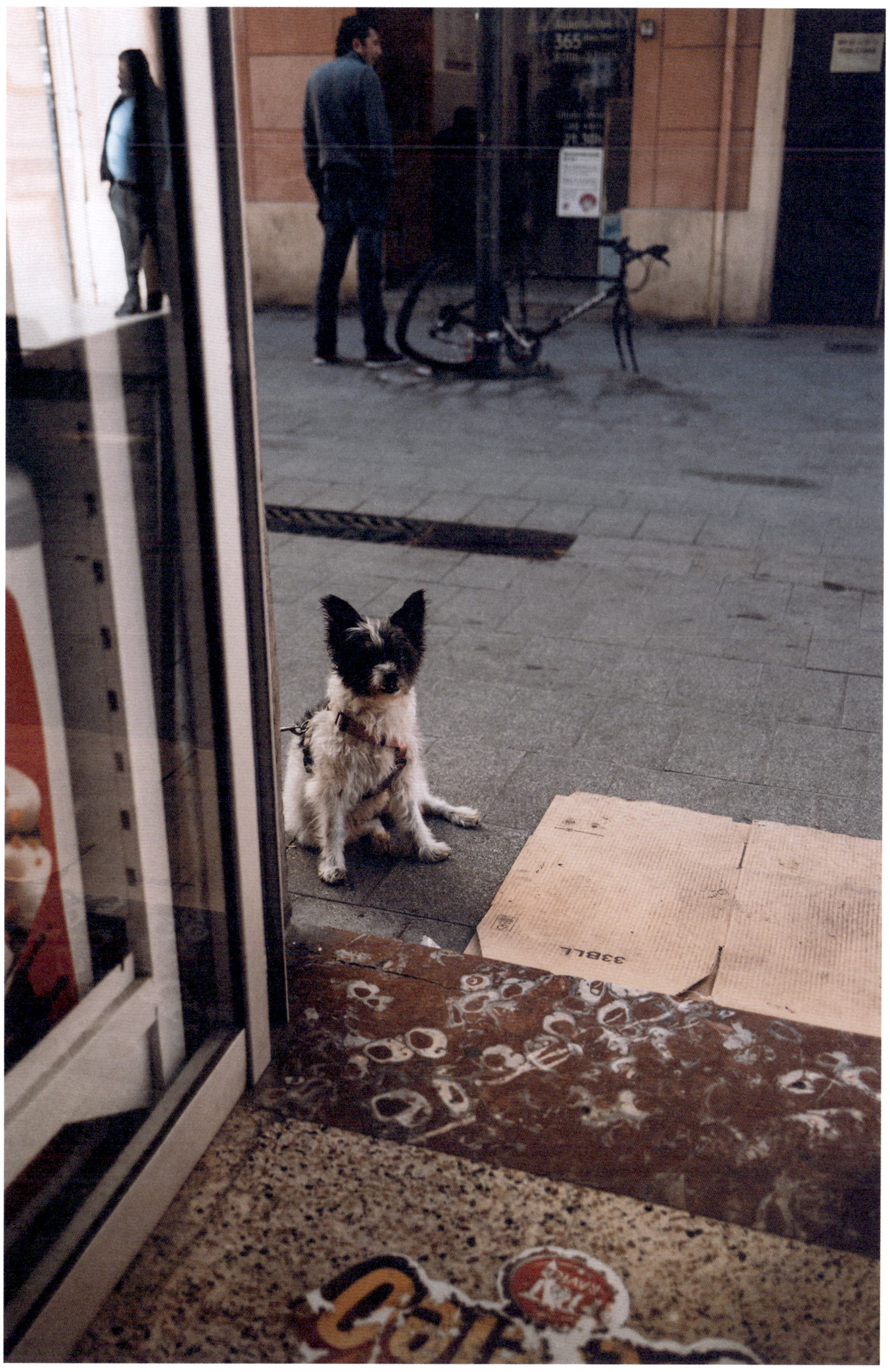
365

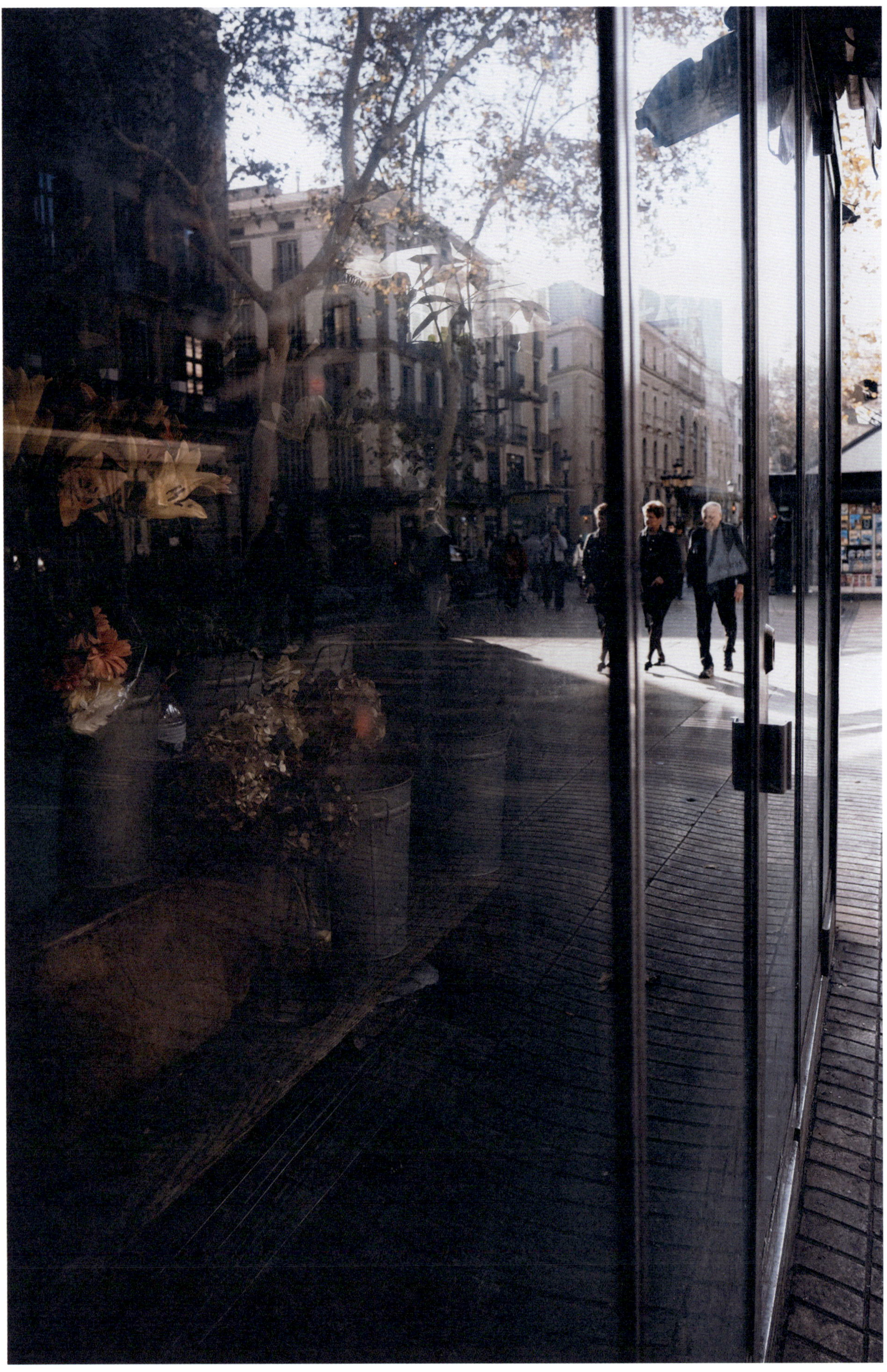

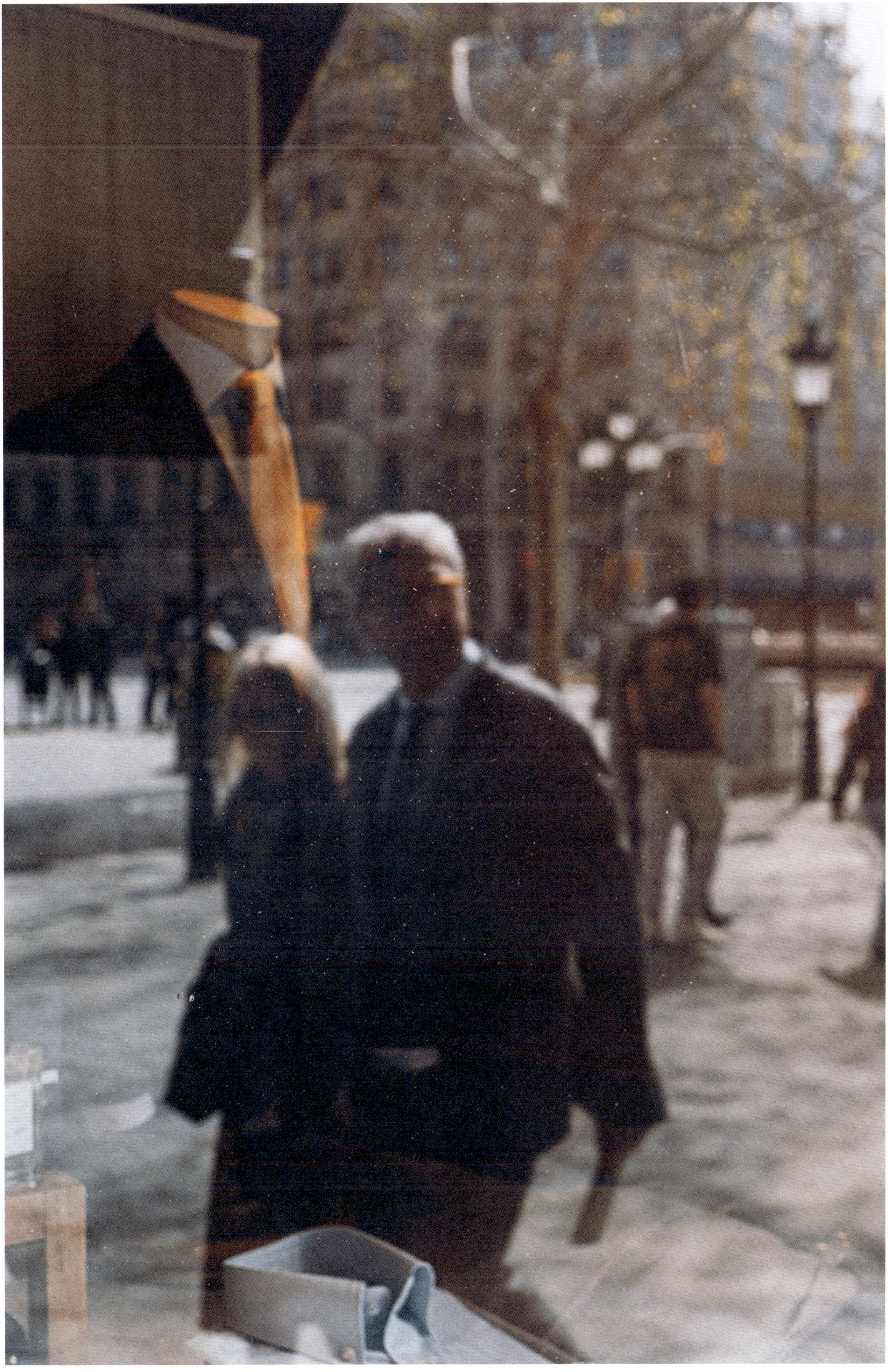

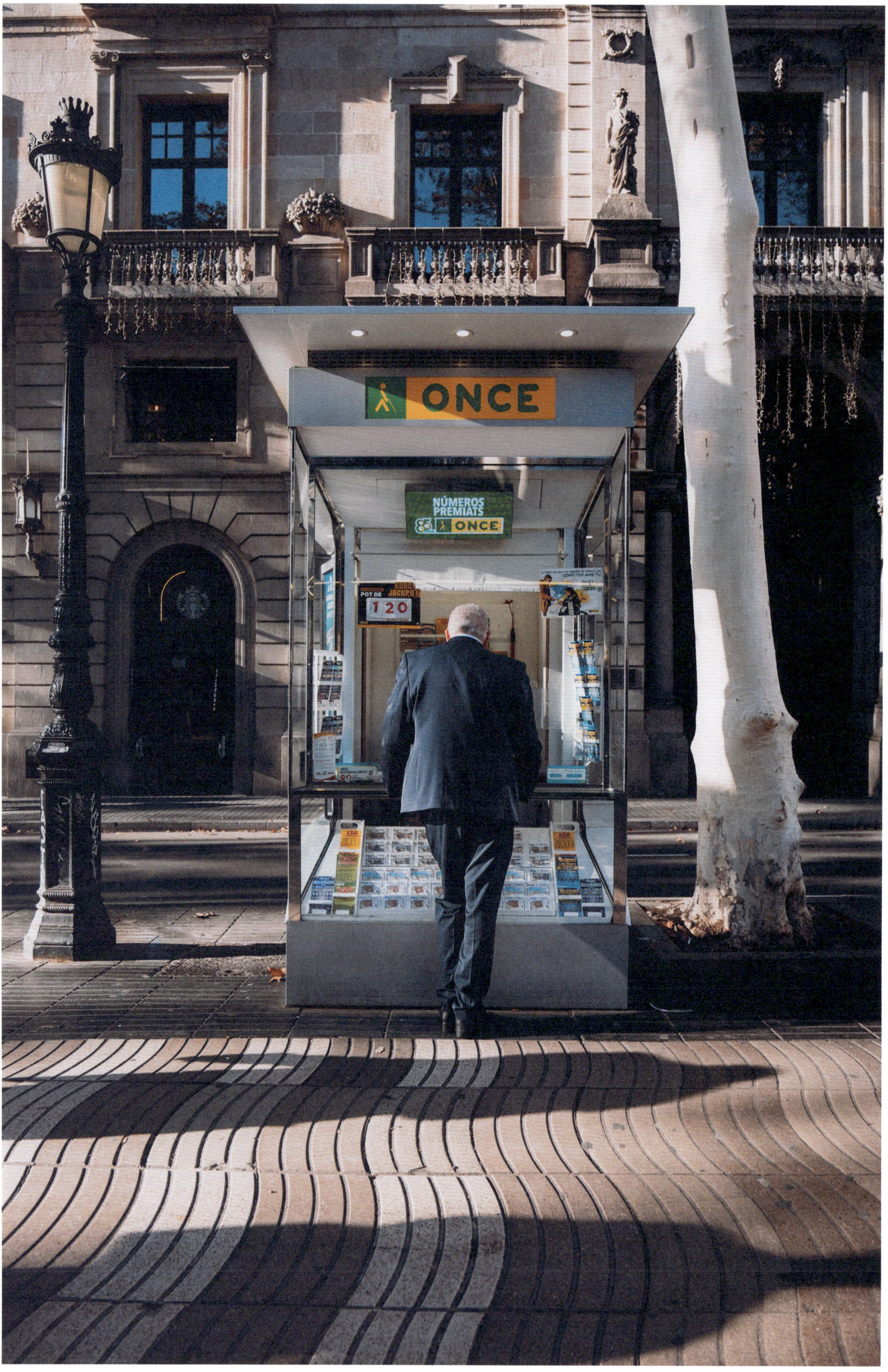
ONCE
NÚMEROS
PREMIATS
ONCE

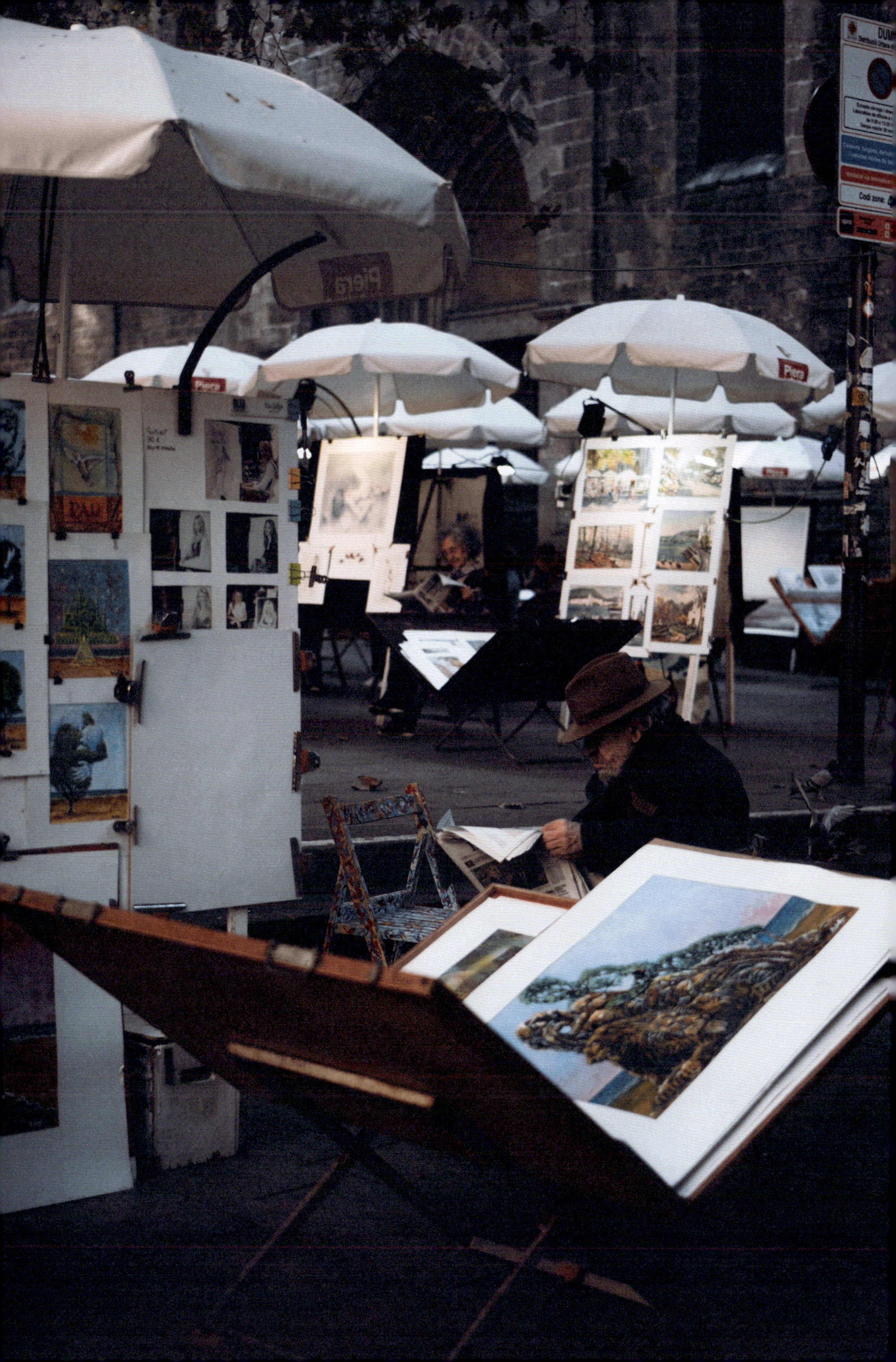
Piera

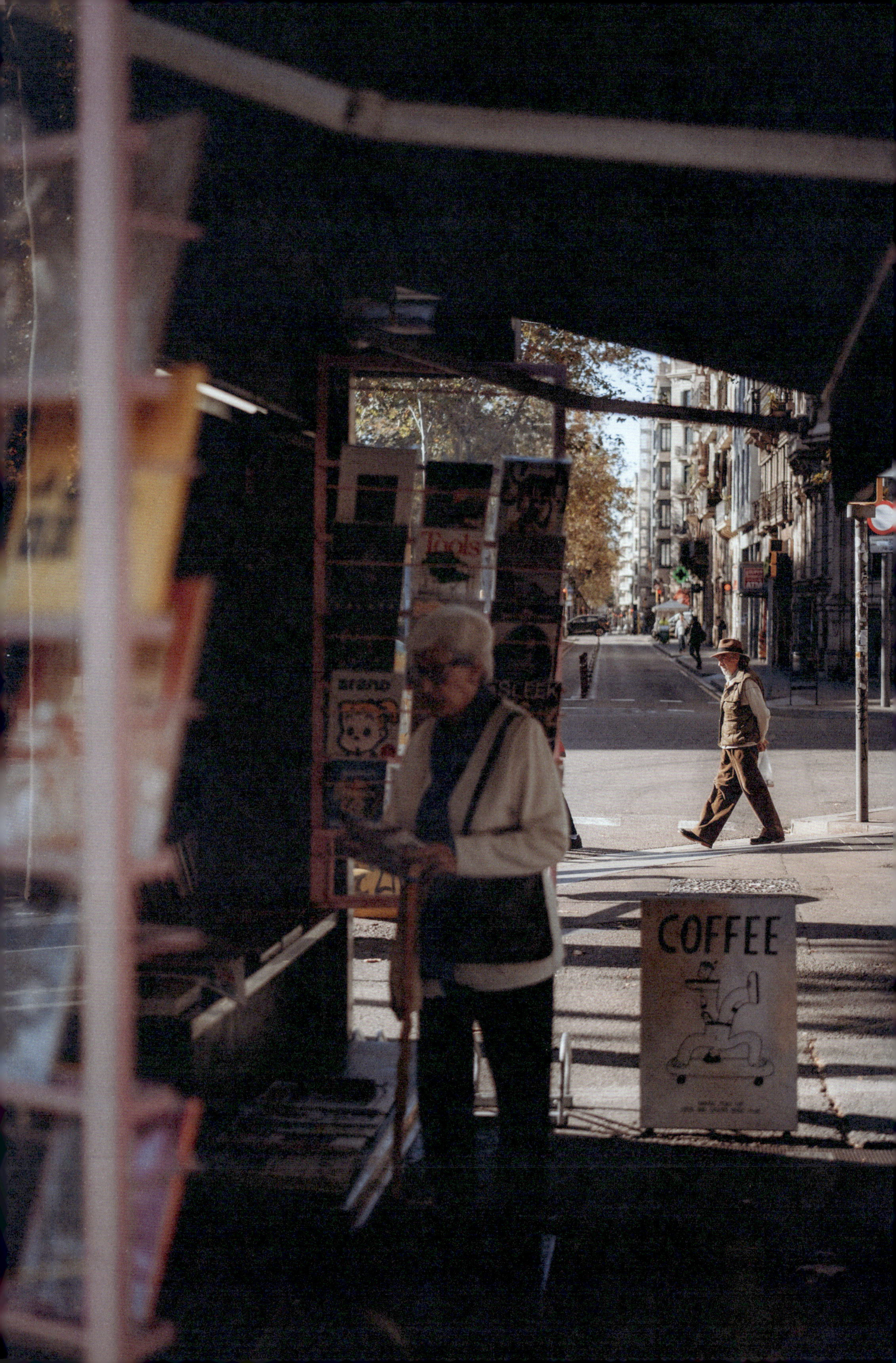
Tools
COFFEE

In Barcelona, every day begins slowly—coffee, light, conversation. Then the city picks up its beat, like a flamenco rhythm sneaking in around noon.

COLM TÓIBÍN

Irish Novelist

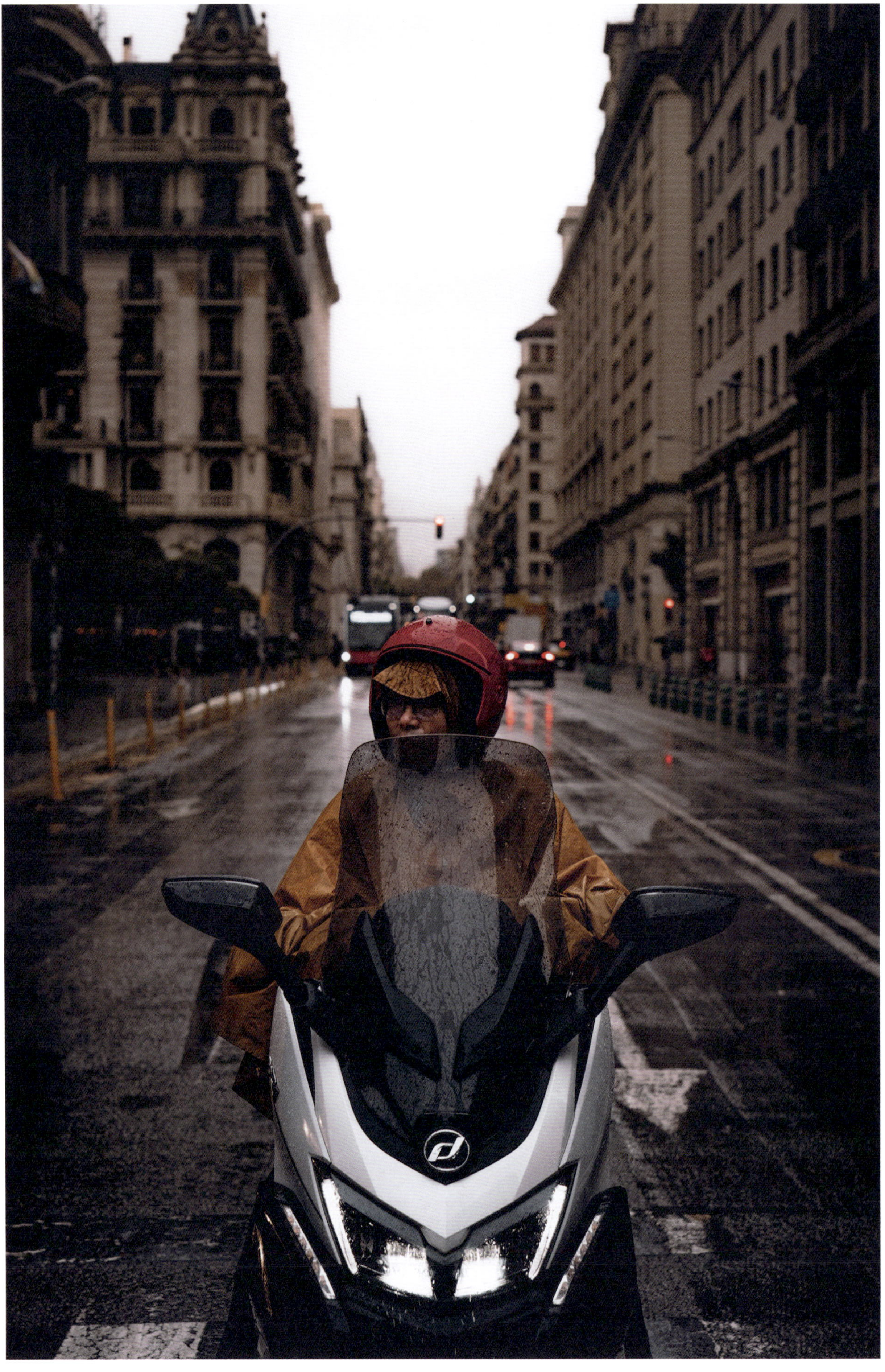

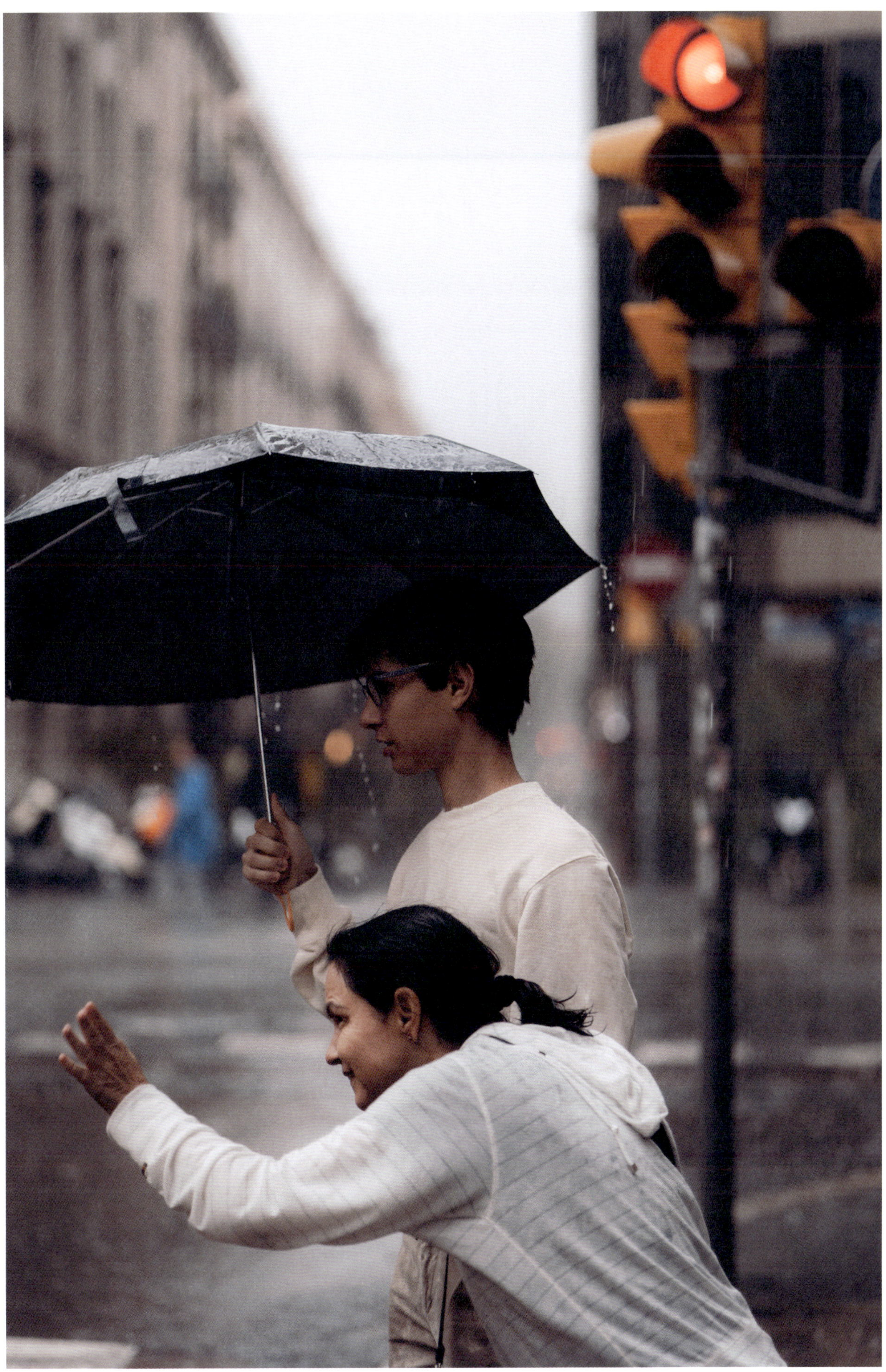

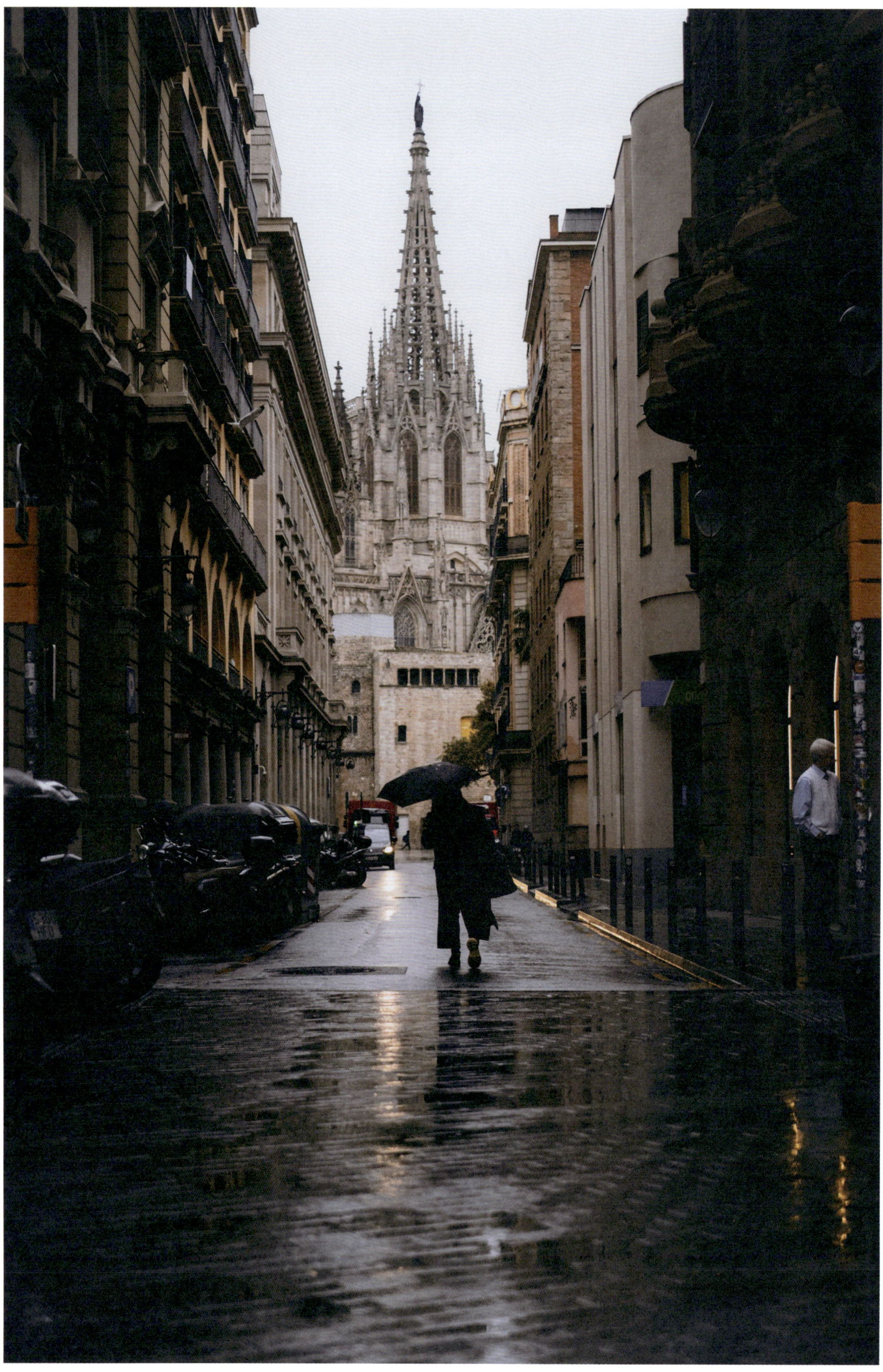

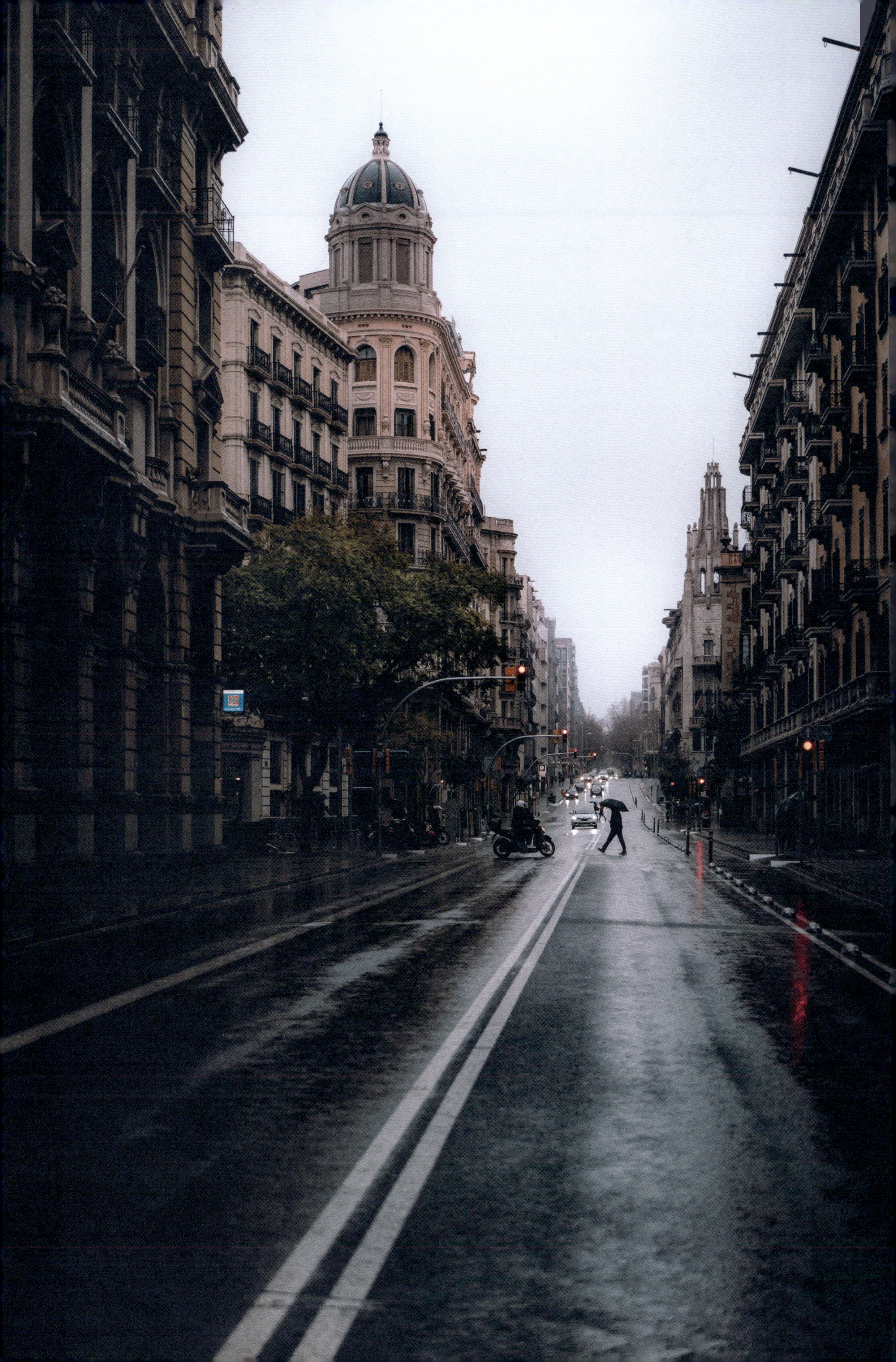

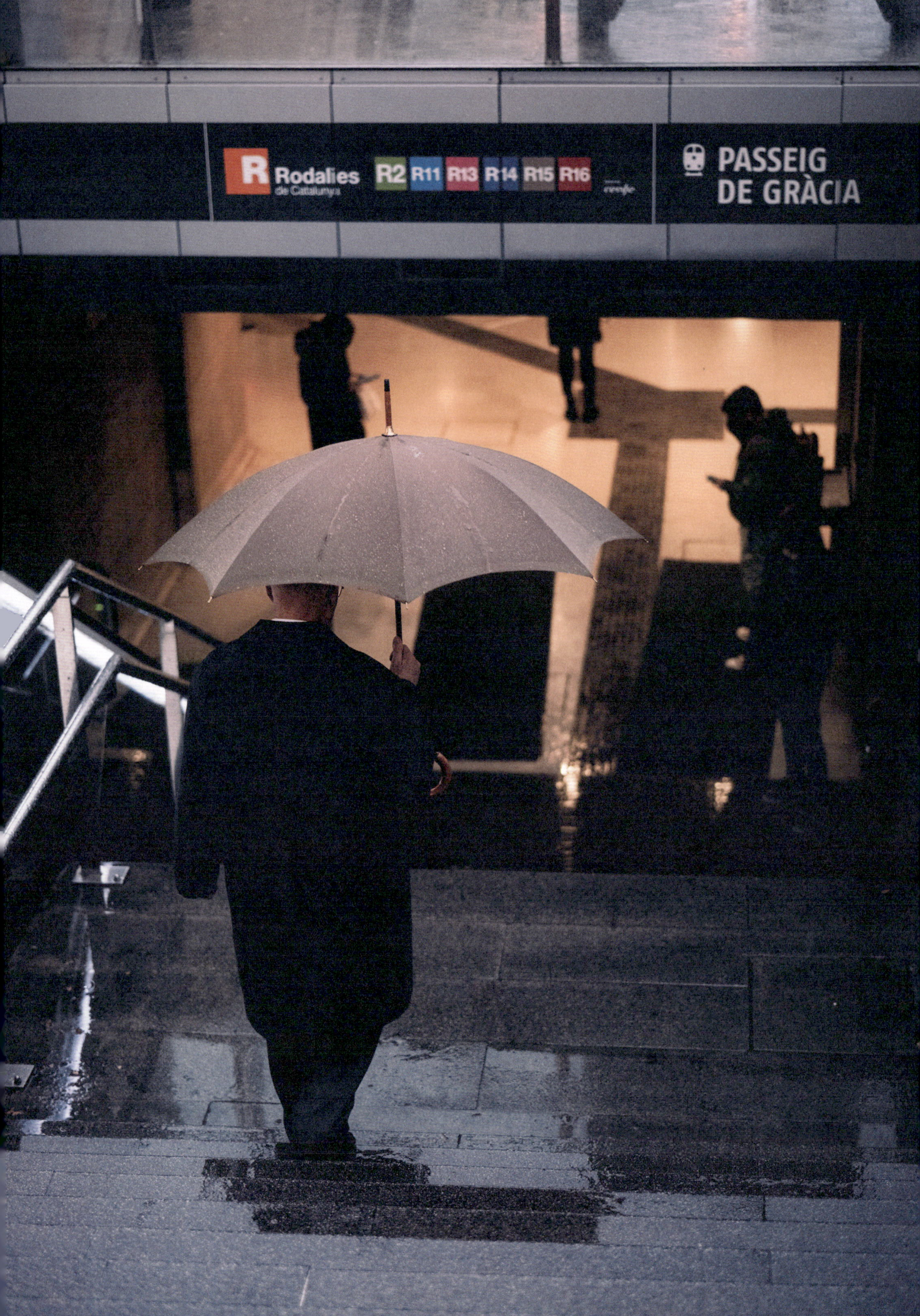
R Rodalies de Catalunya
R2 R11 R13 R14 R15 R16
PASSEIG DE GRÀCIA

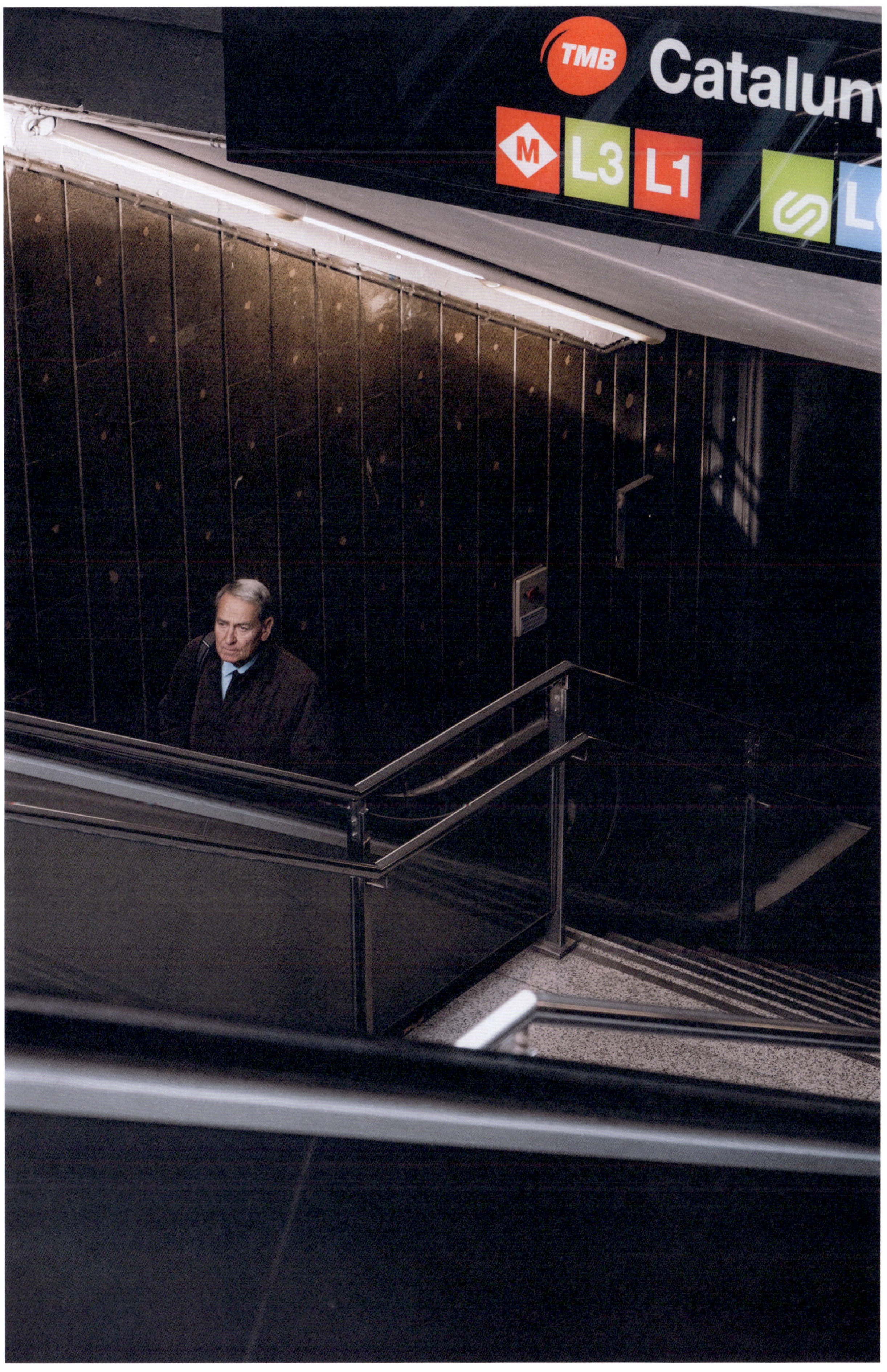
TMB
Catalun
M
L3
L1

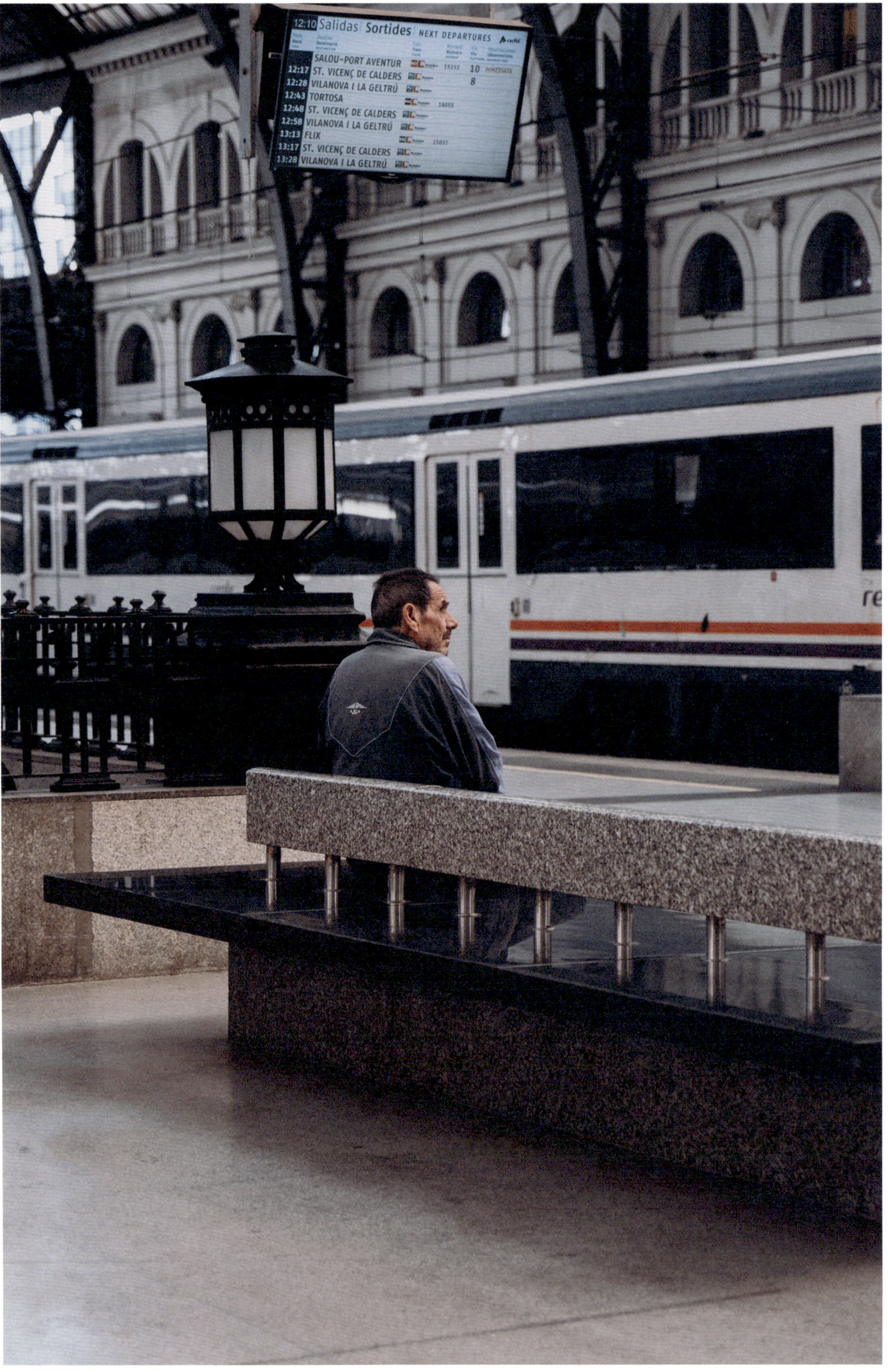
12:10 Salidas | Sortides | NEXT DEPARTURES
adif
SALOU-PORT AVENTUR 15233 10
12:17 ST. VICENÇ DE CALDERS 8
12:28 VILANOVA I LA GELTRÚ
12:43 TORTOSA 18055
12:48 ST. VICENÇ DE CALDERS
12:58 VILANOVA I LA GELTRÚ
13:13 FLIX 15037
13:17 ST. VICENÇ DE CALDERS
13:28 VILANOVA I LA GELTRÚ

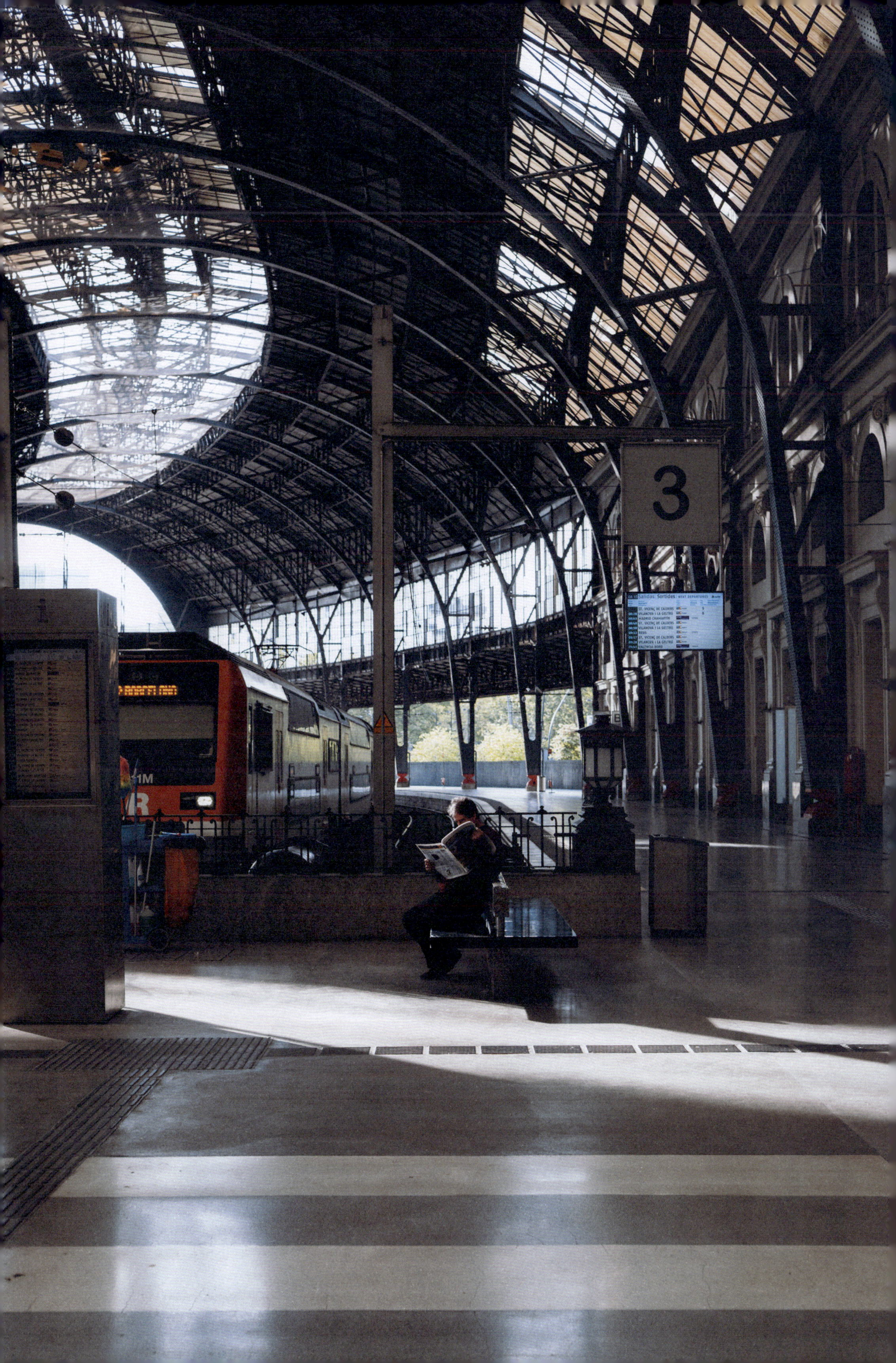
3

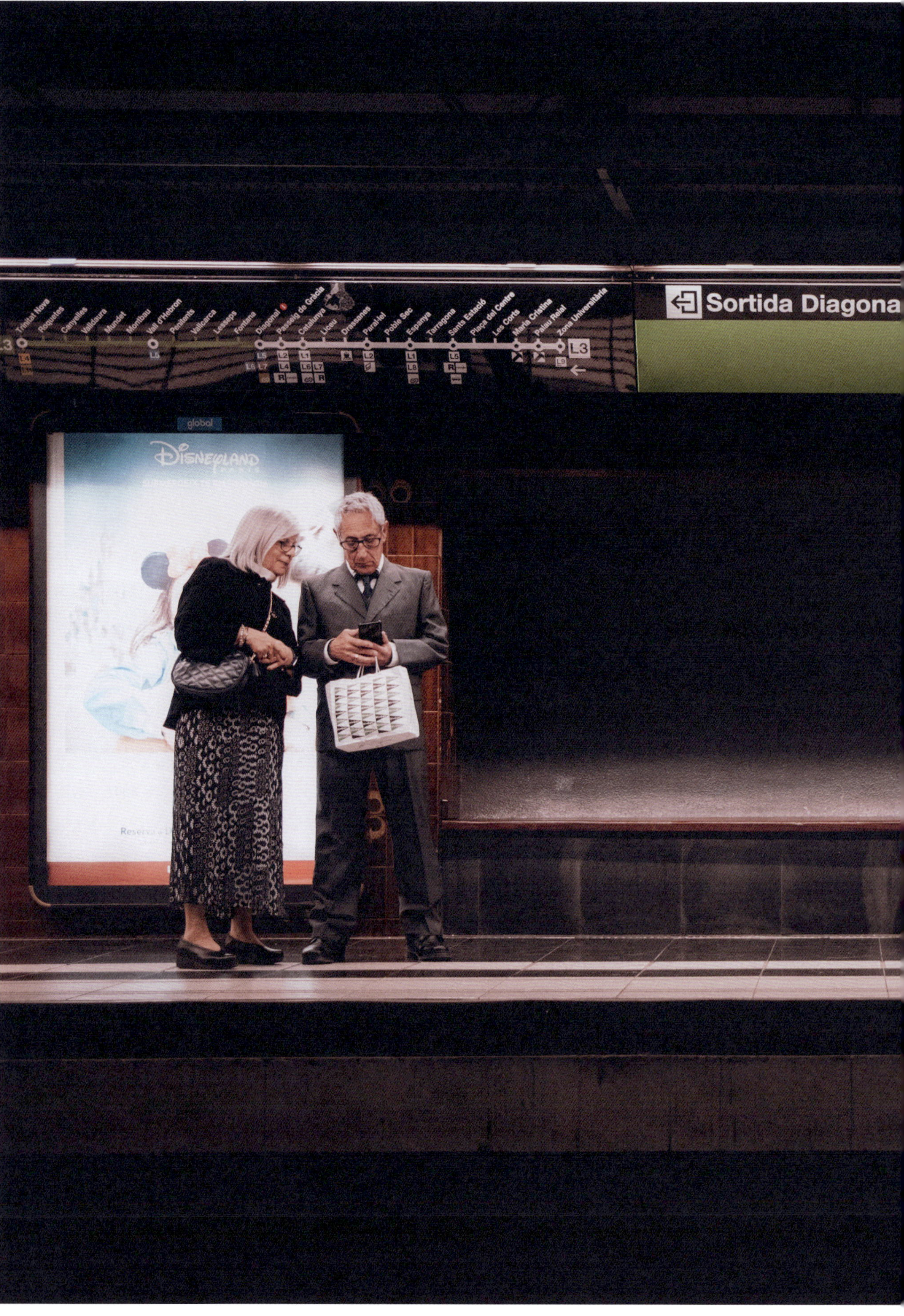

Sortida Diagona
L3
global
DISNEYLAND

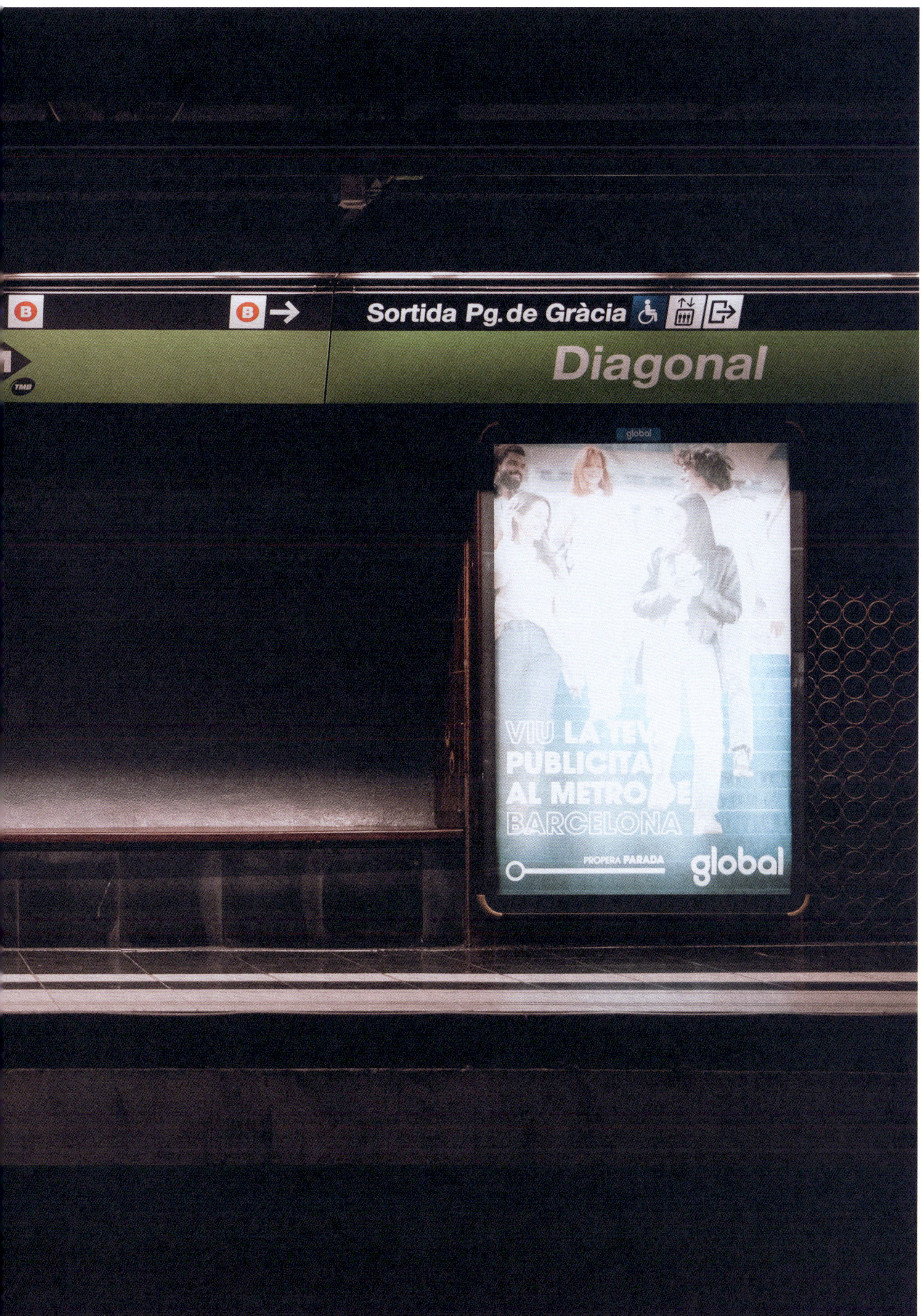
Sortida Pg.de Gràcia
Diagonal
TMB
global
VIU LA TEV
PUBLICITA
AL METRO
BARCELONA
PROPERA PARADA
global

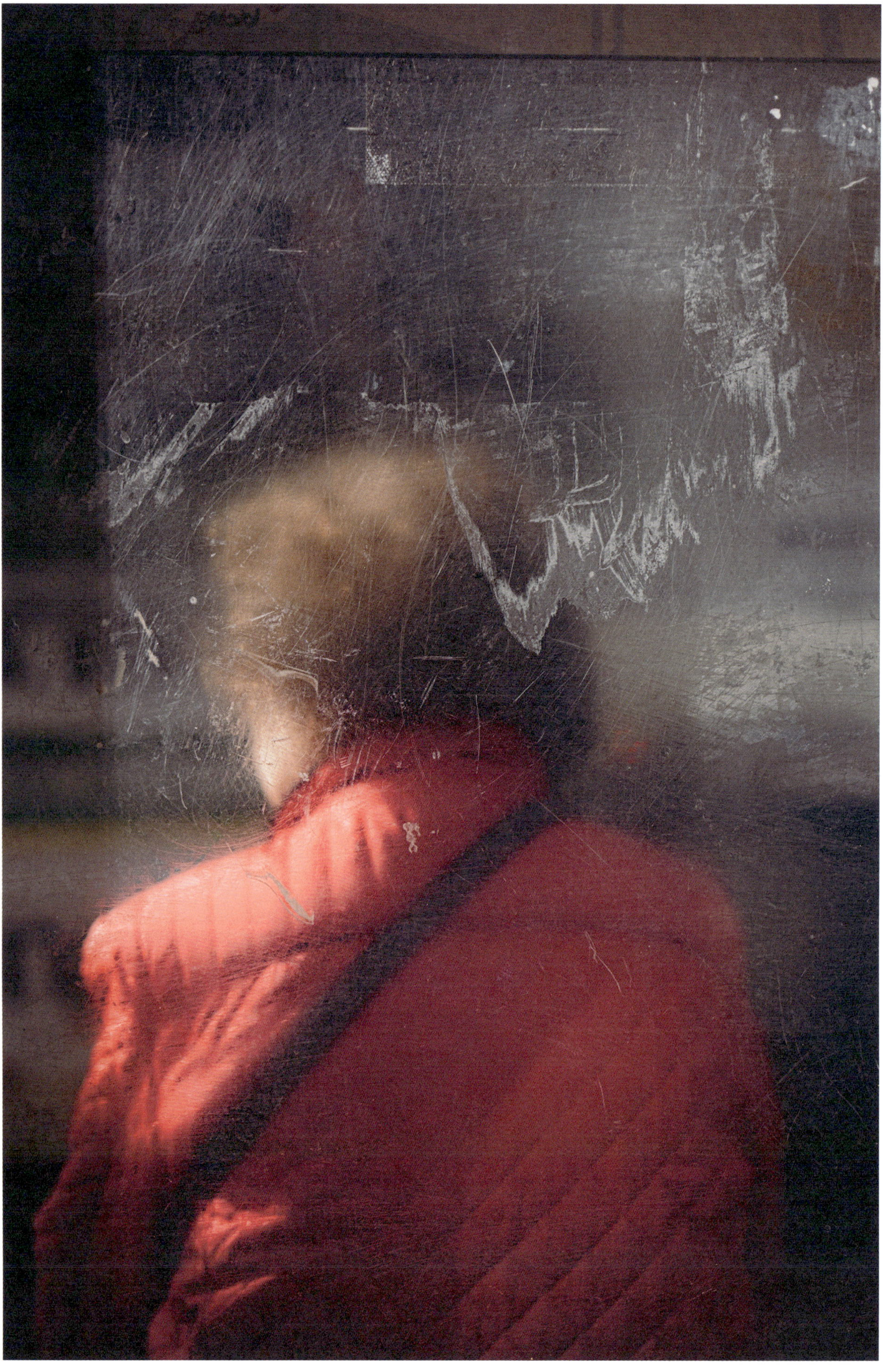

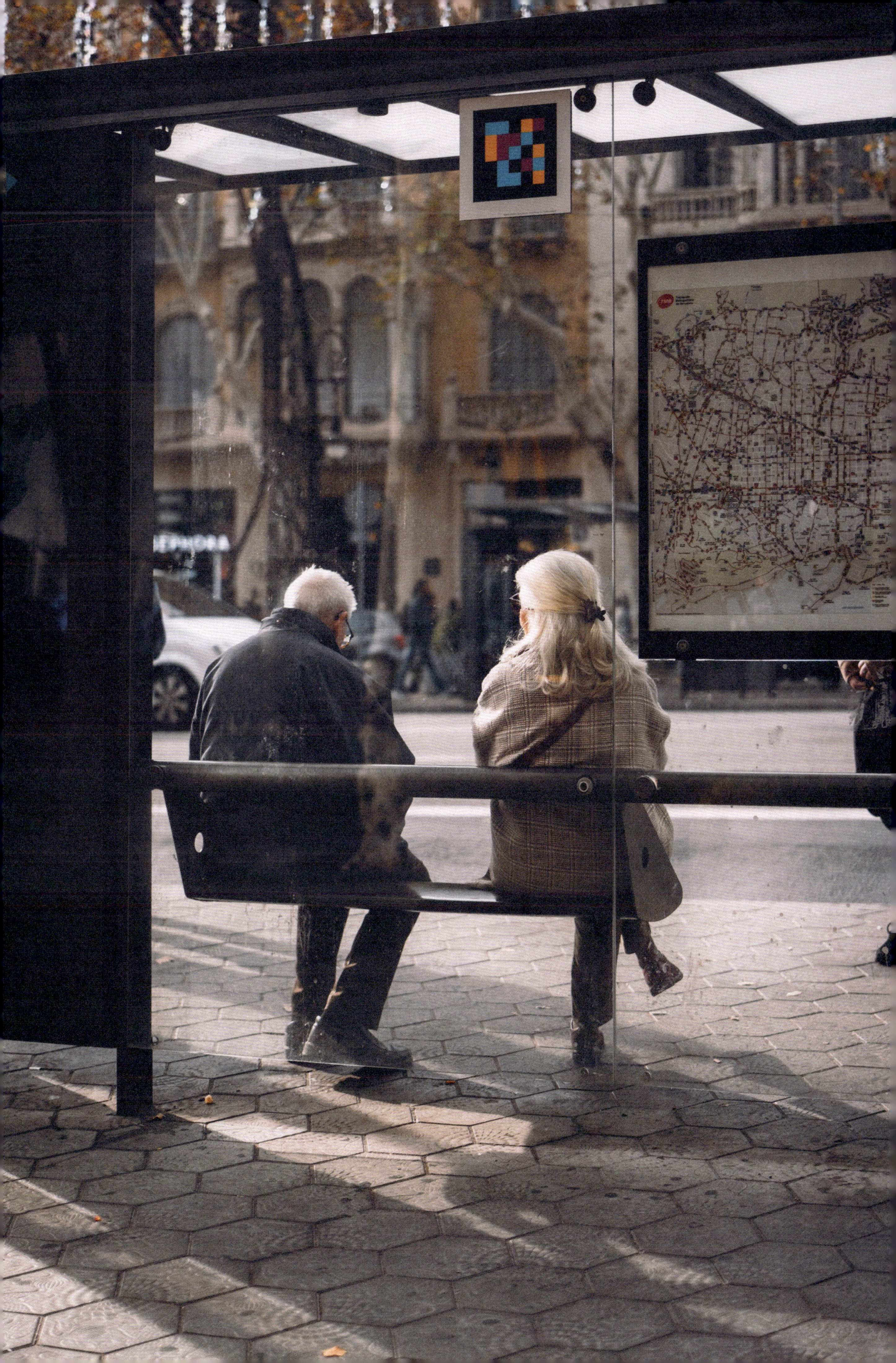

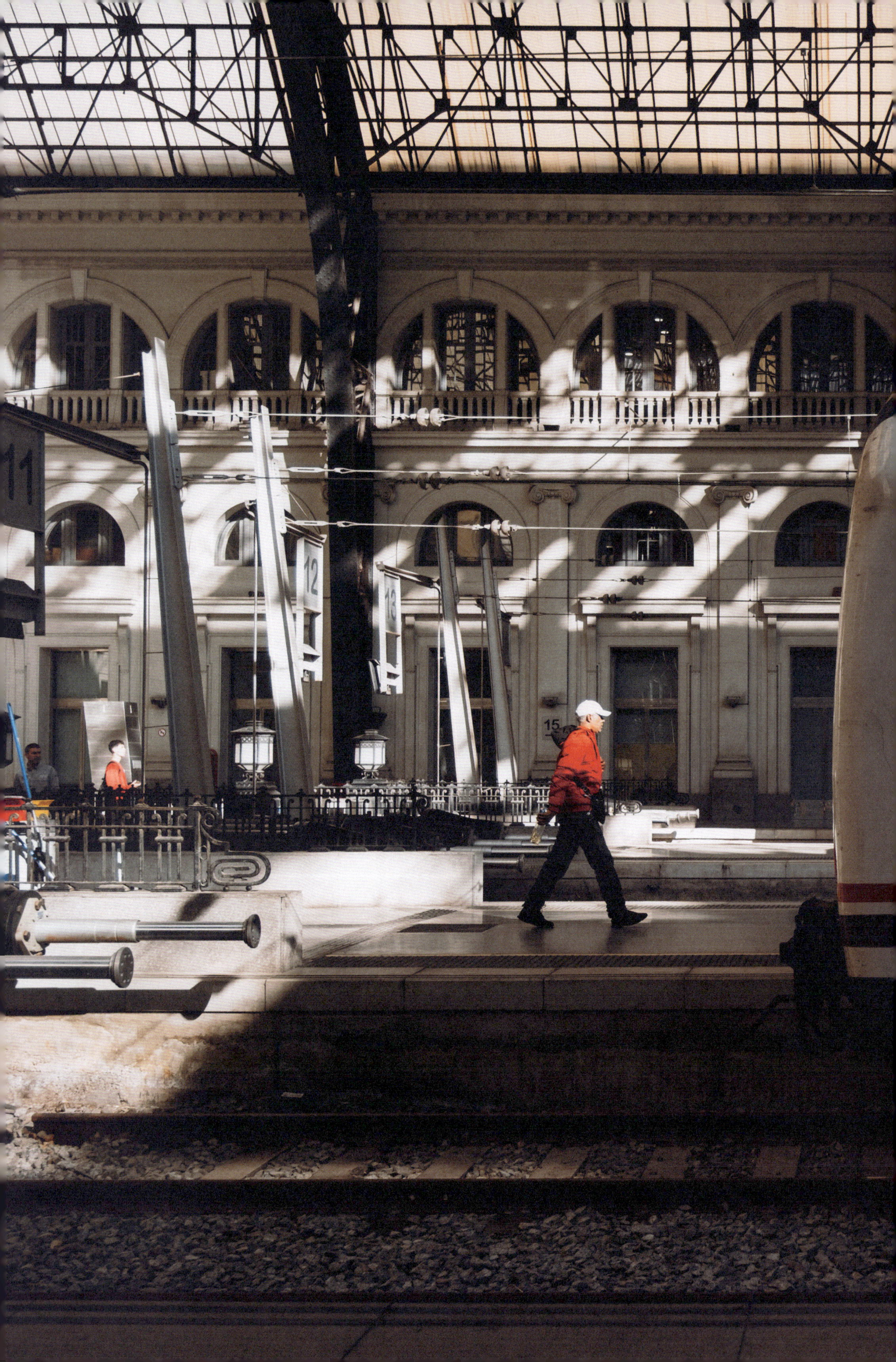
11
12
13
15

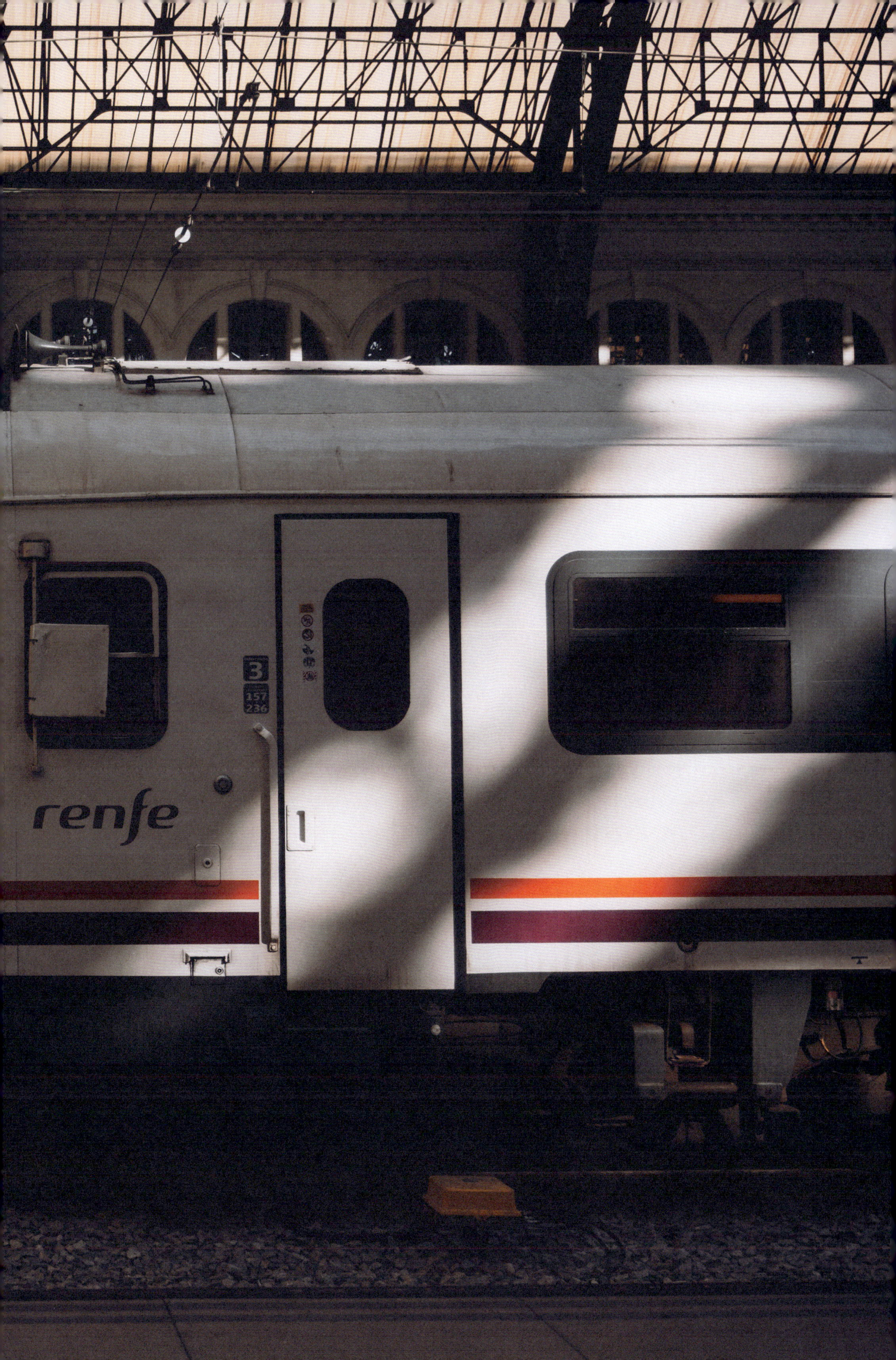
renfe
3
157
236

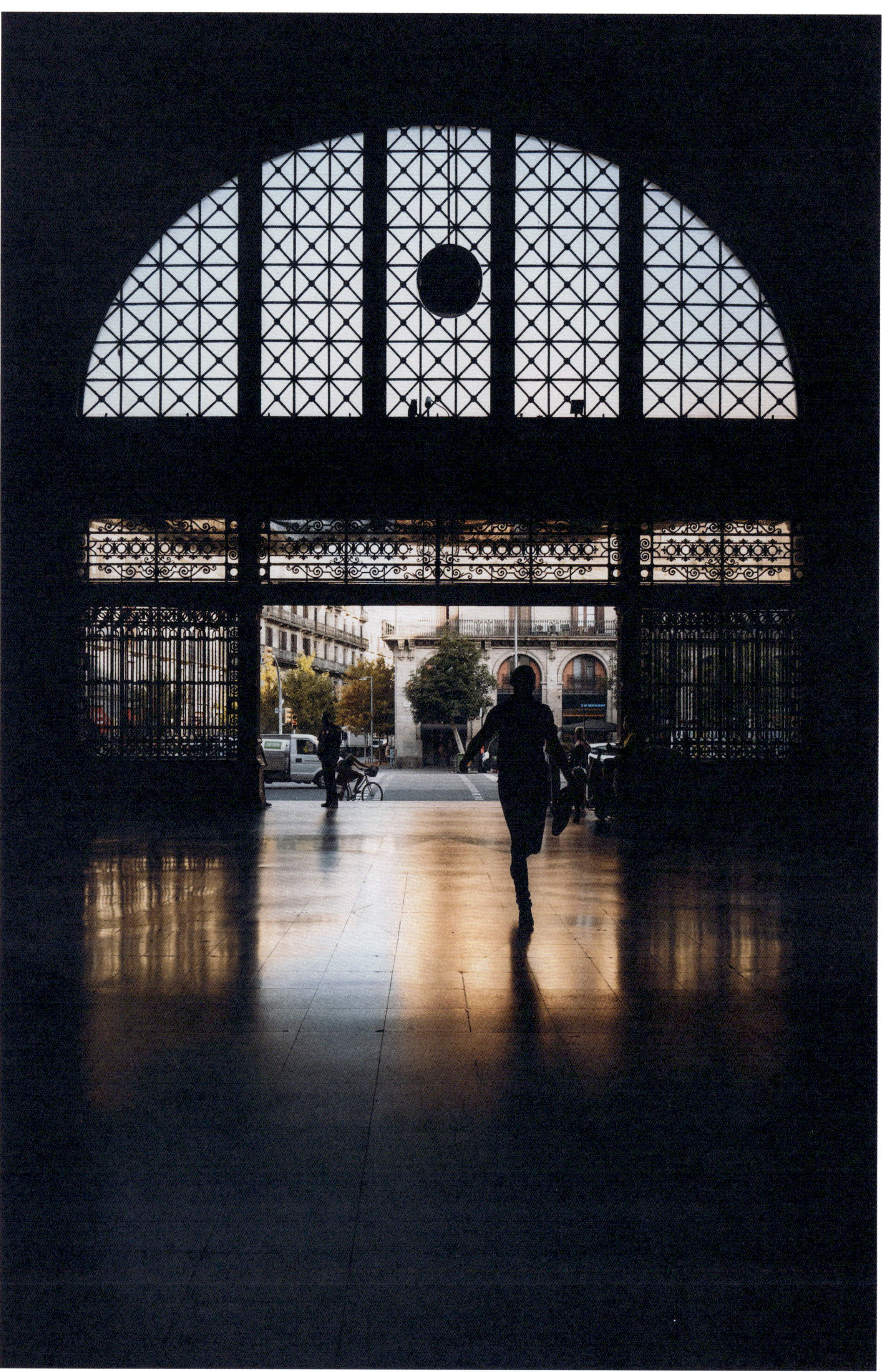

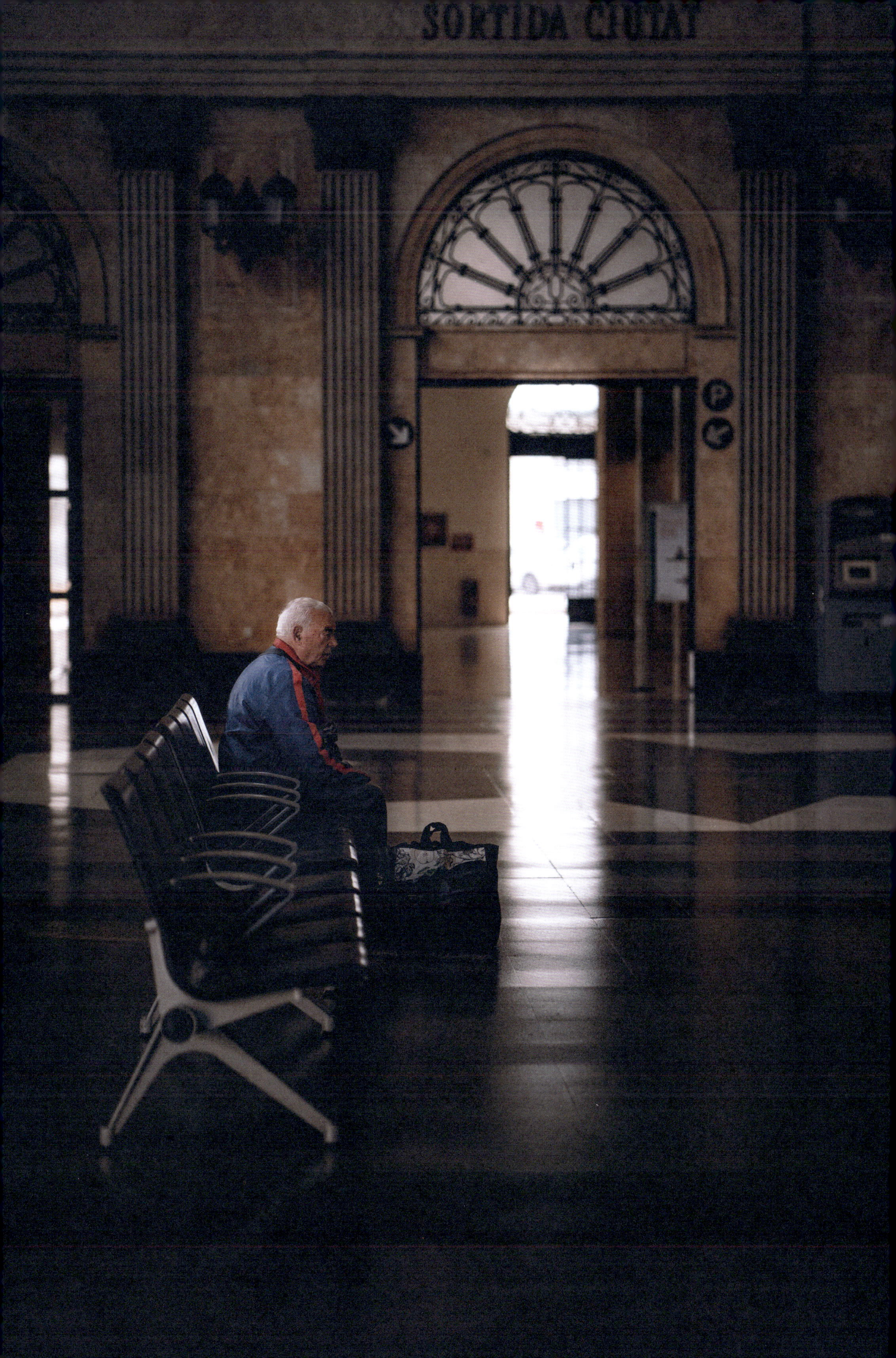
SORTIDA CIUTAT

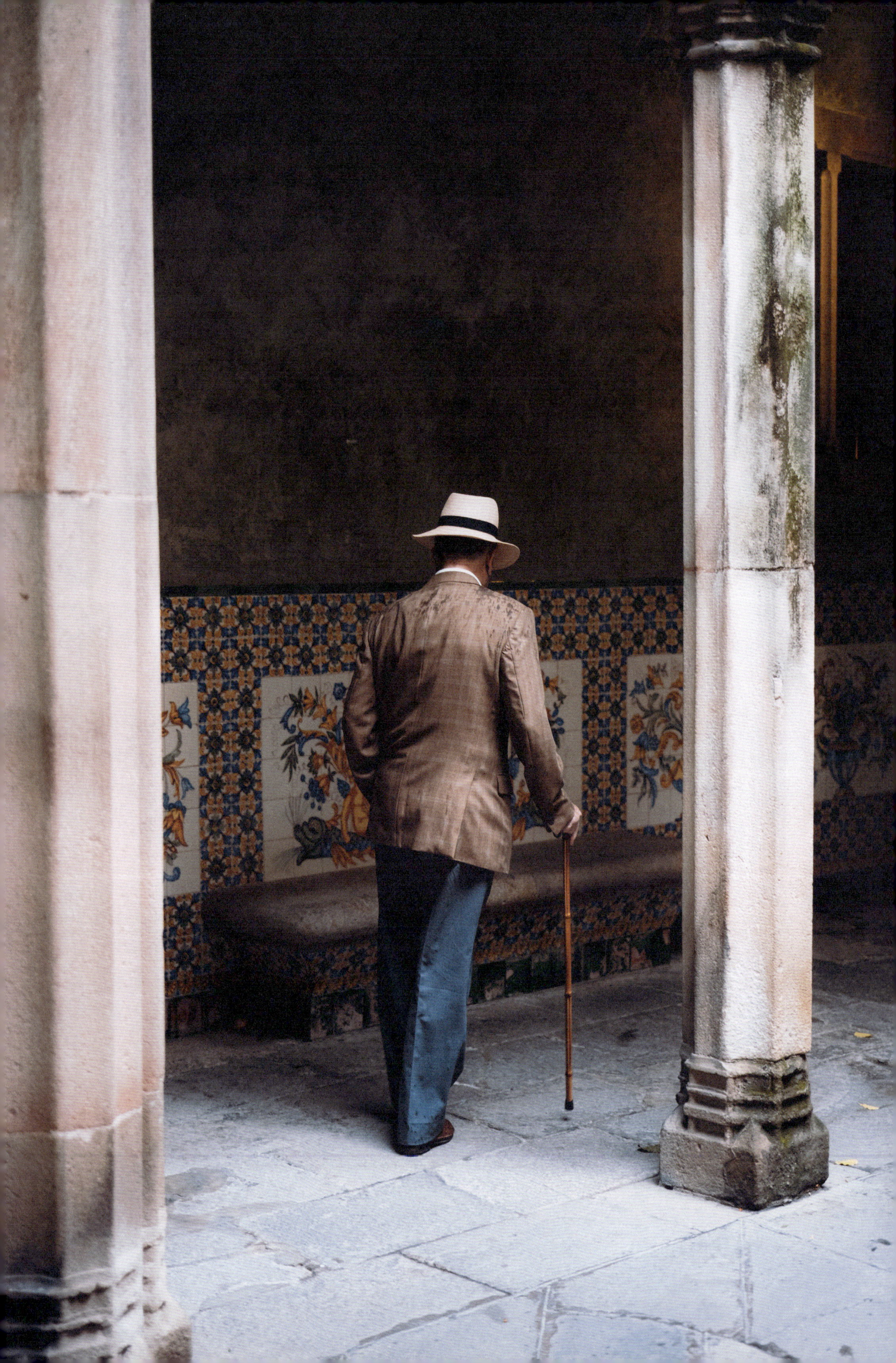

To travel across Spain and finally to reach Barcelona is like drinking a respectable red wine and finishing up with a bottle of champagne.

JAMES A. MICHENER

American Writer

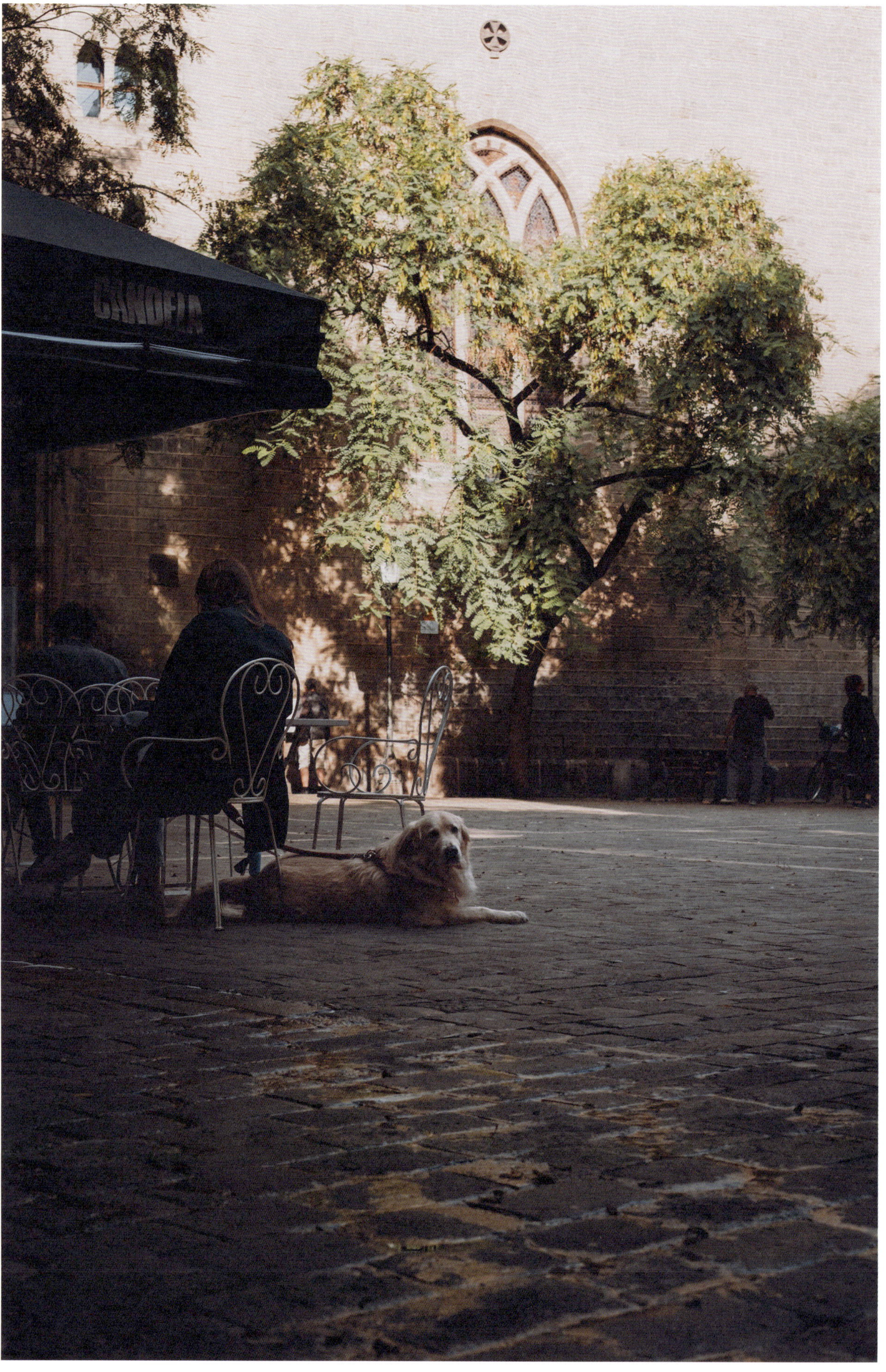

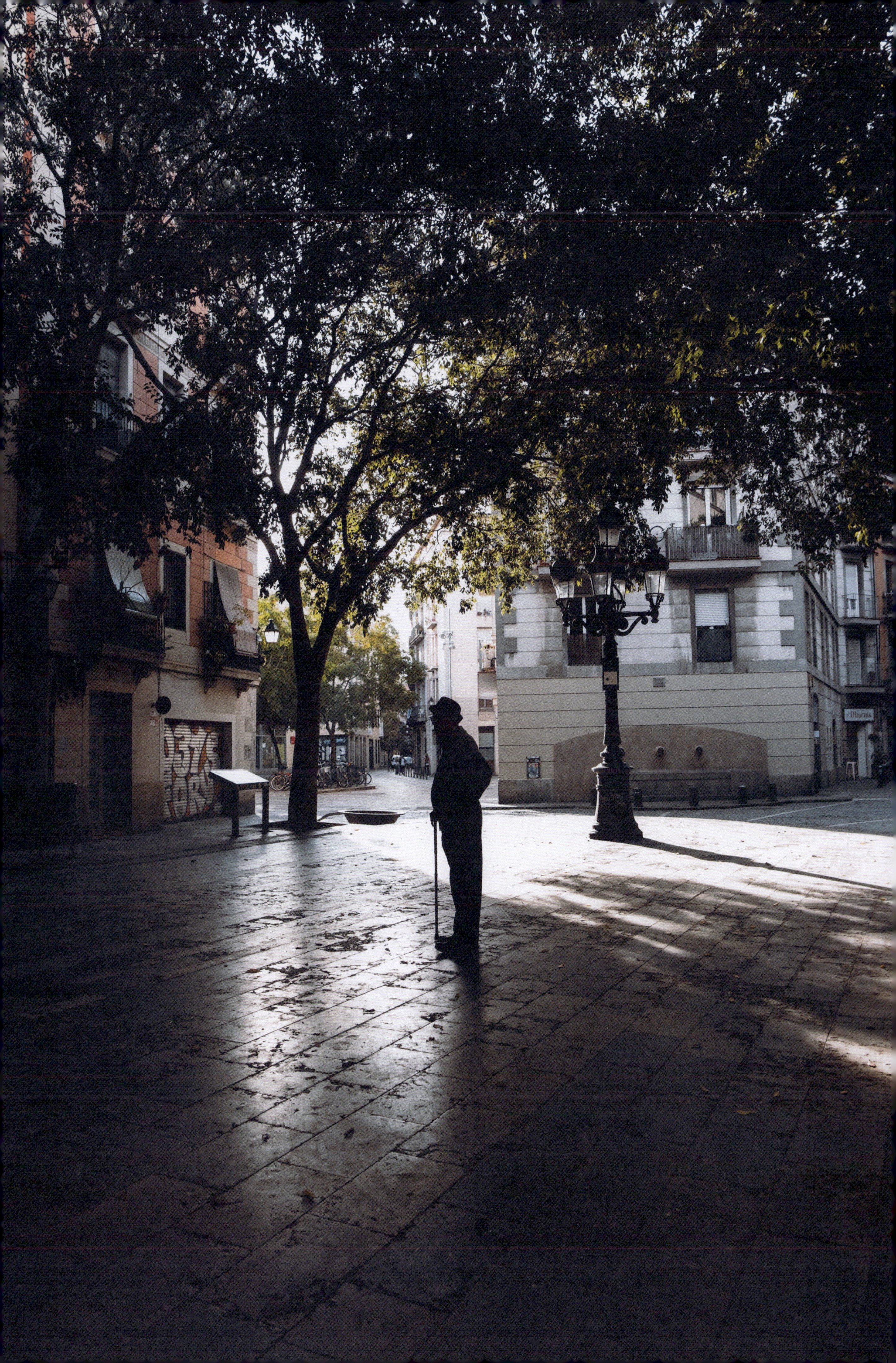

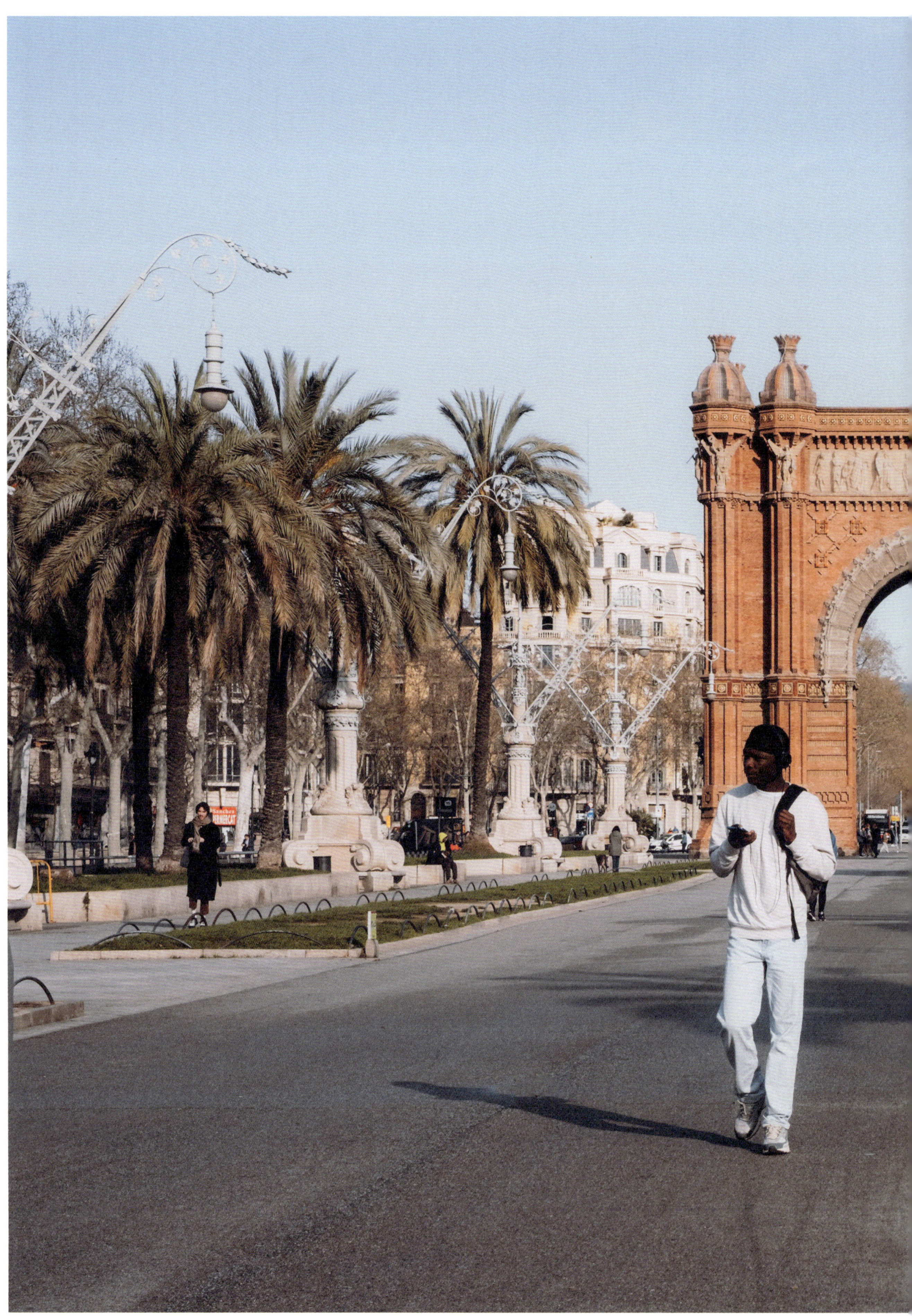

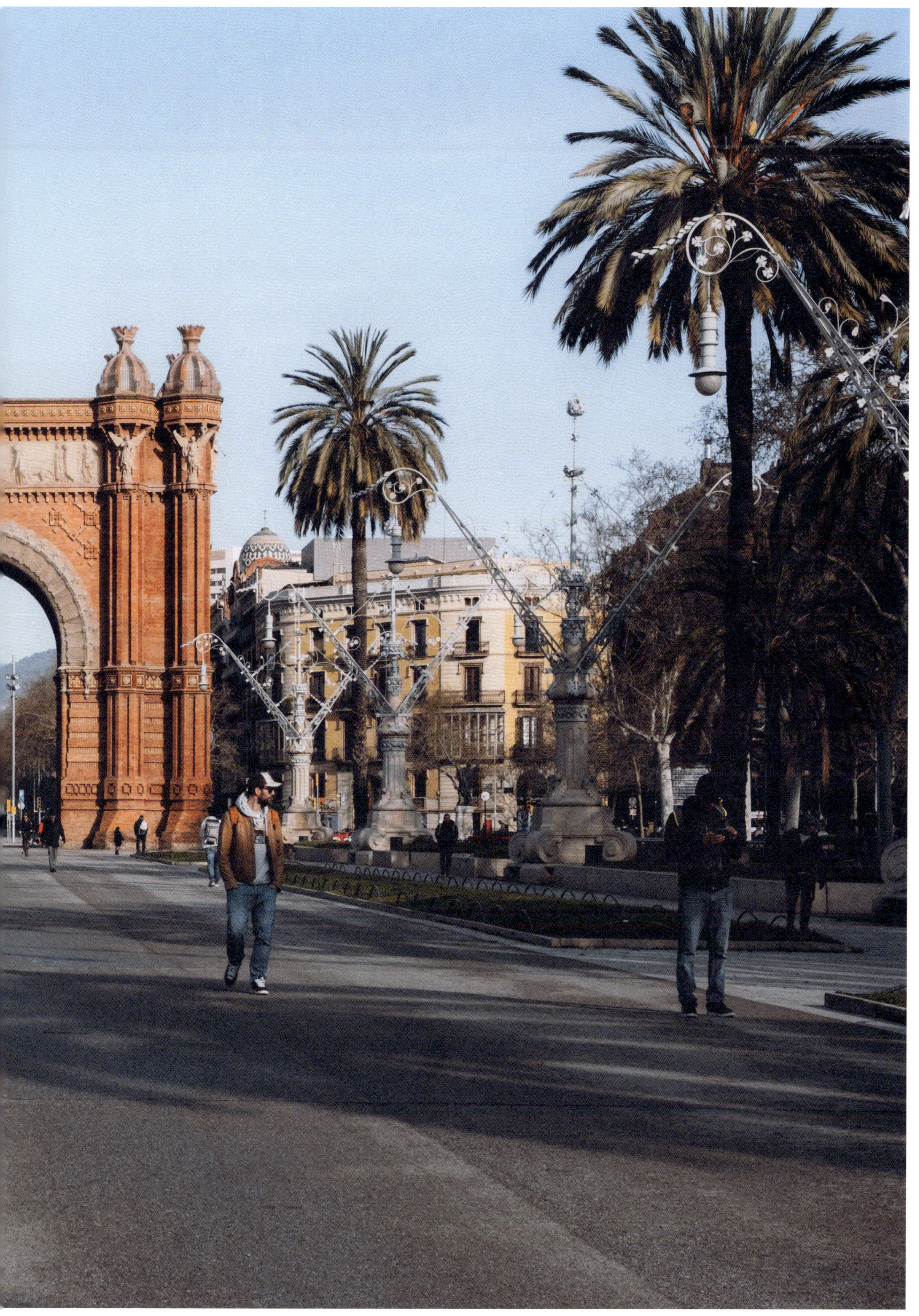

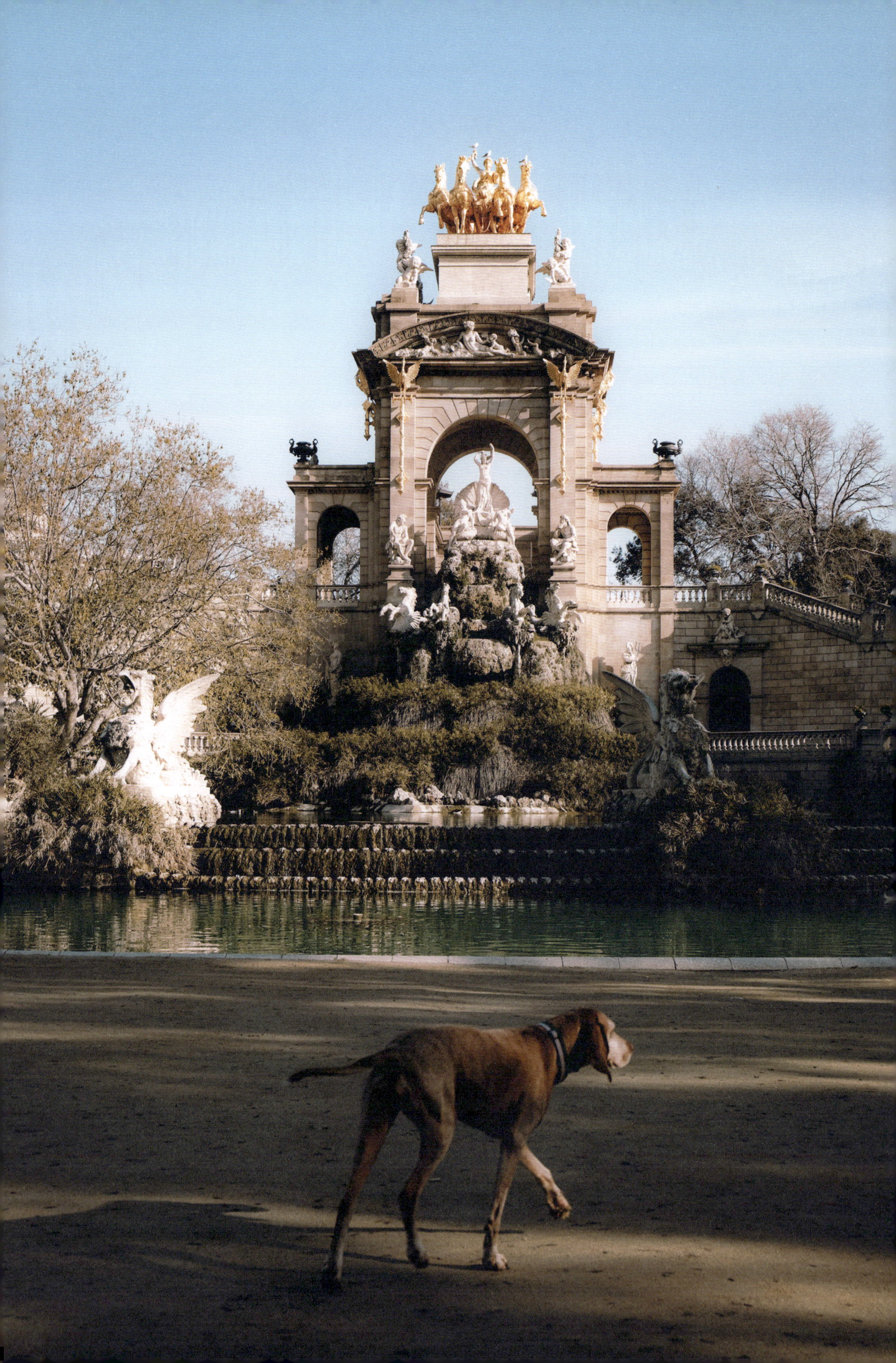

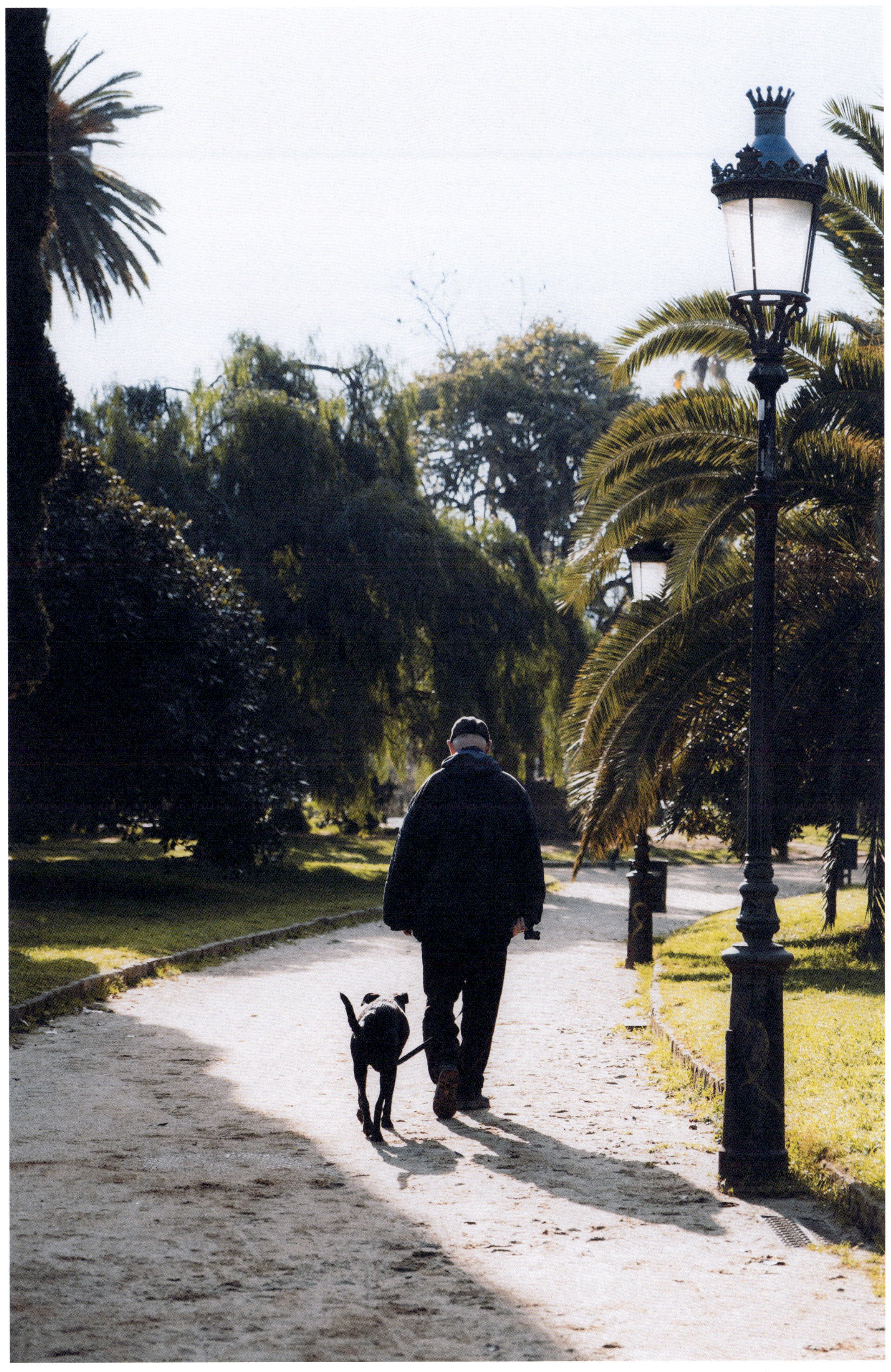

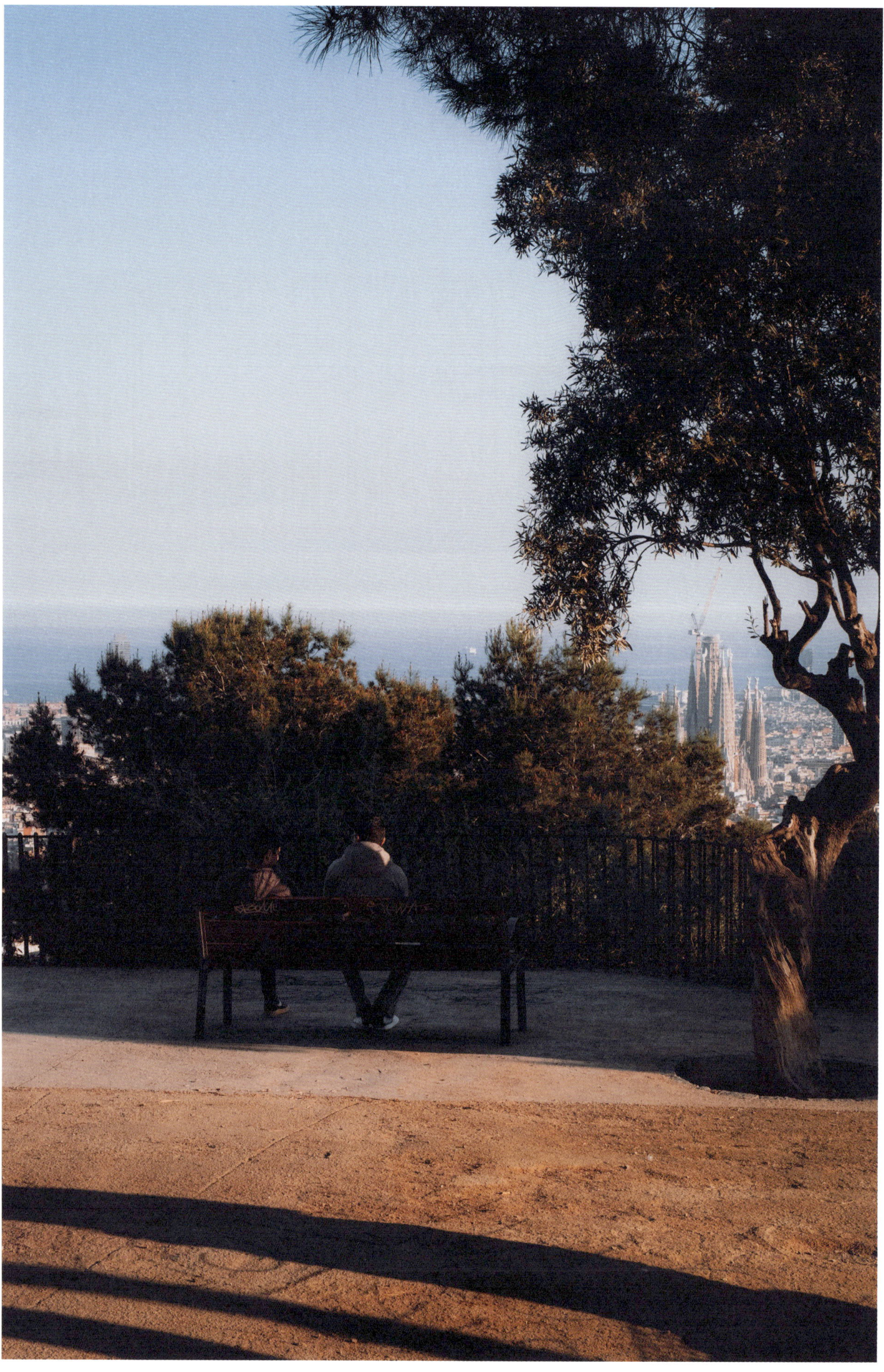

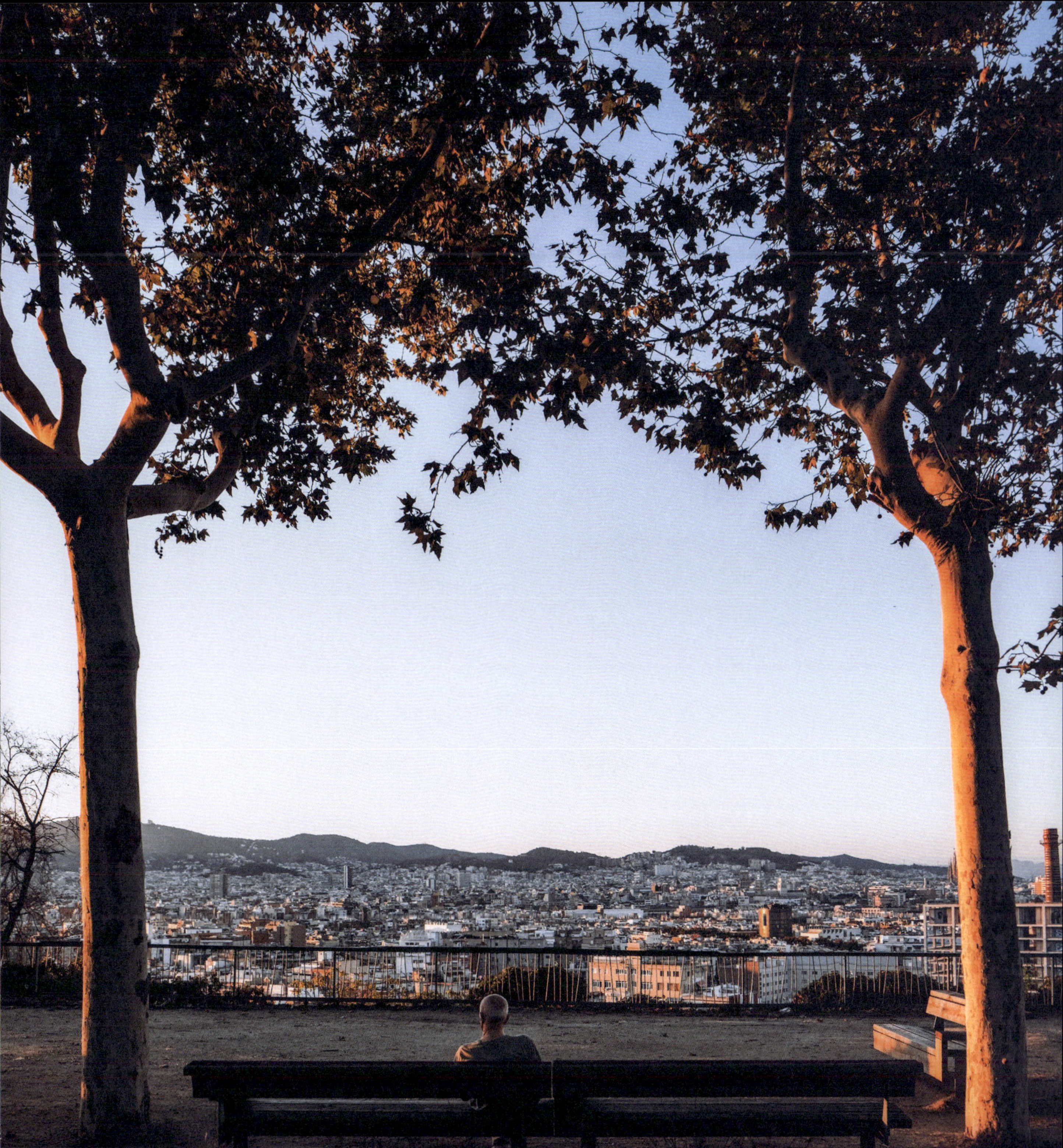

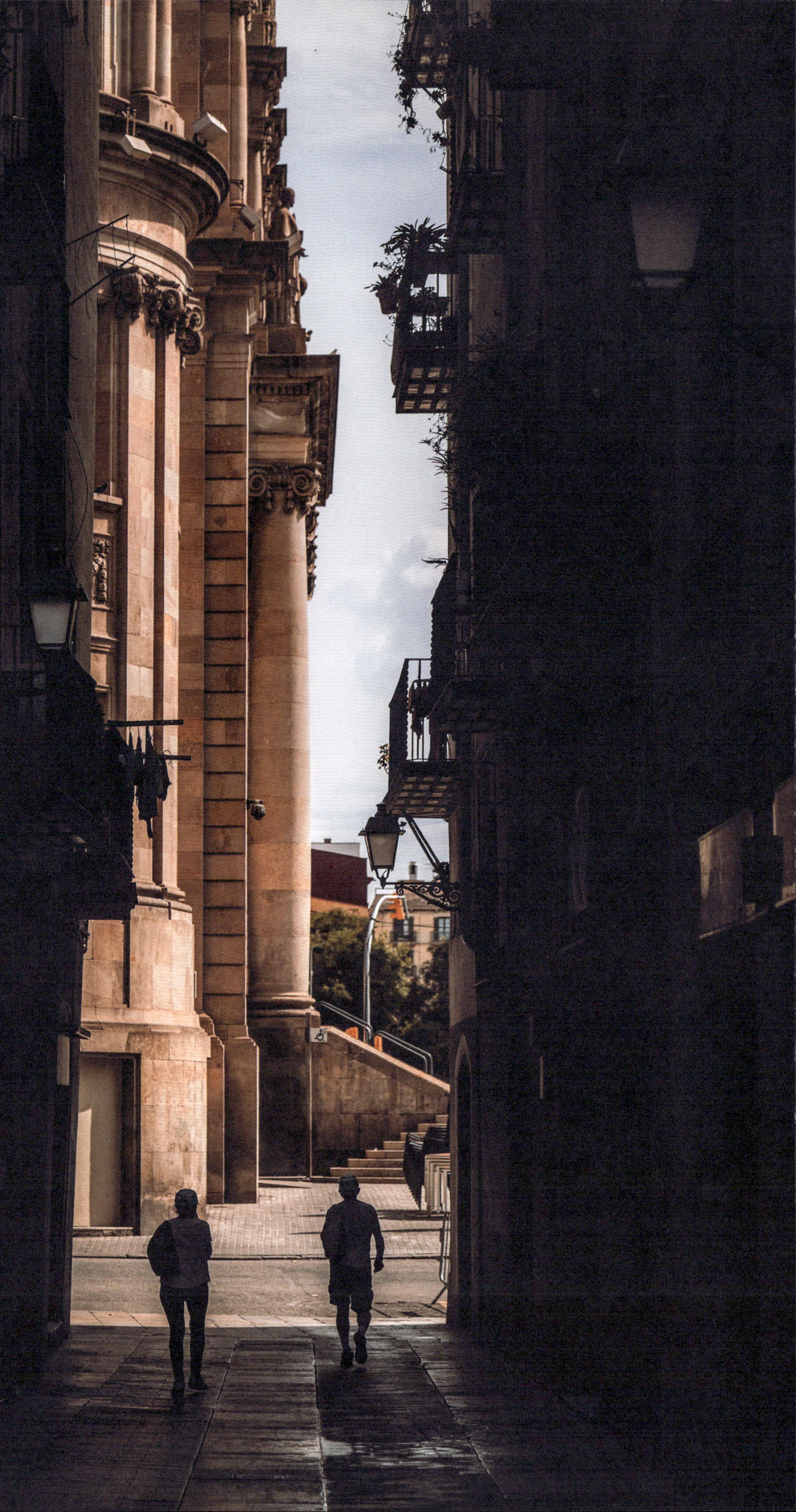

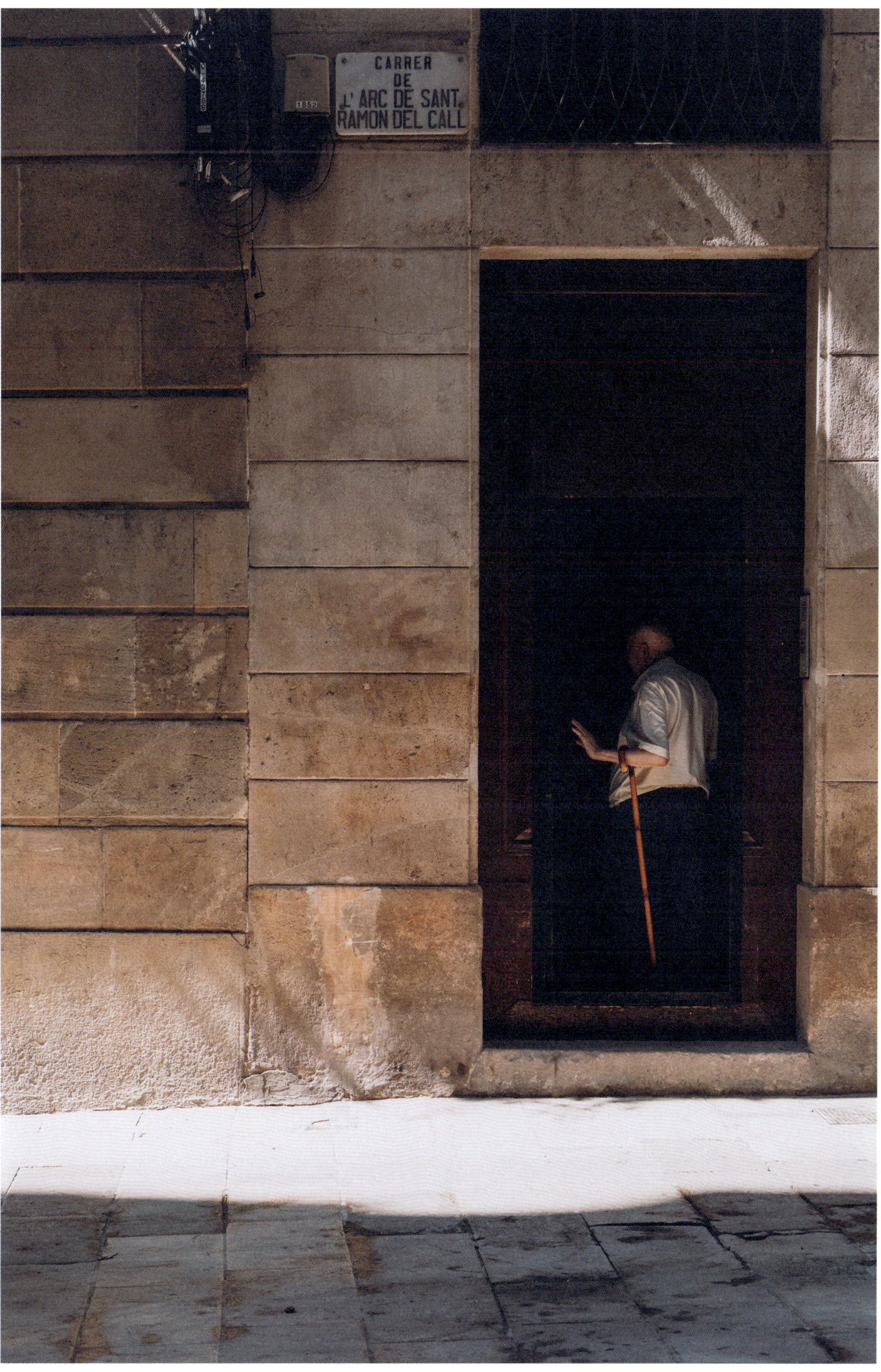
CARRER
DE
L' ARC DE SANT
RAMON DEL CALL

Barcelona is an open and multicultural city. It's brimming with a very special creative energy. If you pay attention, you may be easily inspired by the places and people living there.

ROSALÍA
Spanish Singer

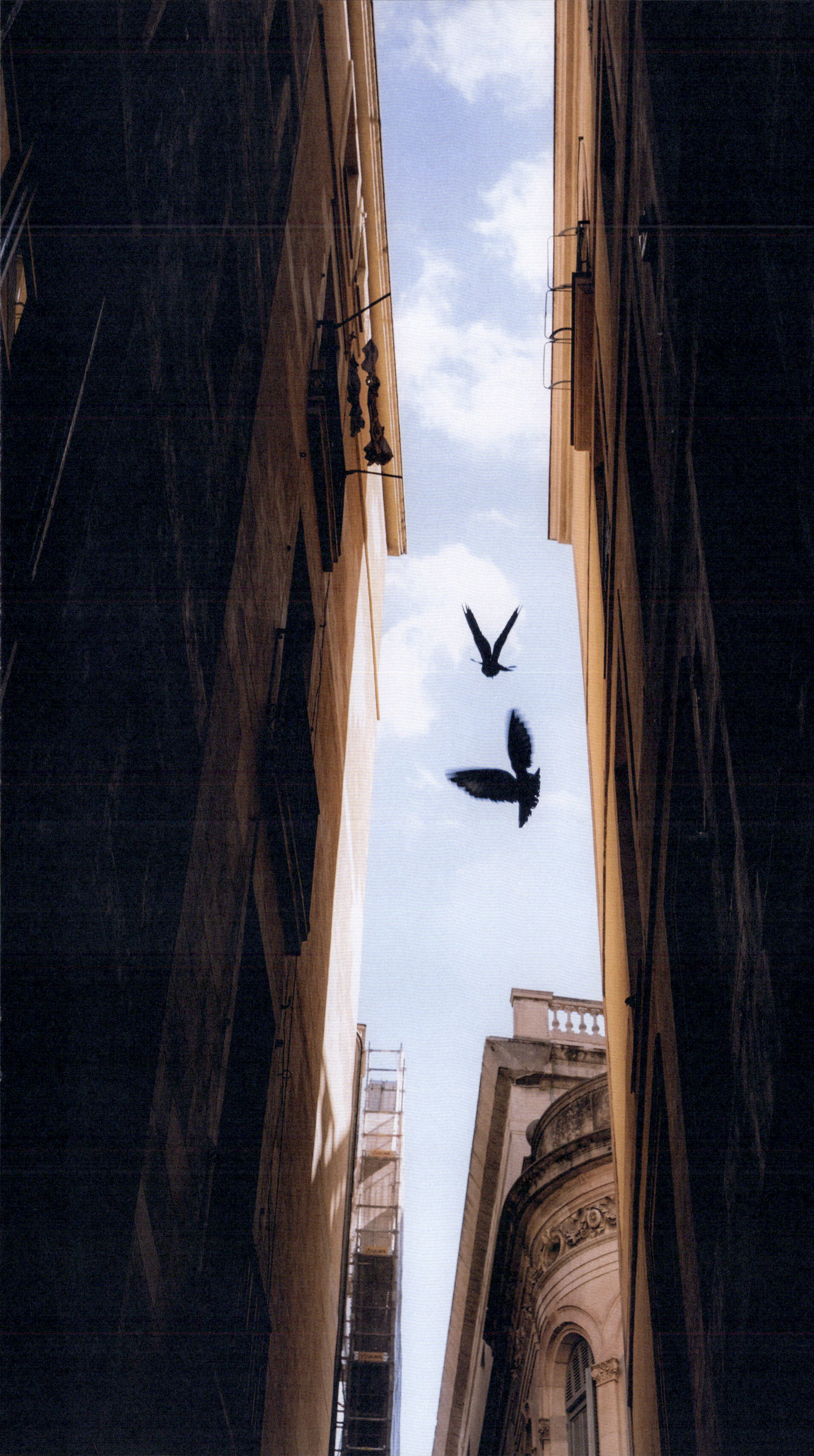

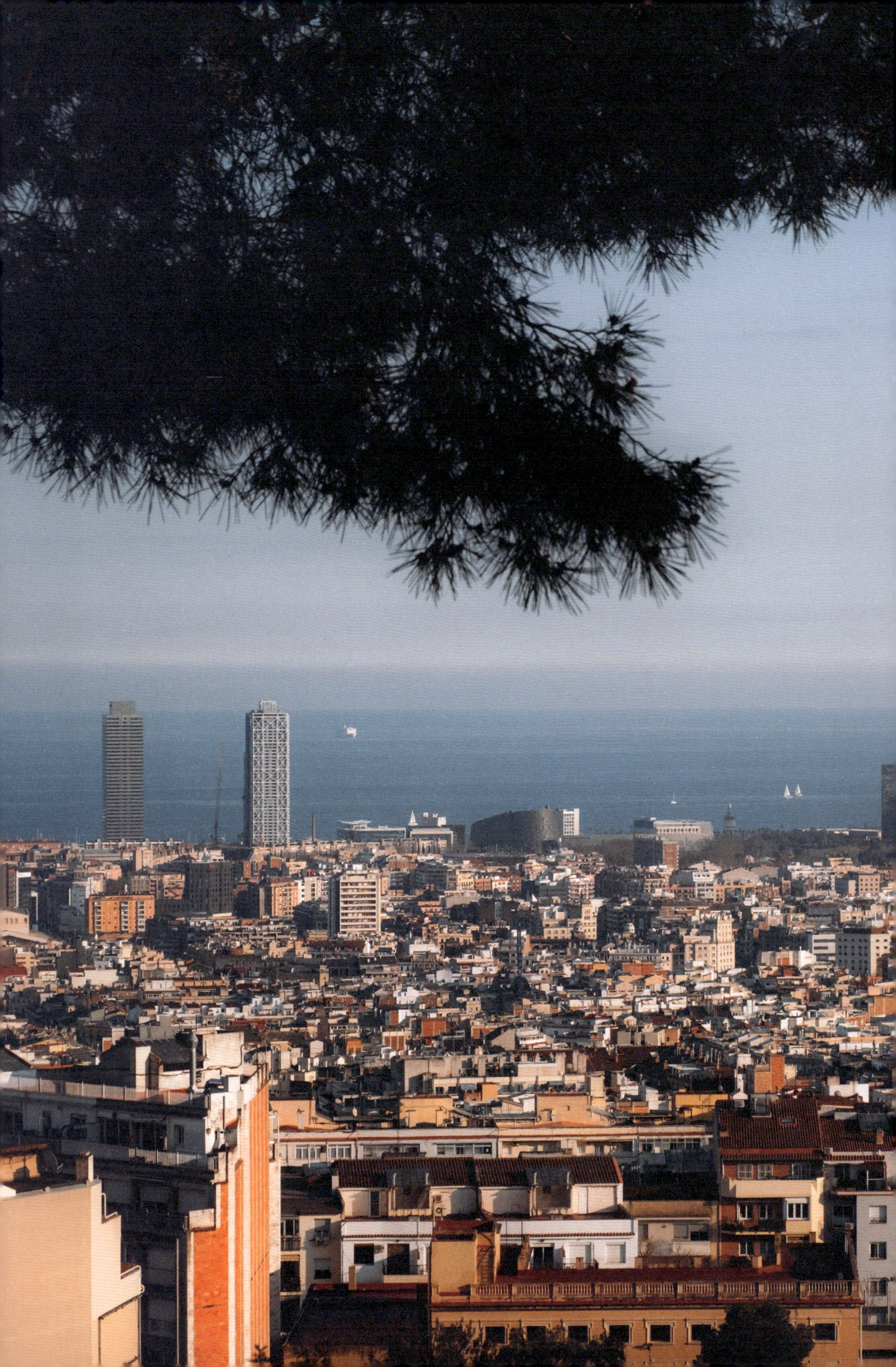

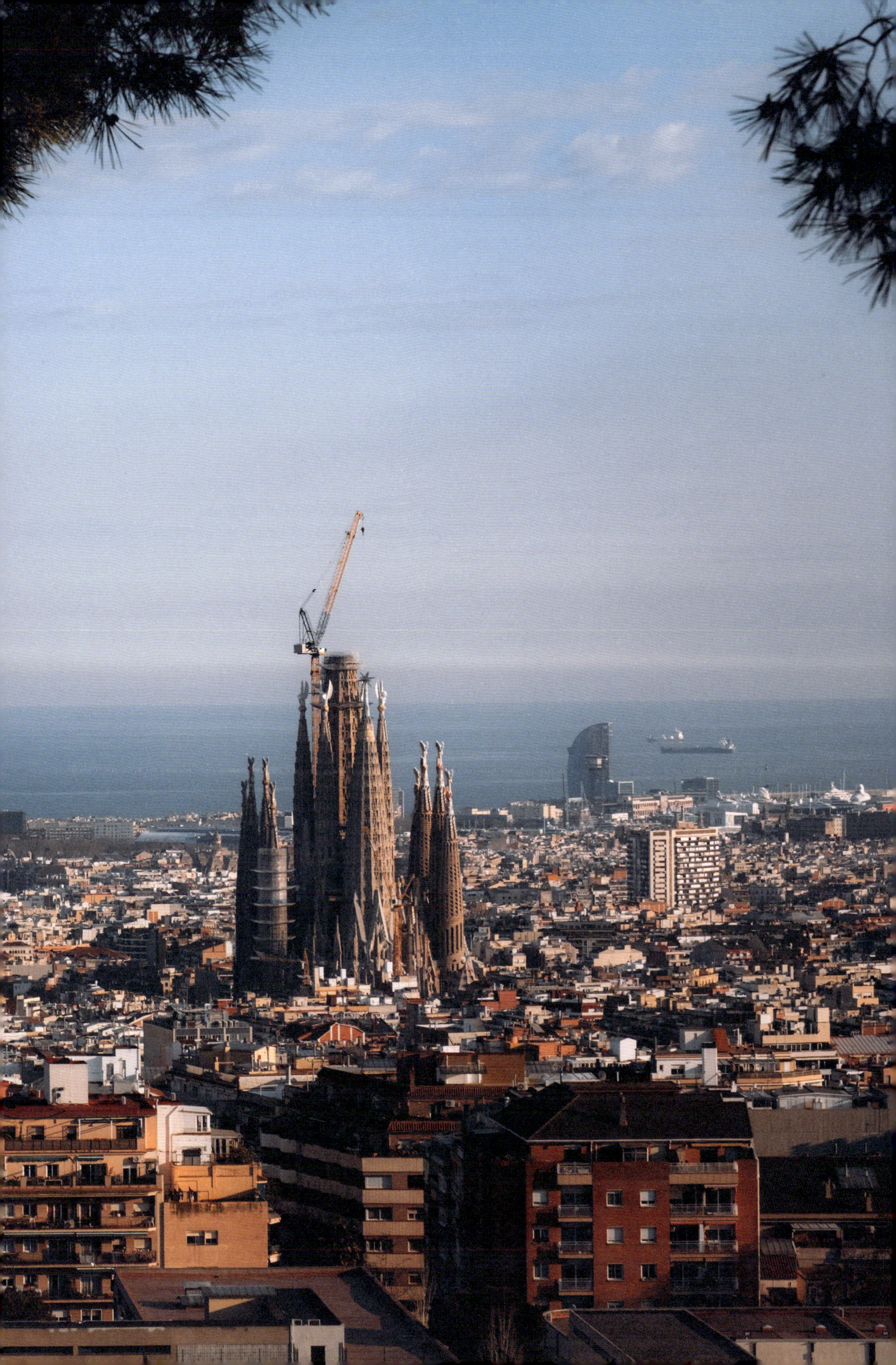

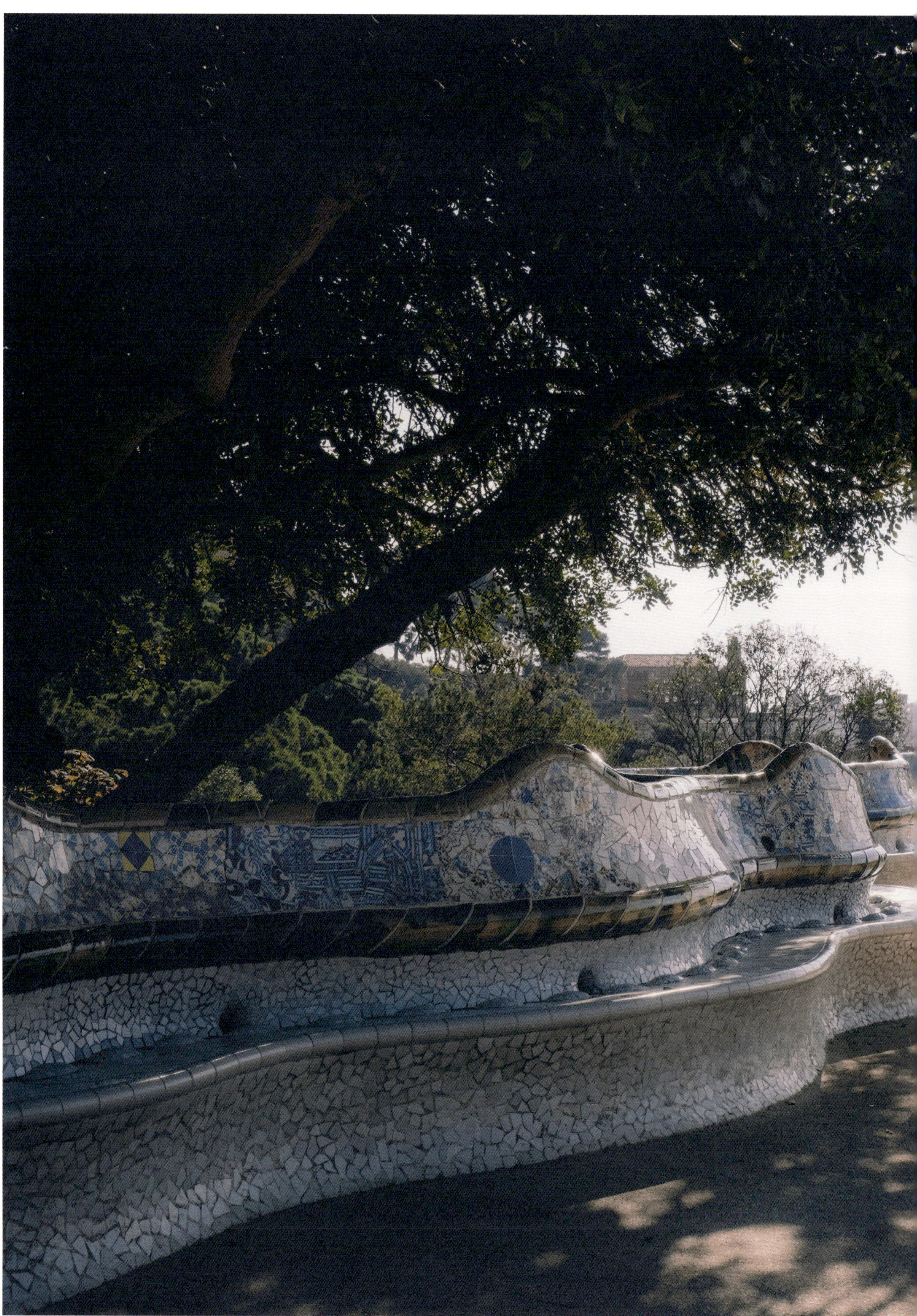

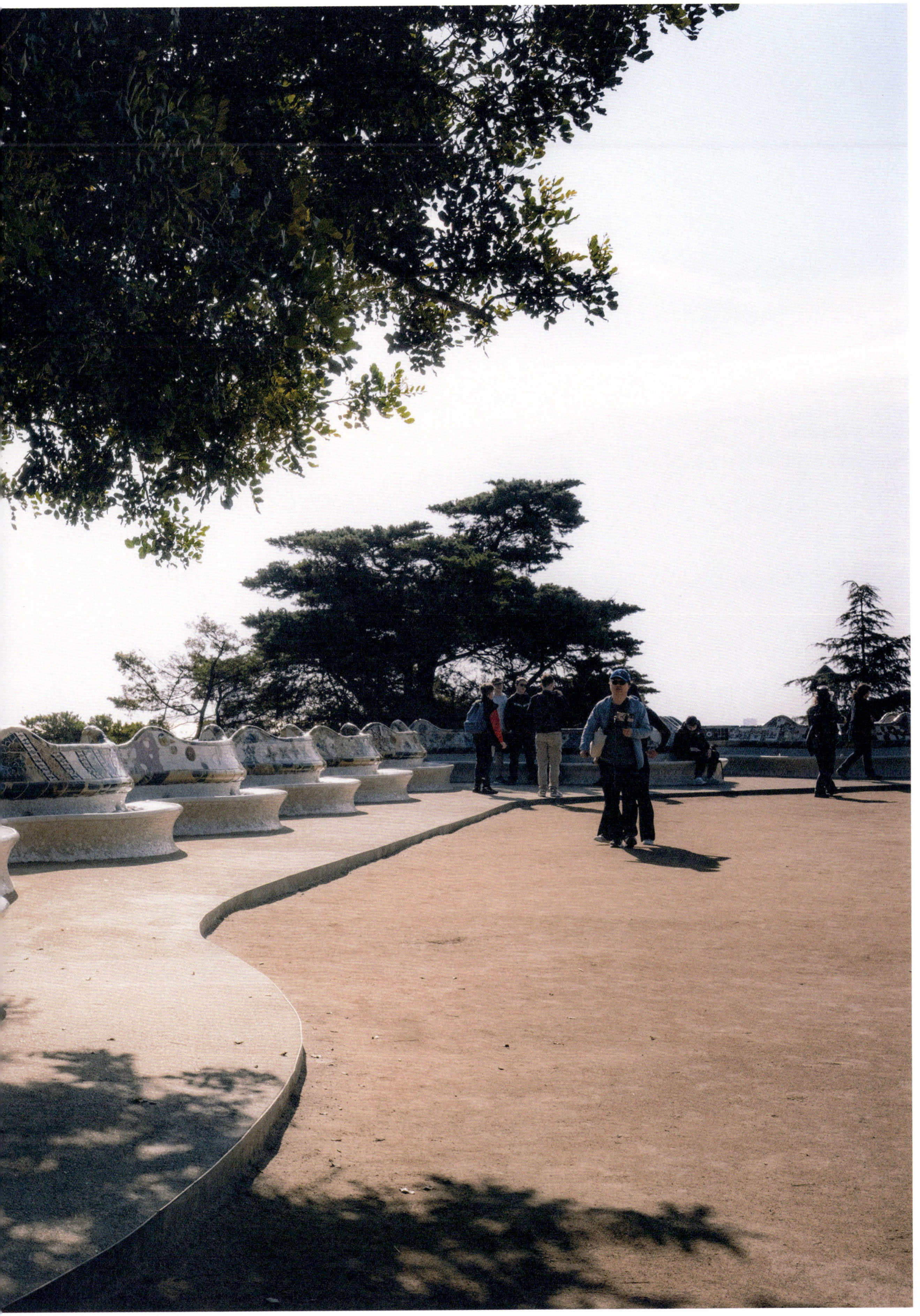

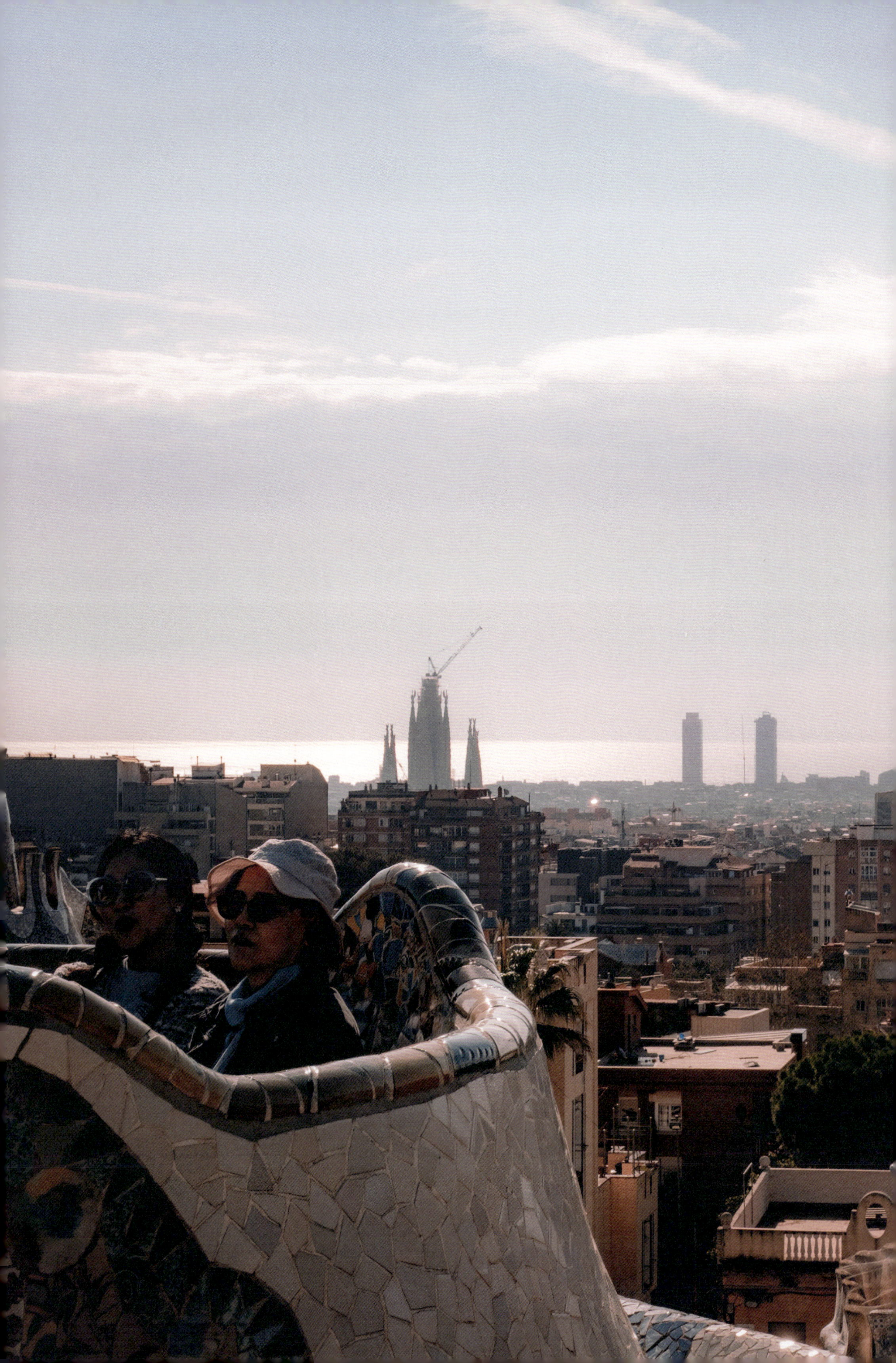

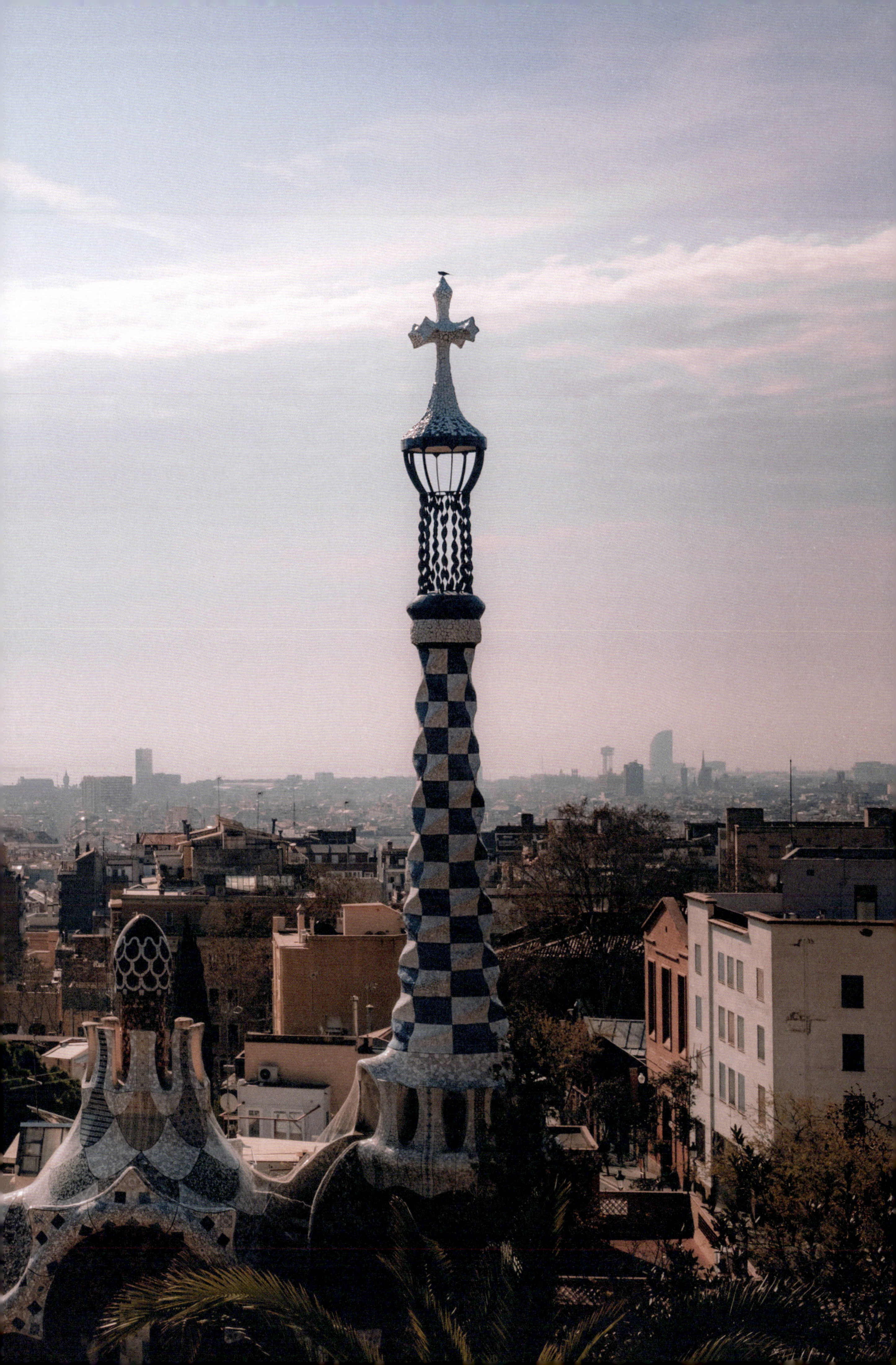

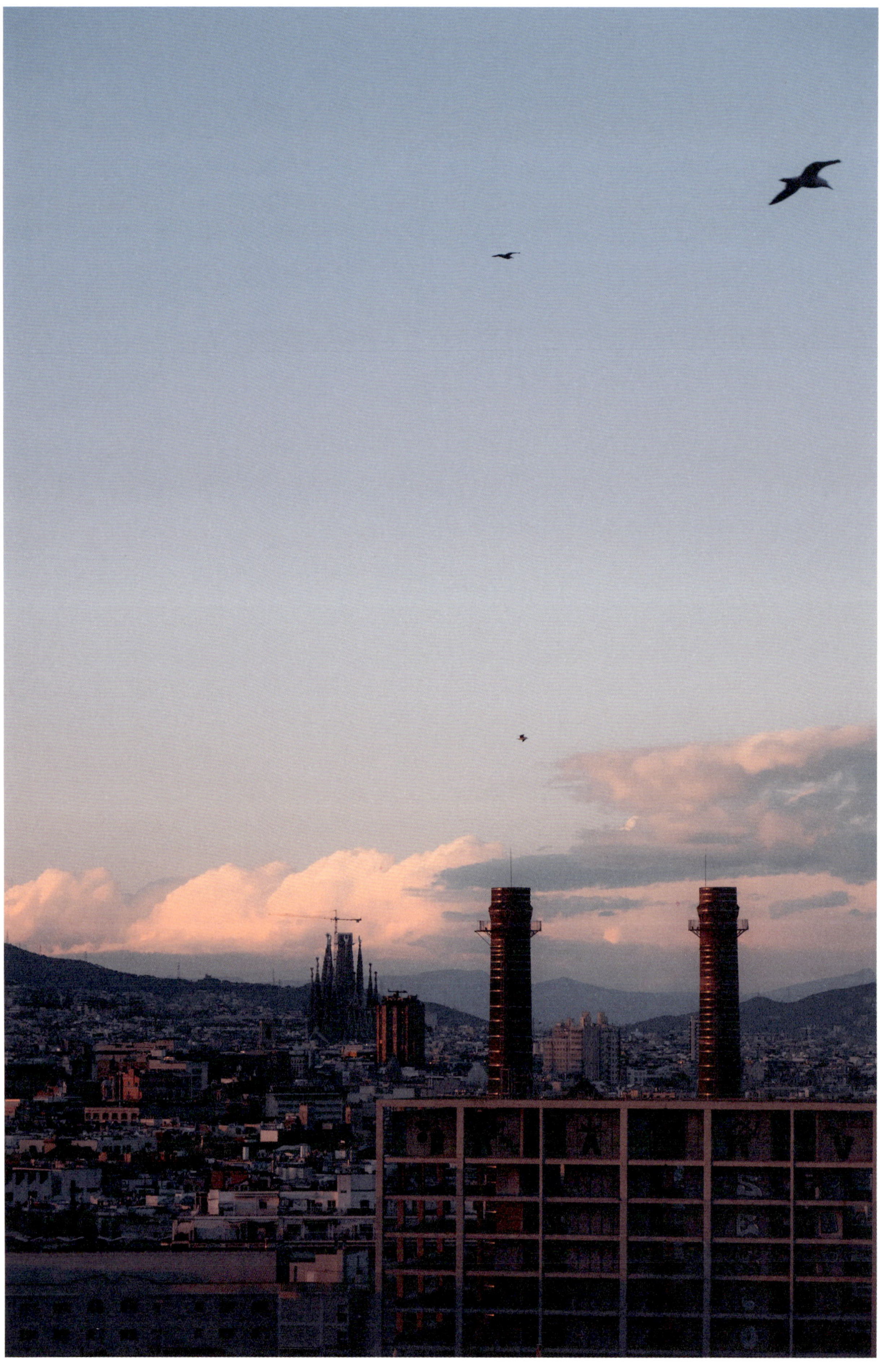

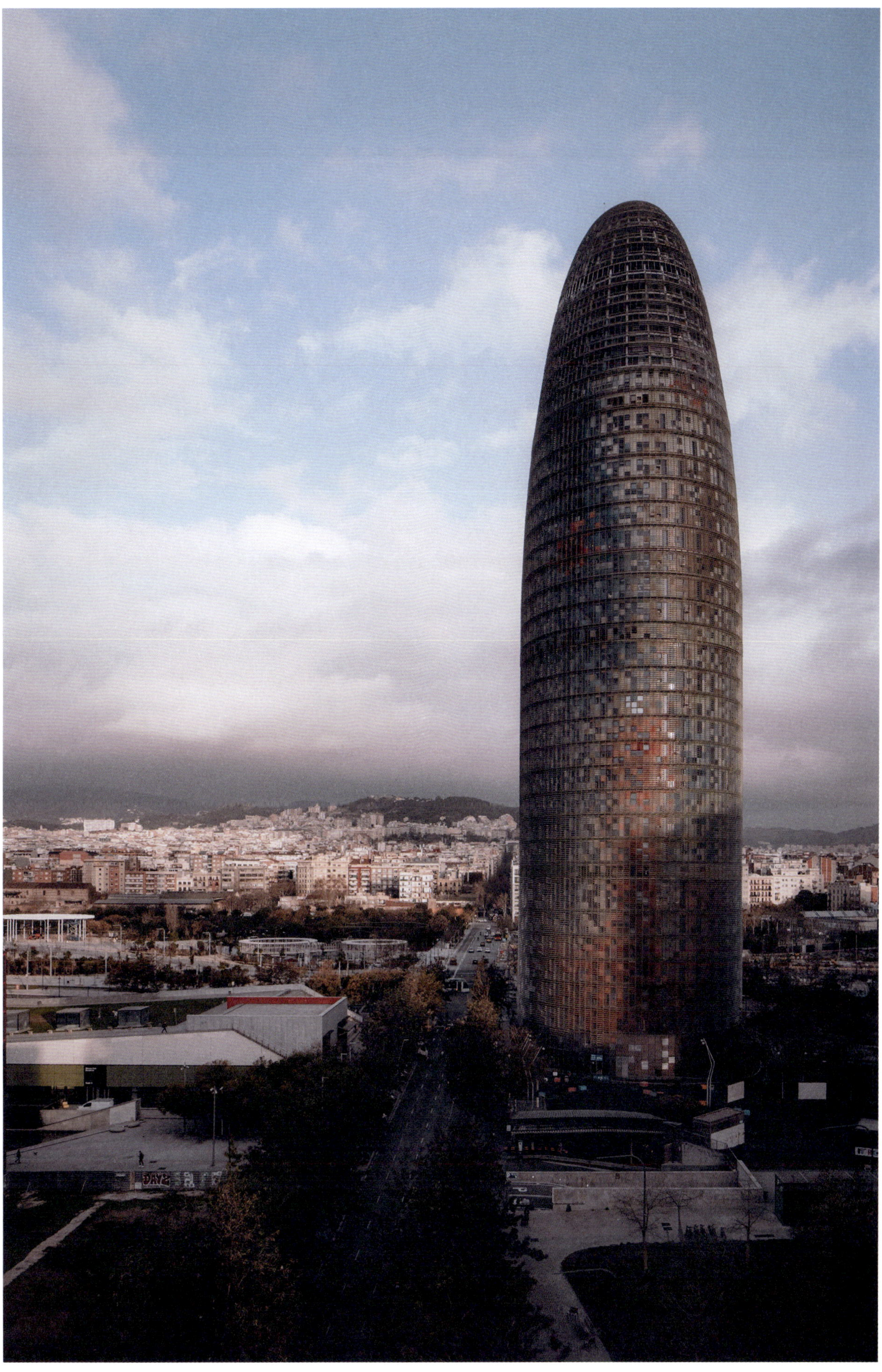

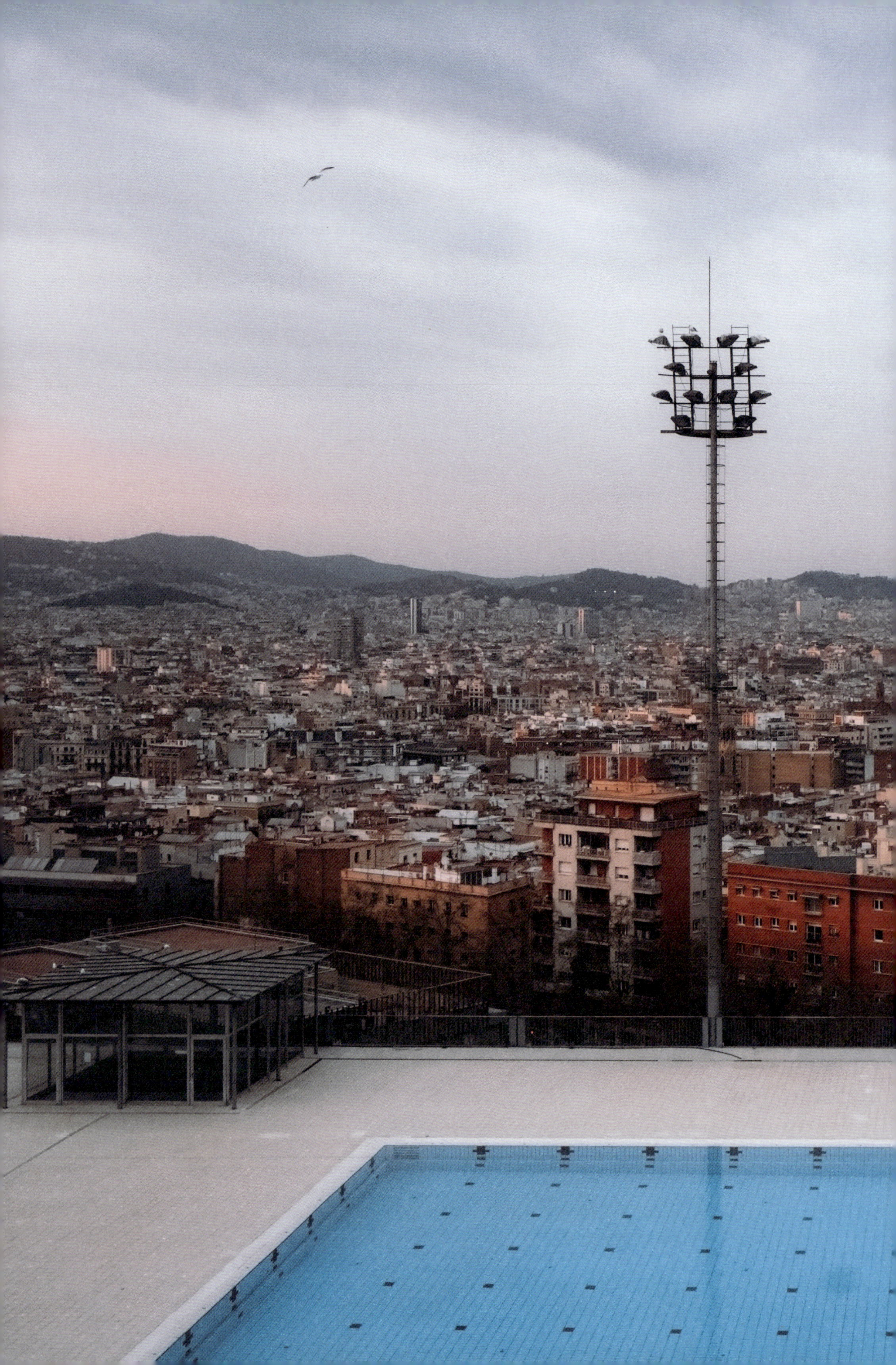

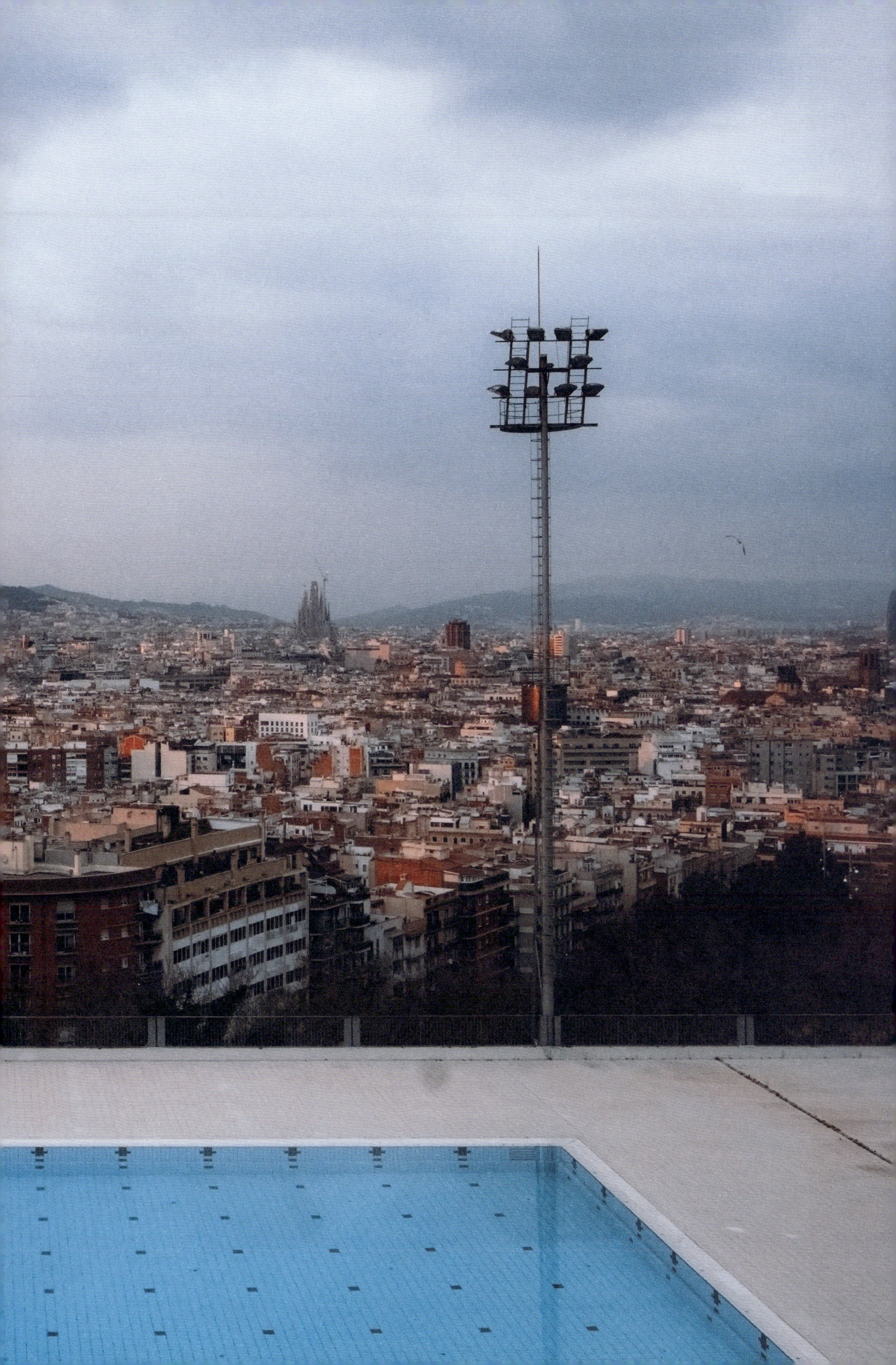

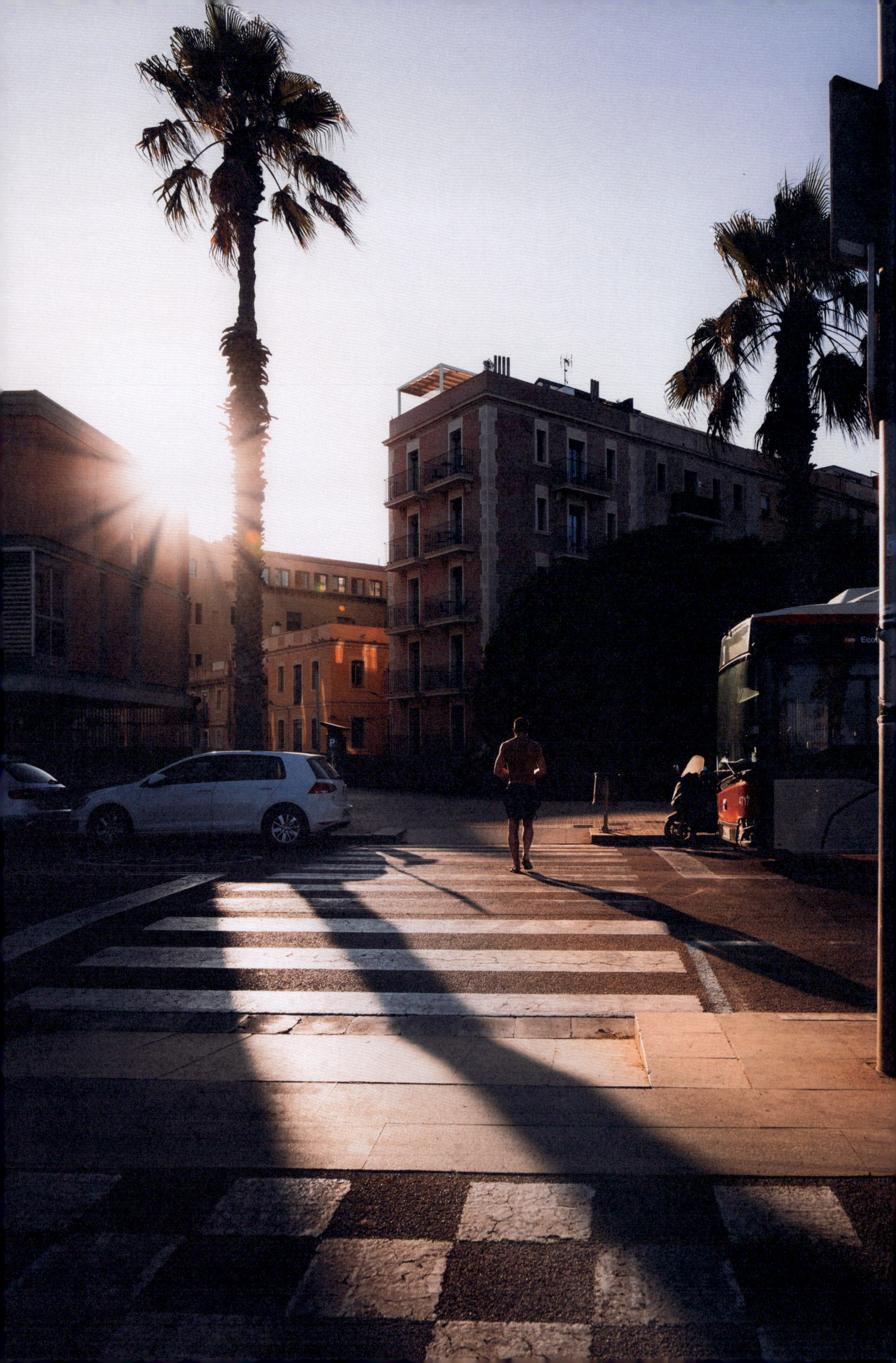

Barcelona is an enchanting seaside city with boundless culture, fabled architecture, and a world-class drinking and dining scene.

TYLER COWEN

American Economist and Columnist

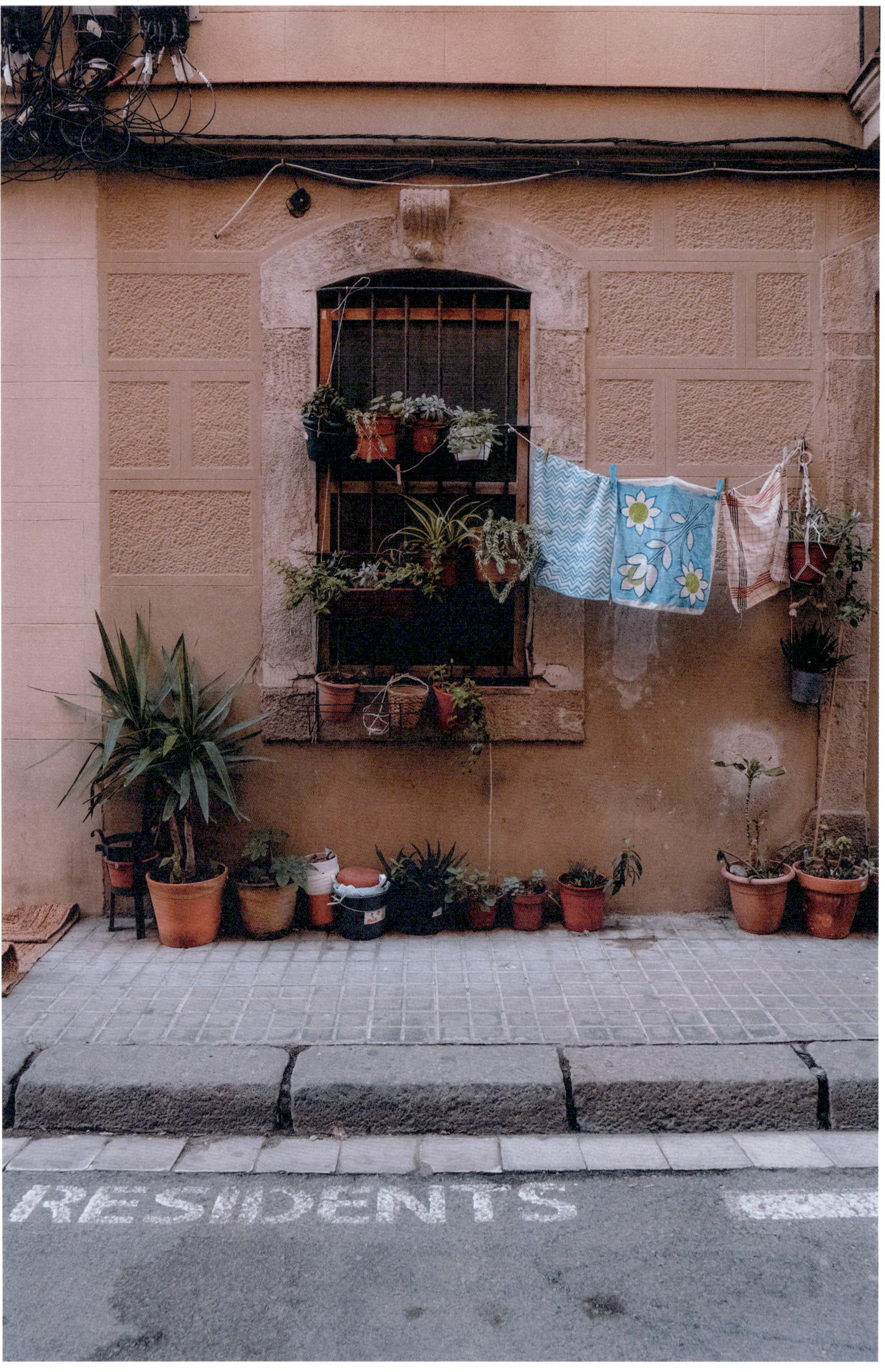
RESIDENTS

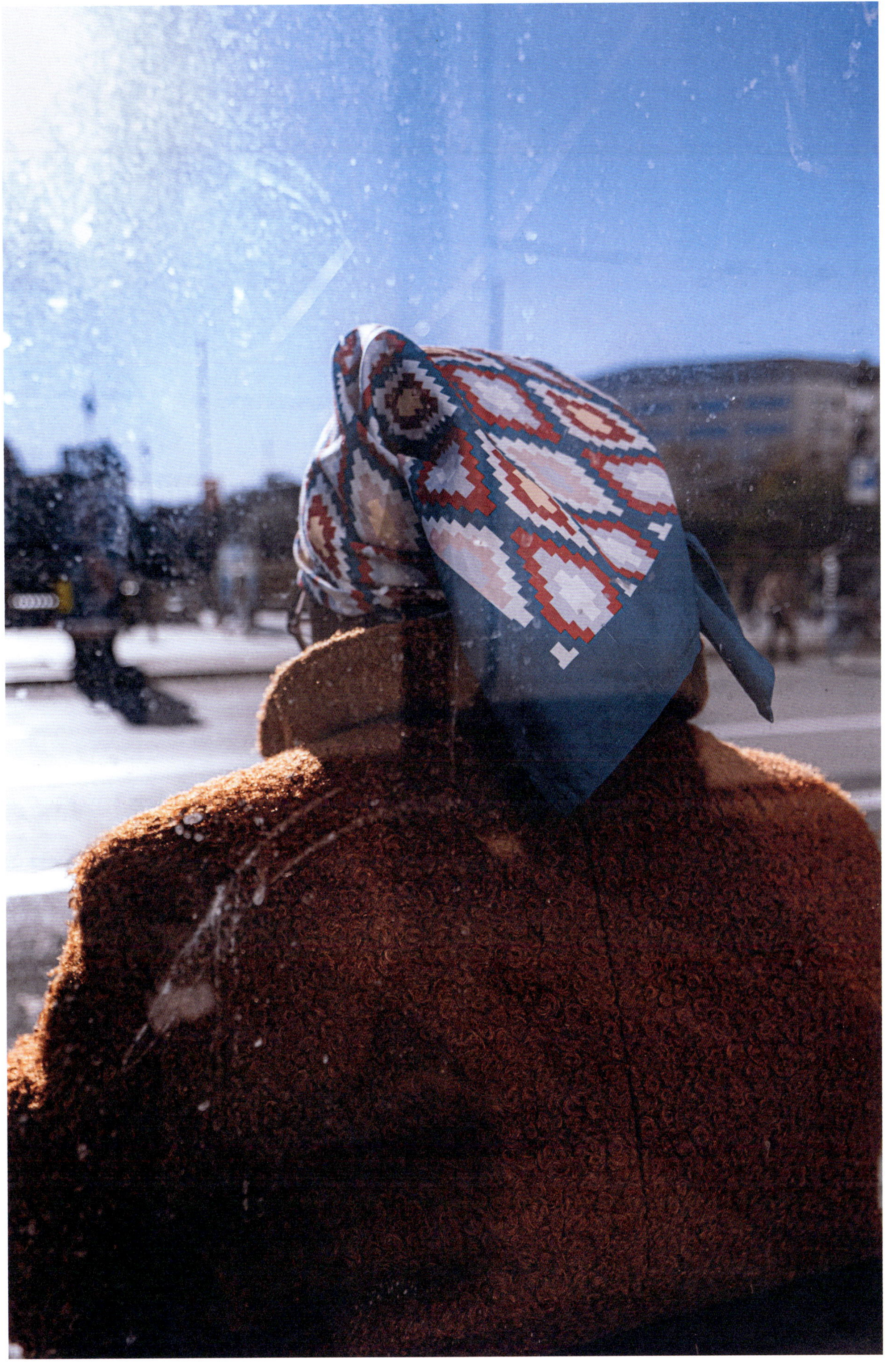

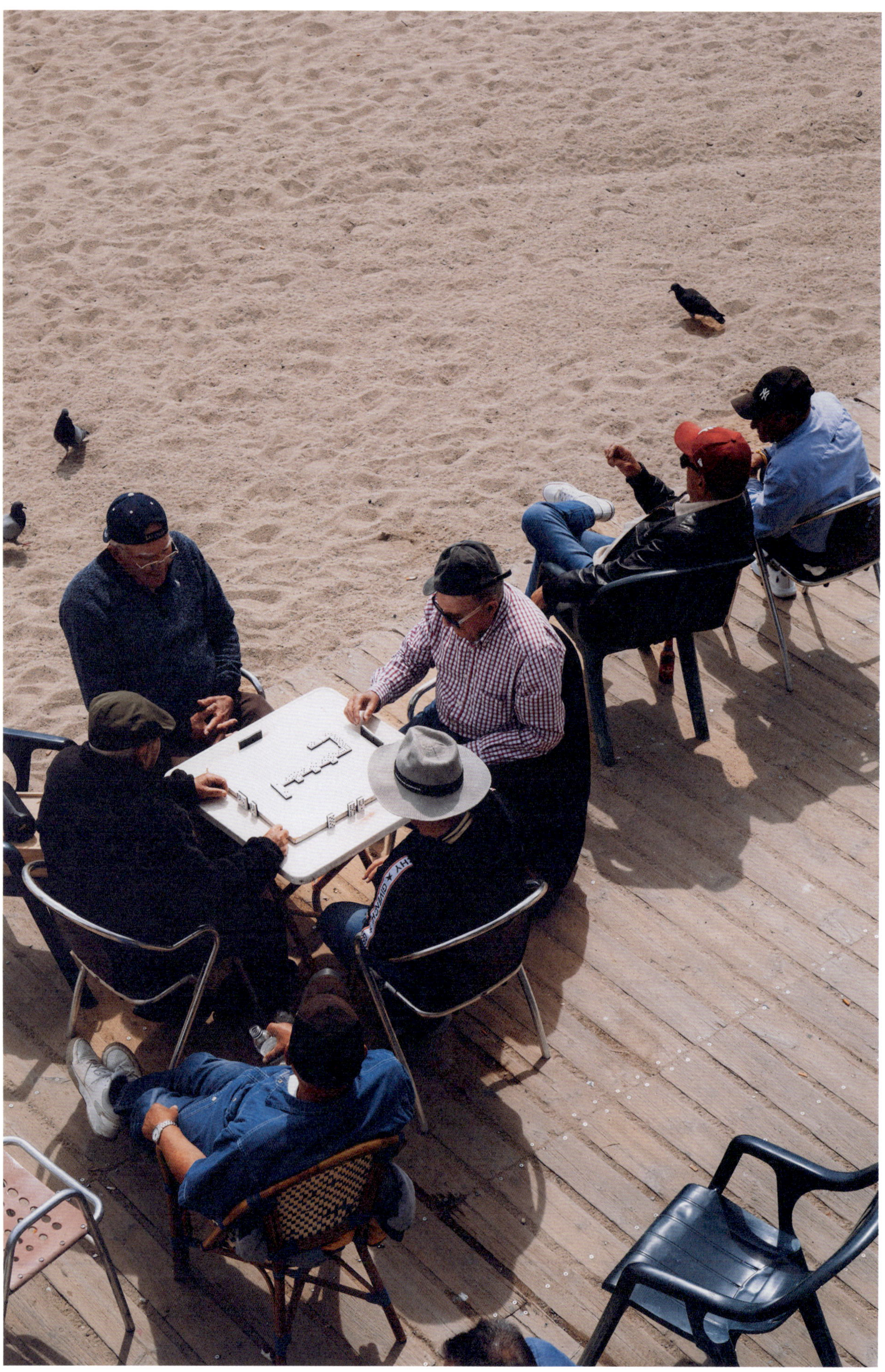

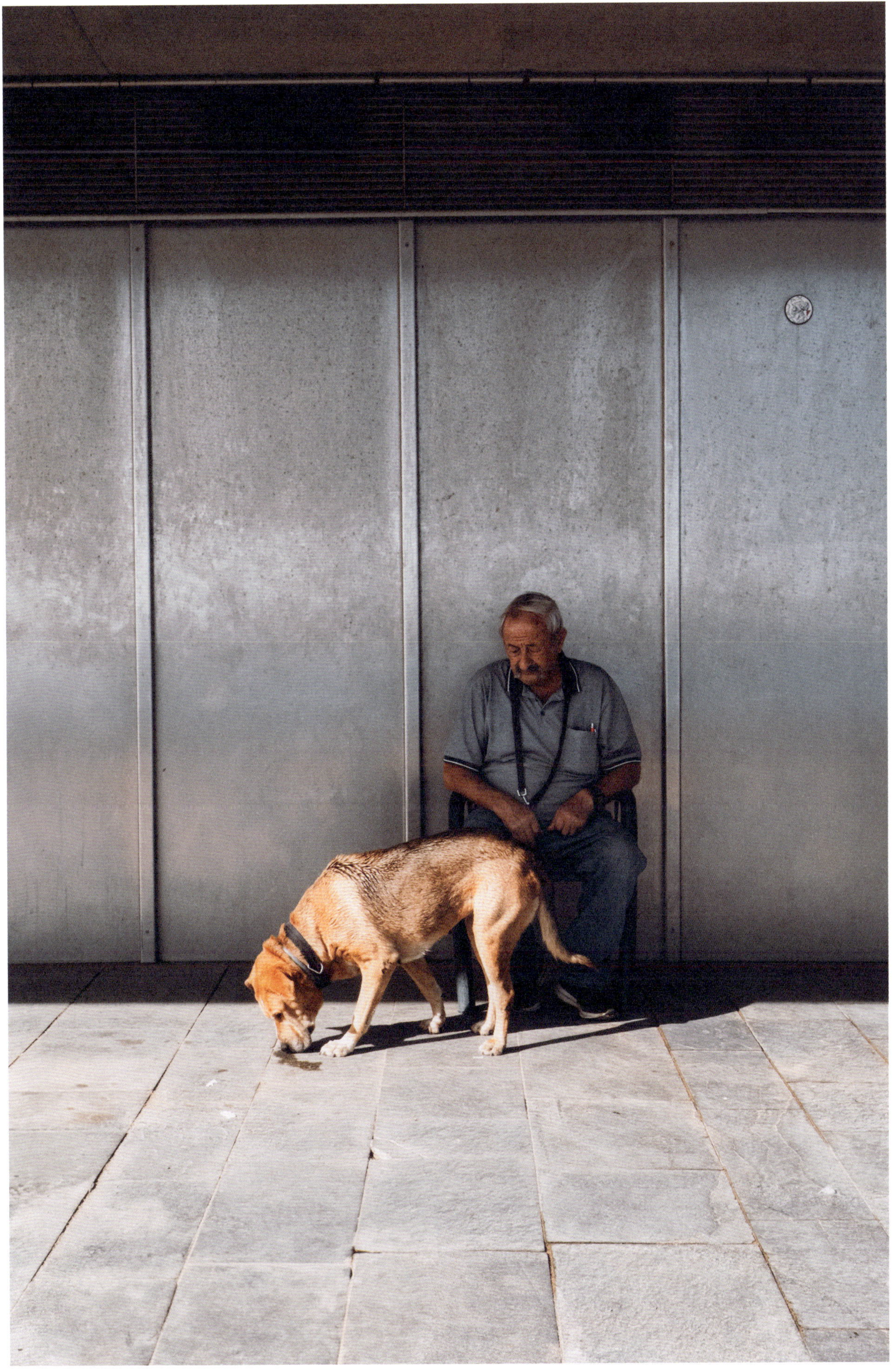

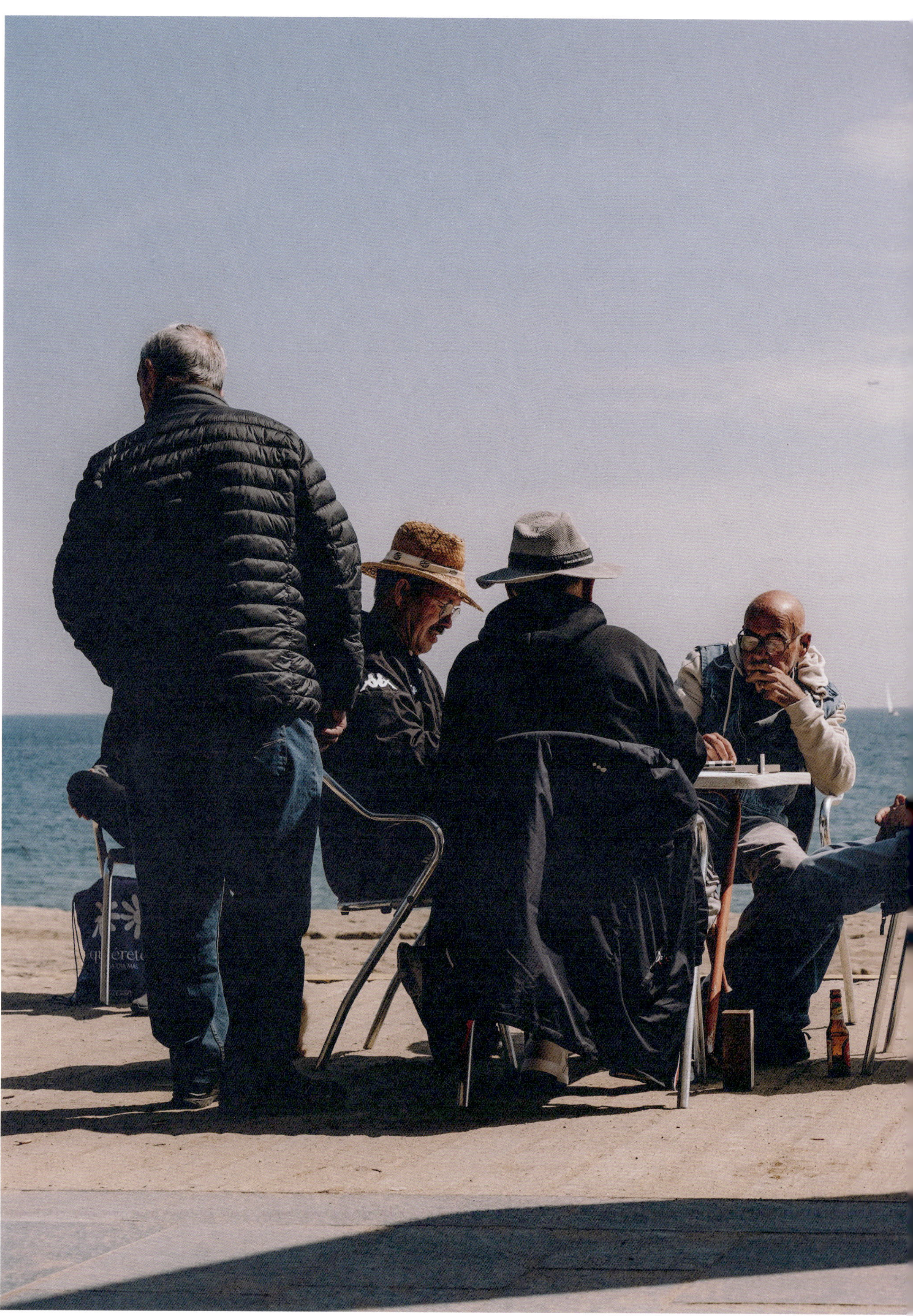

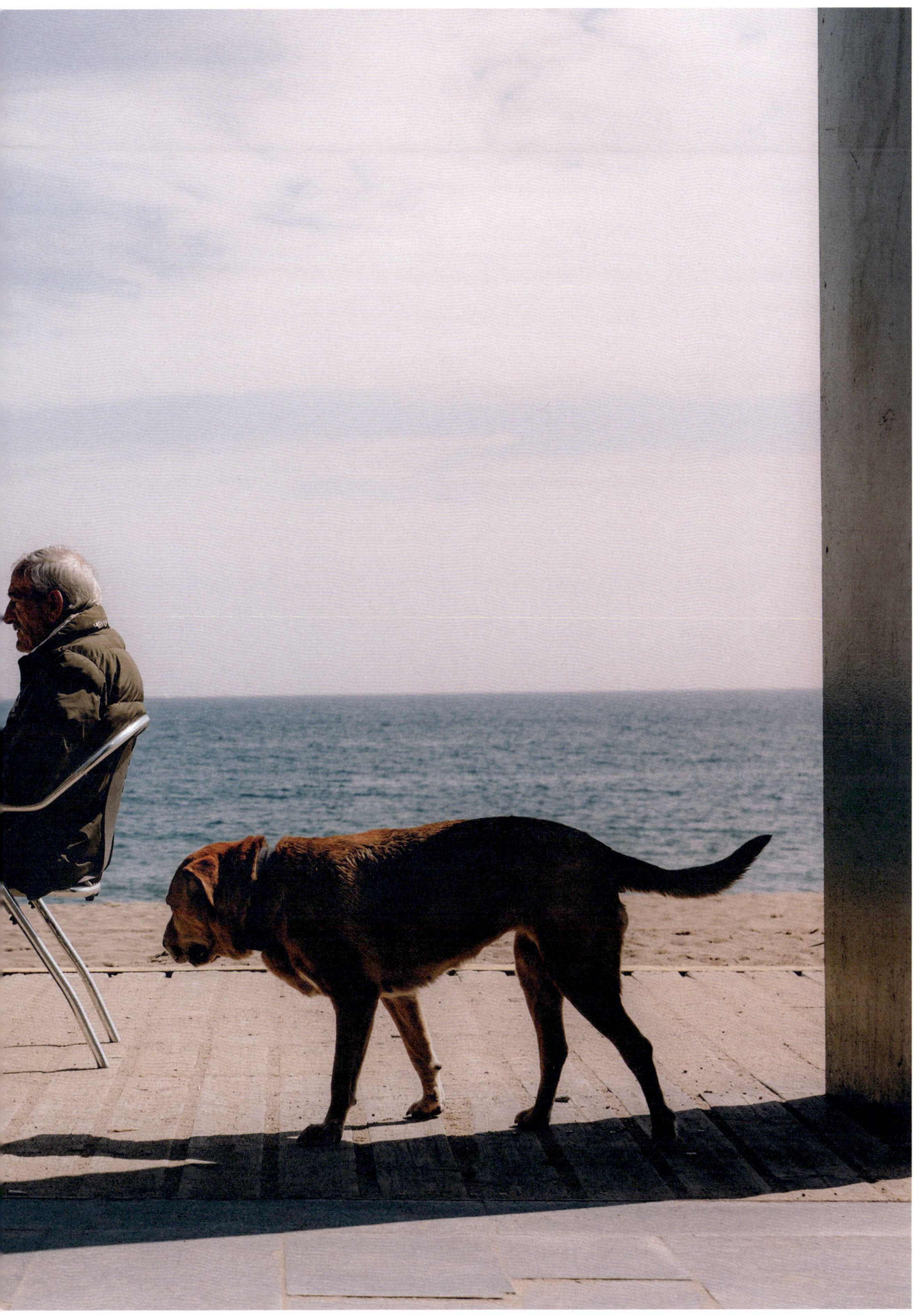

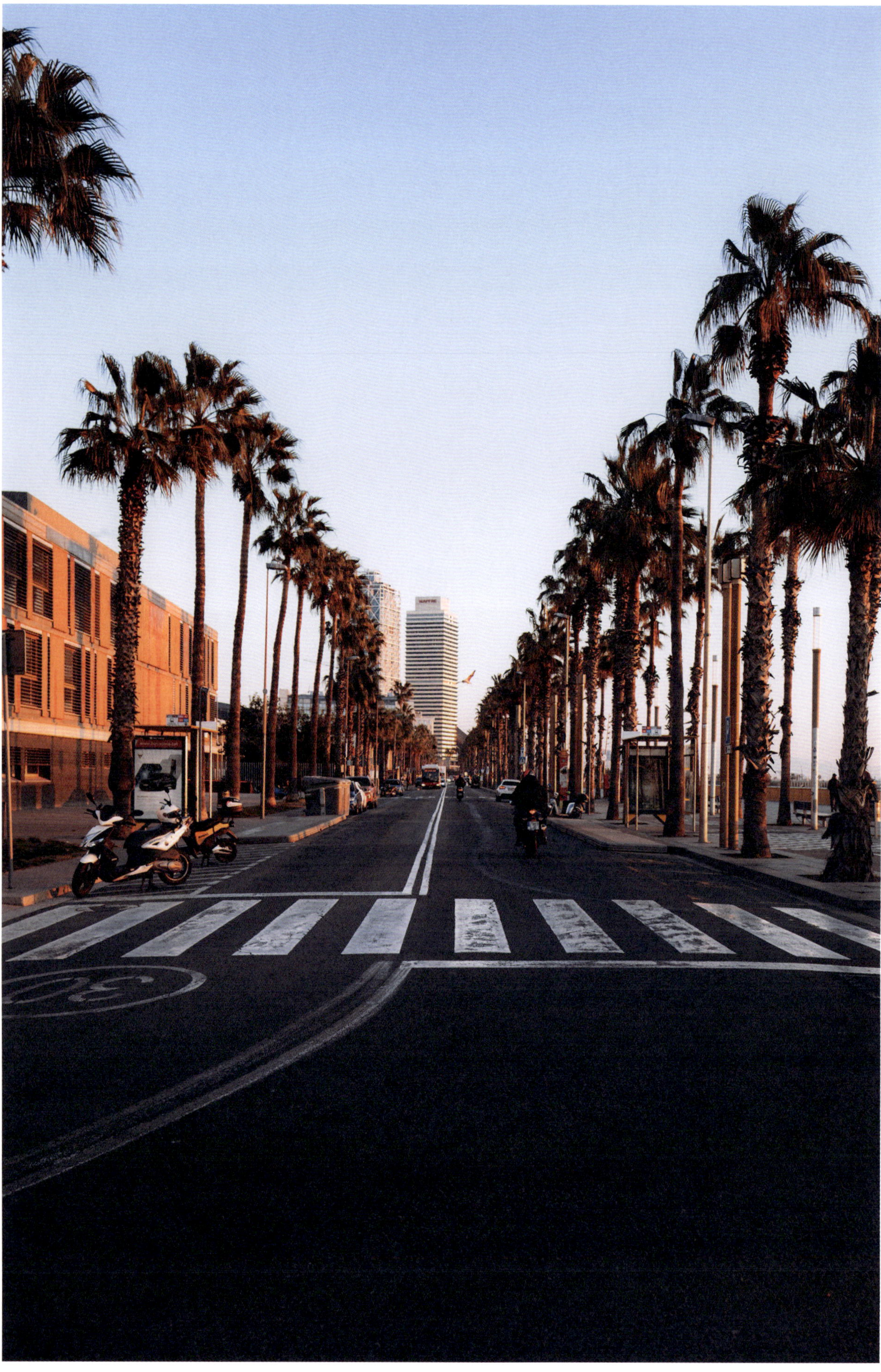

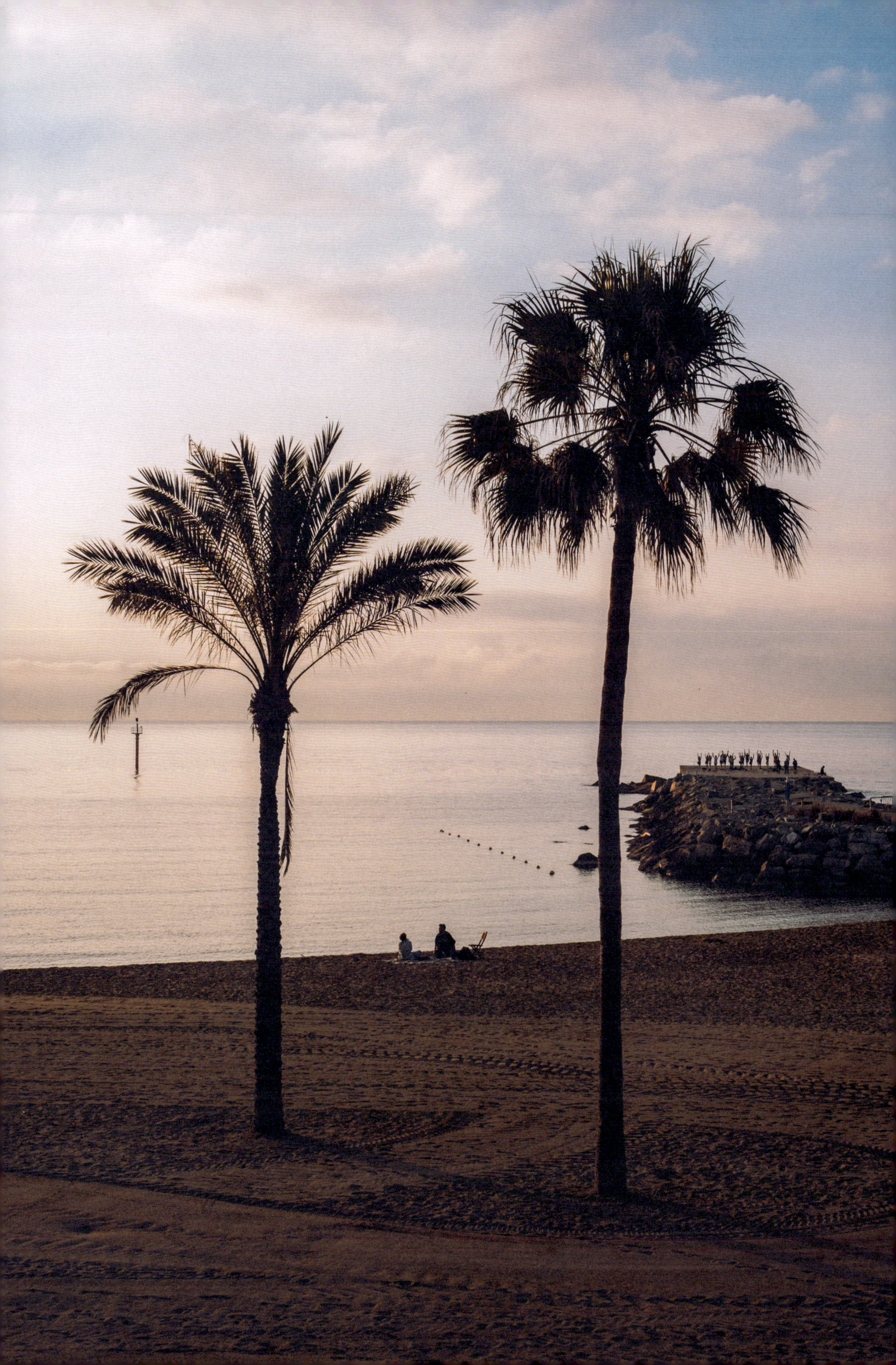

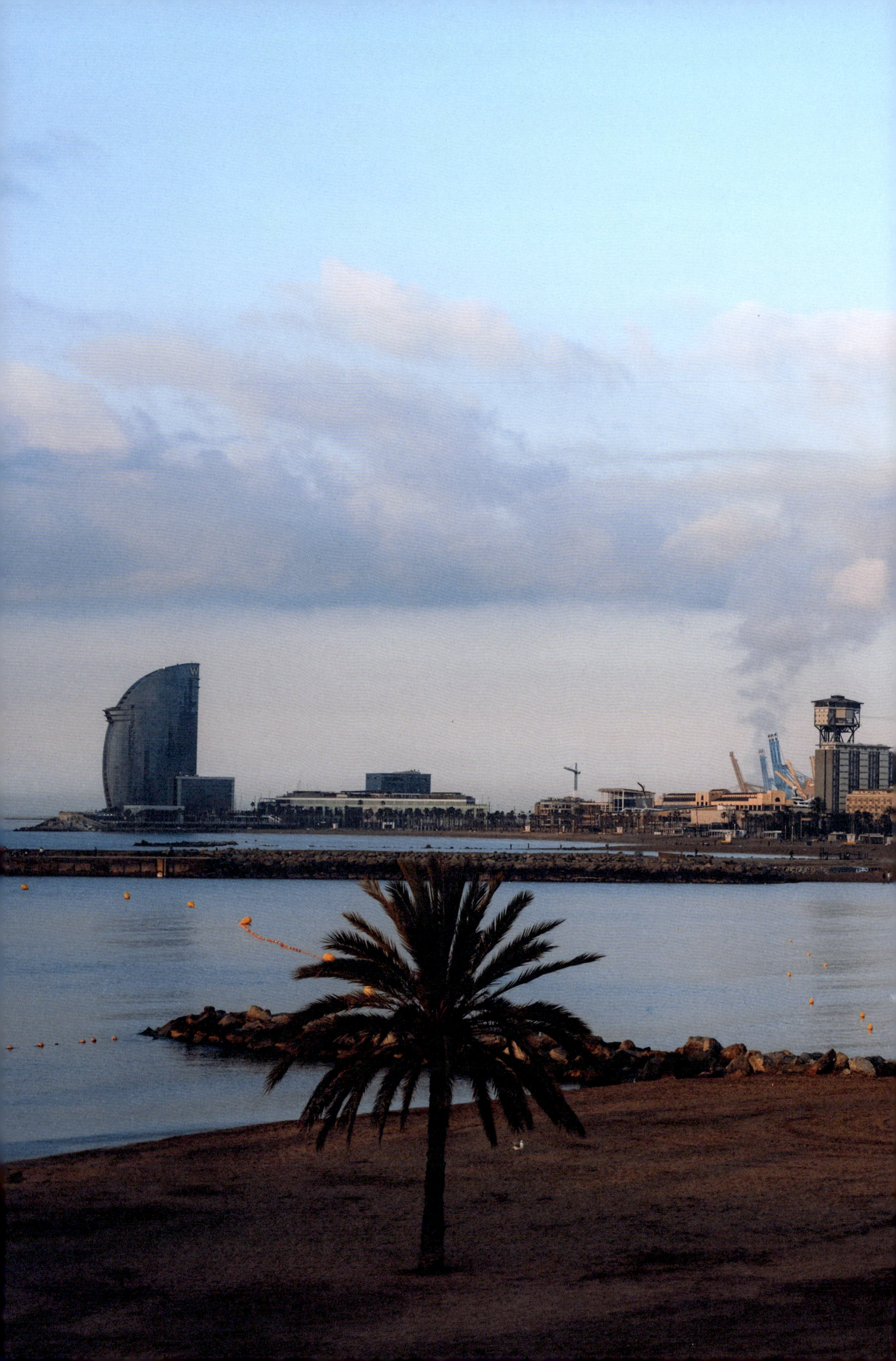

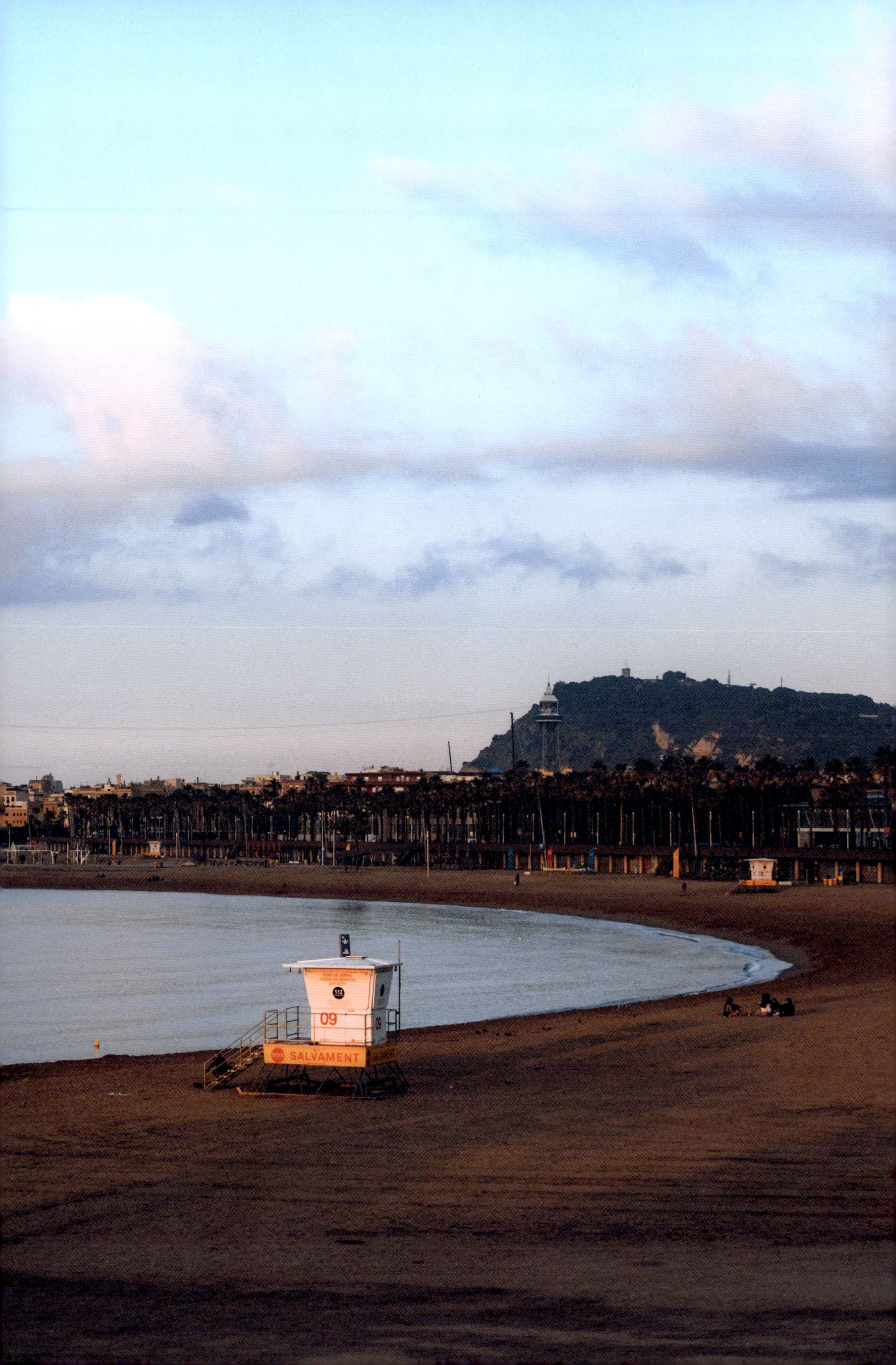
09
SALVAMENT

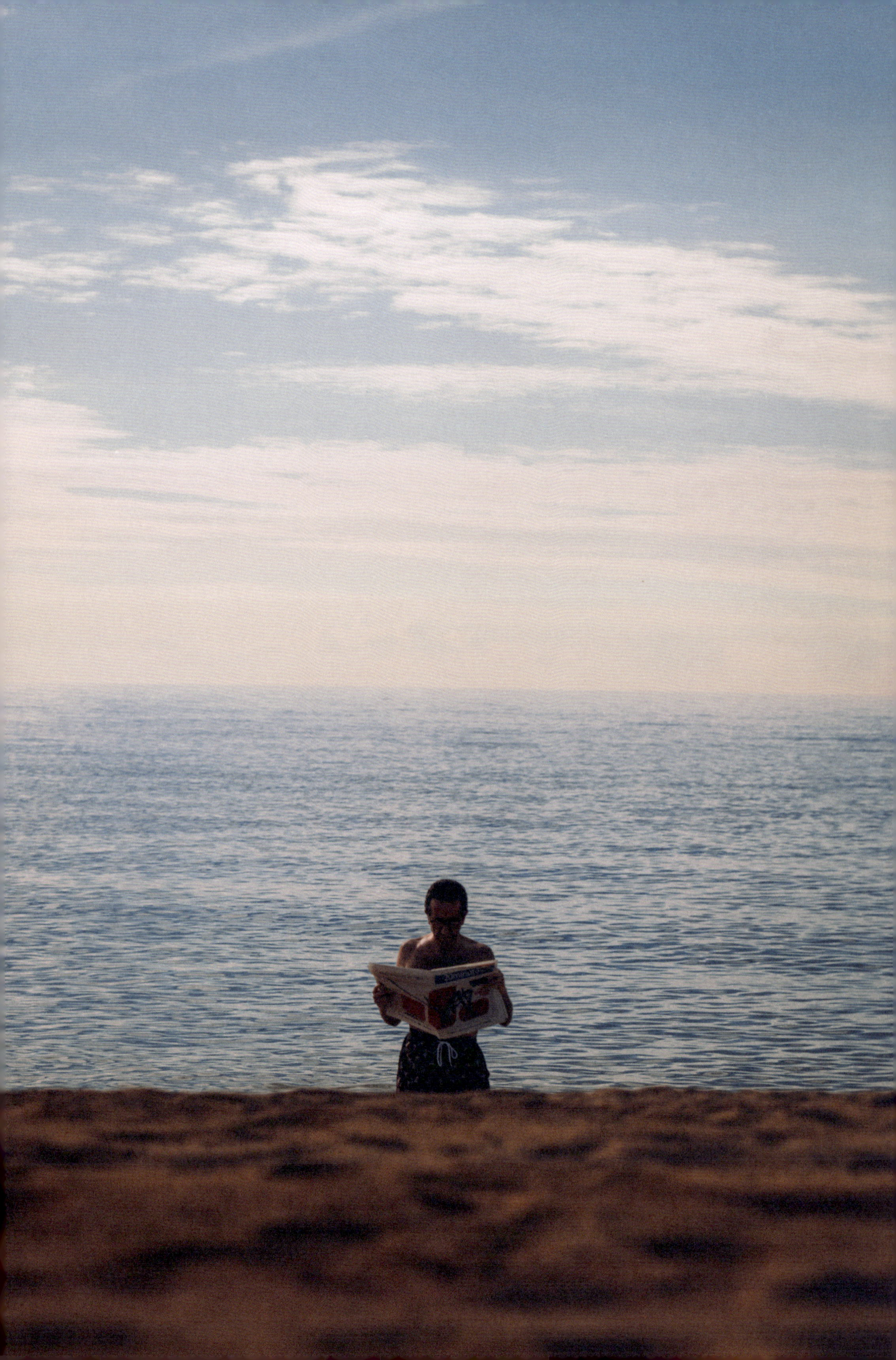

Allow me to state here how much
I love Barcelona, an admirable city,
a city full of life, intense, a port open
to the past and future.

LE CORBUSIER
Swiss-French Architect

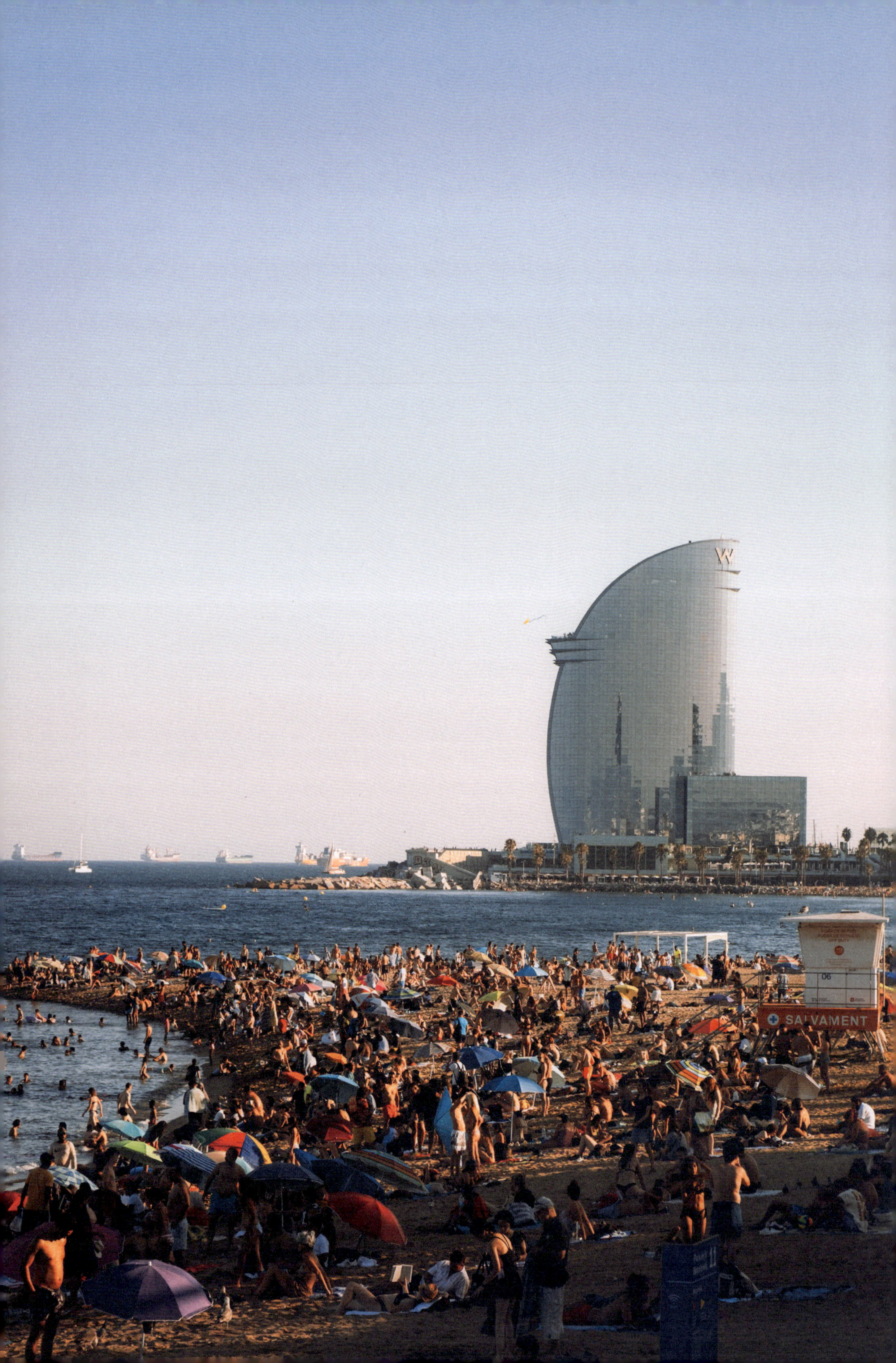
SALVAMENT

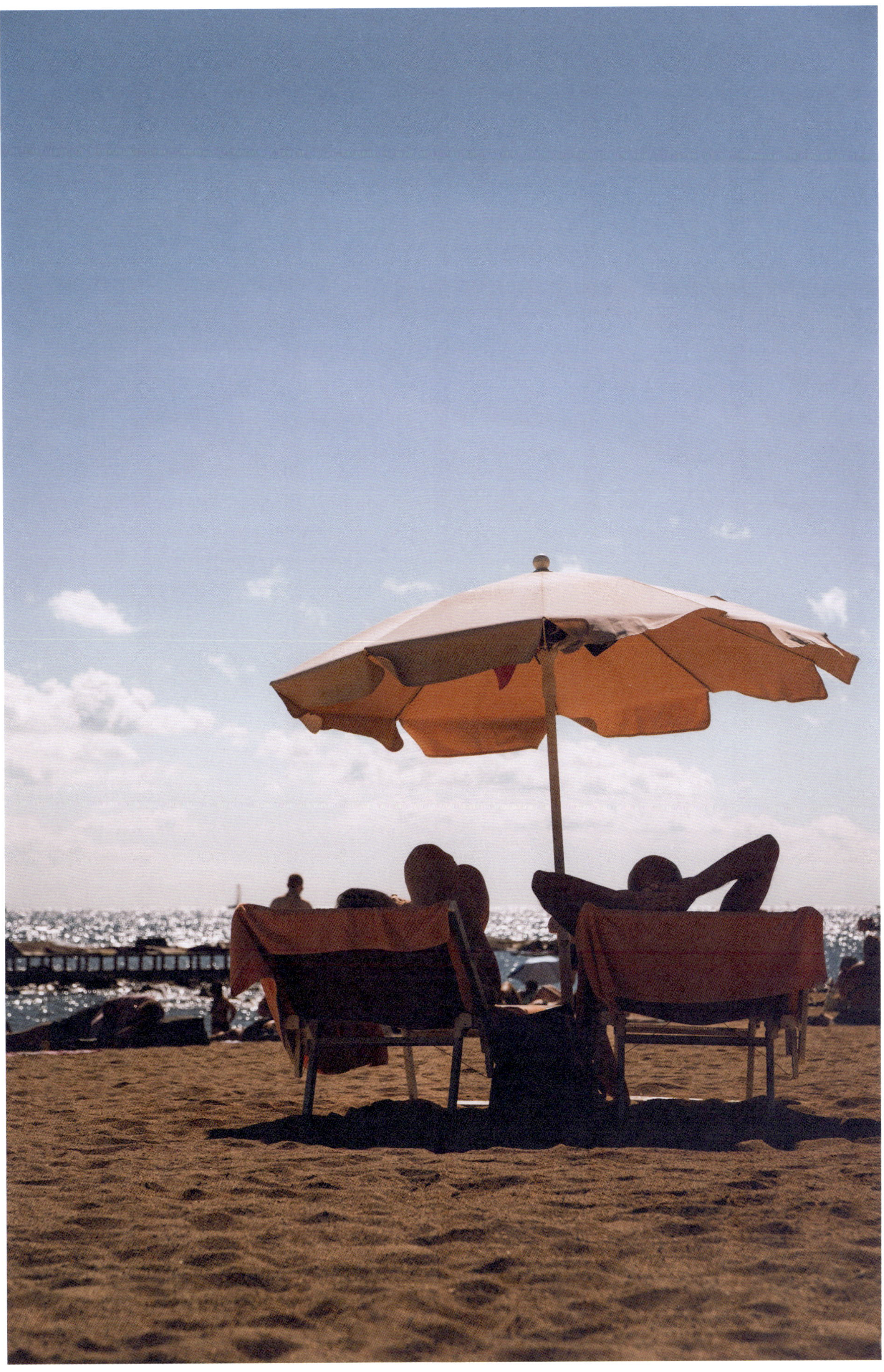

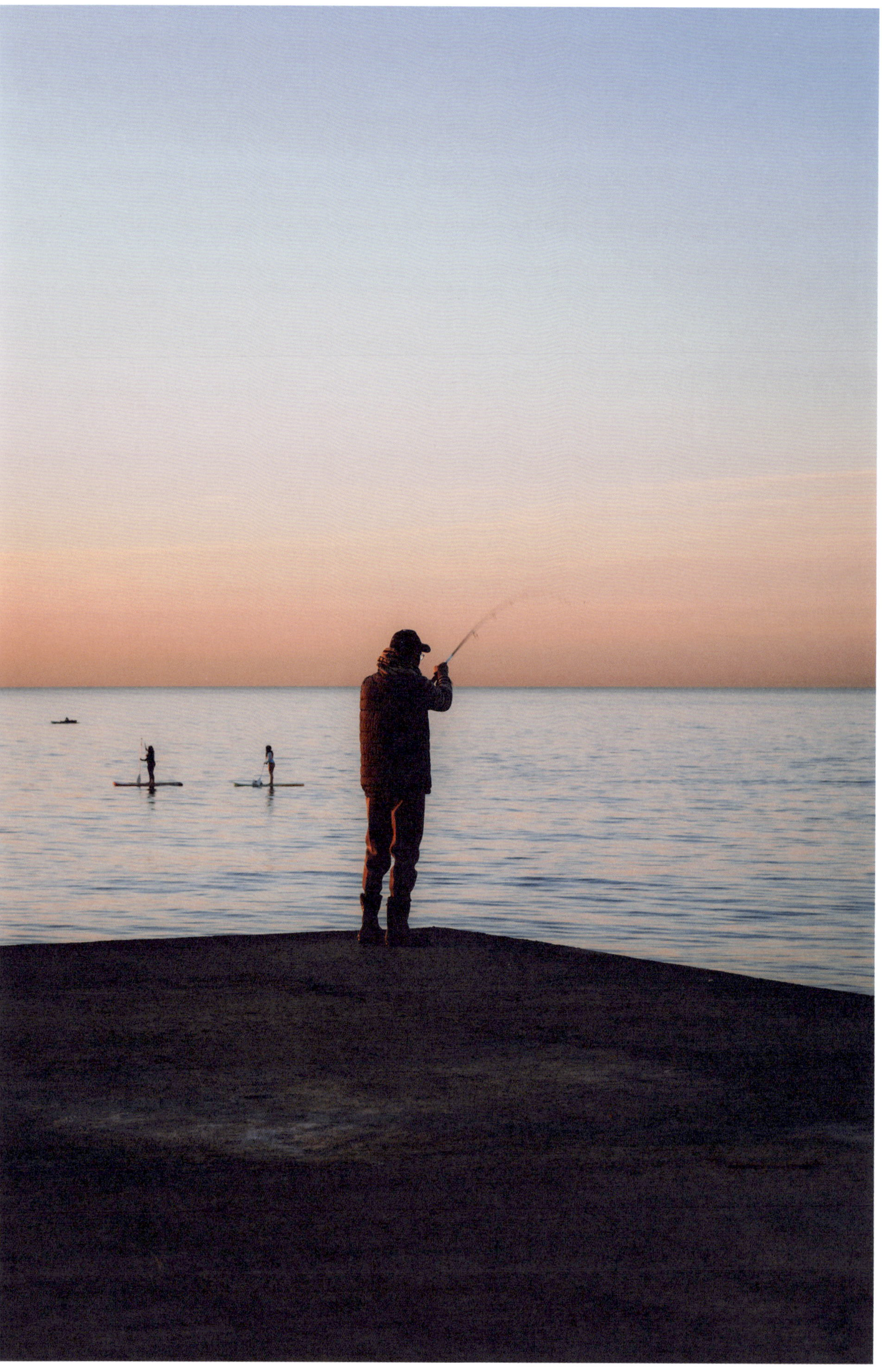

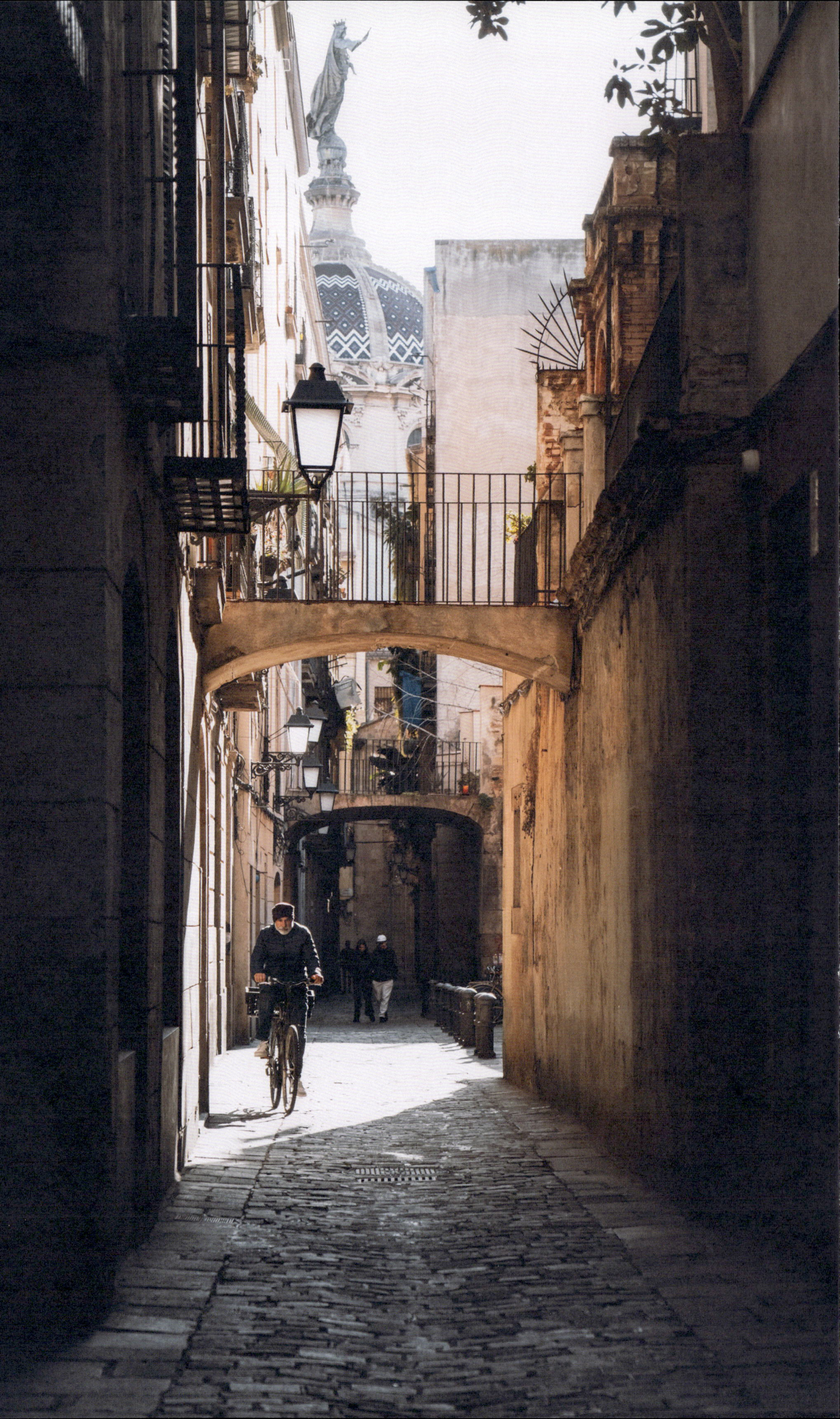

ARTIST'S STATEMENT

For me, photography is about capturing beauty in the everyday – how people live, how the city feels. Its textures, light, and tones. I'm drawn to ordinary scenes that often go unnoticed.

Right after I moved to Barcelona in 2022, I started documenting the city with my camera. Its culture, warmth, and atmosphere have shaped my style significantly. The way early morning light moves through the narrow streets, the contrast between old architecture and everyday routines. This is what I love photographing the most.

As in many cities and regions in Spain, Barcelona's culture is about living outside at a slower pace. It's about enjoying life. Near the seaside, in a bar sharing tapas, or on a terrace sipping a cortado. It's a place where tradition and community still play an important role in everyday life. These are all things I'm trying to display in my work.

I draw inspiration from photographers who've mastered the art of visual storytelling. Català Roca's historical work across Spain is a key influence on my photography. He reminds me of both the documentary and artistic power of photography. Saul Leiter's use of light, texture, and composition has impacted my way of seeing. I can walk the same street for the 20th time but still find something new to photograph.

The collection in this book showcases some of my favorite photos from my time in Barcelona. I hope these images give you a sense of the rhythm of the city – the beauty of its streets, people, and everyday life.

A special thanks to everyone close to me who have always supported me during my creative journey. Also, to the Trope team, for their belief in this project. It's an honor to be part of the community among such inspiring photographers.

PETER JONKER

@peterjonkero

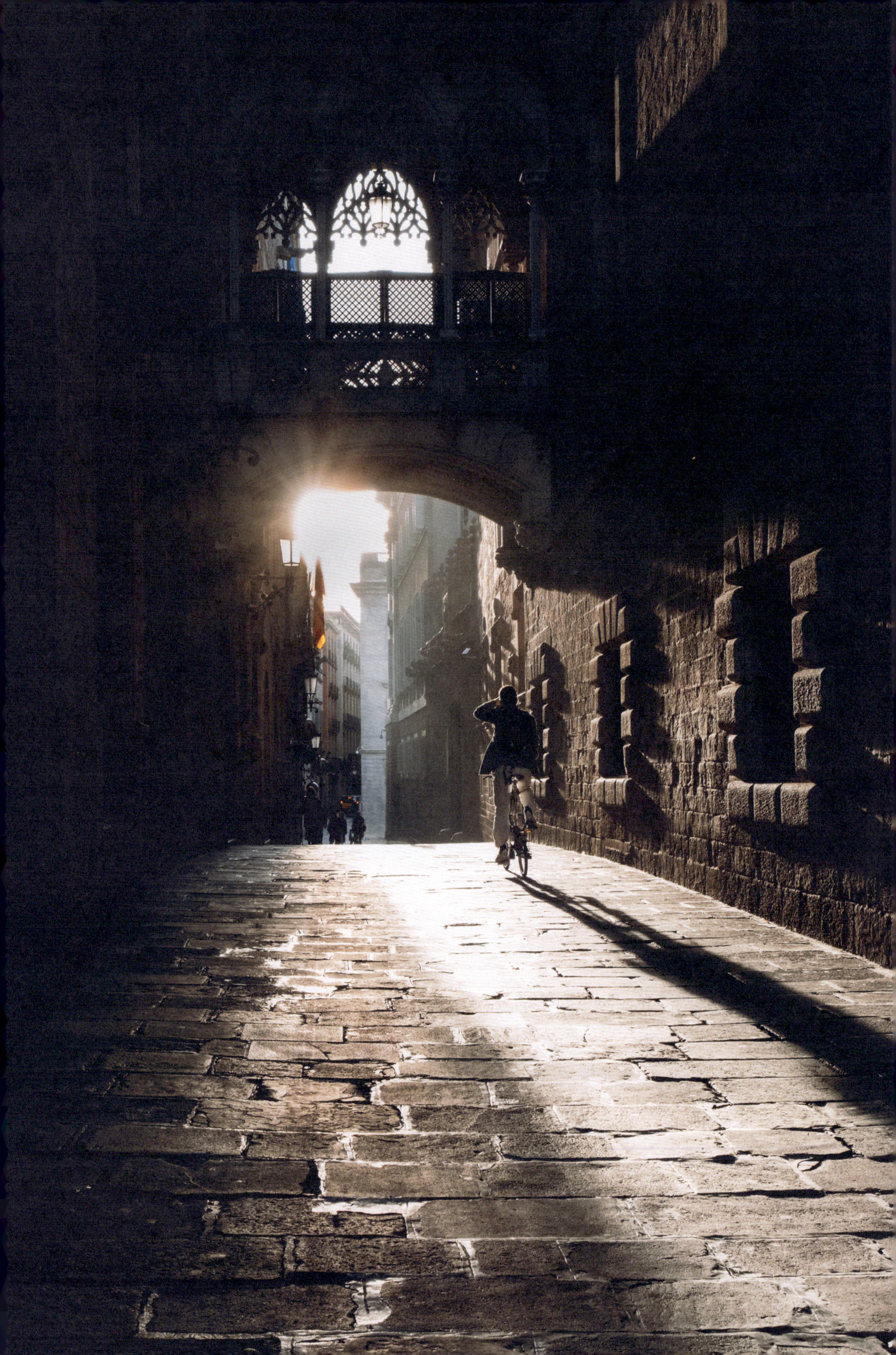

PETER JONKER

Peter Jonker is a Dutch photographer documenting daily life in the city.

His love for photography started during travels through Asia and Latin America. After moving to Barcelona, this started to become a true passion. The city's vibrant street life, the constant presence of good light, and the experience of being exposed to a new culture, gave him a fresh source of inspiration. He started using photography as a way to slow down and document the world around him.

Peter's work centers on timeless street and travel photography, with a strong focus on light, composition, and colors. While photographing cities like Barcelona, Madrid, Sevilla, and Valencia, he's been drawn to everyday scenes that show the culture, tradition, and personality of Spanish life. Moments that tell something about the place and the people in it.

"What drives me is trying to capture something simple in a creative way. Framing it so the story is felt, not explained."

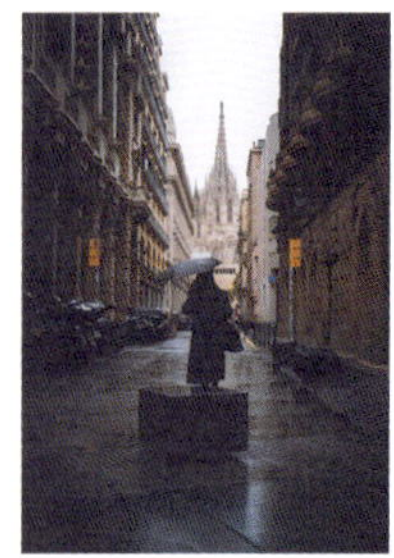
Cover Gothic Quarter

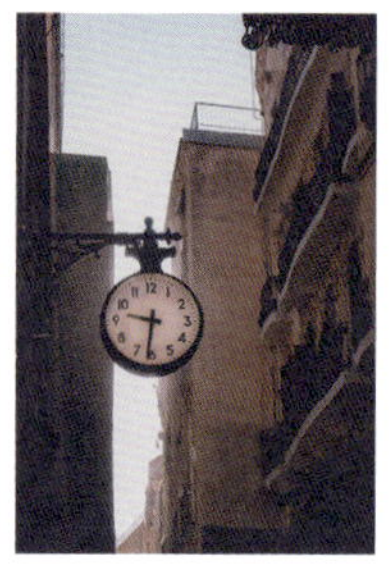
2 Gothic Quarter

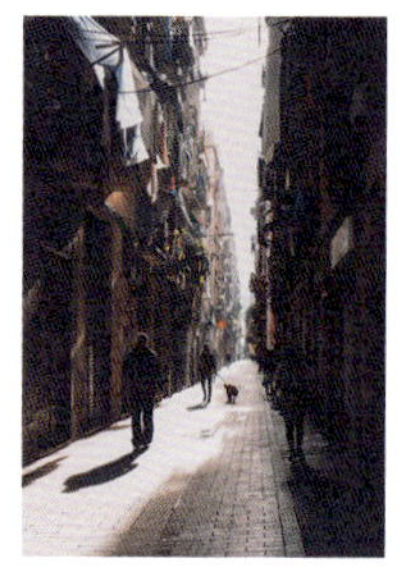
4 El Raval

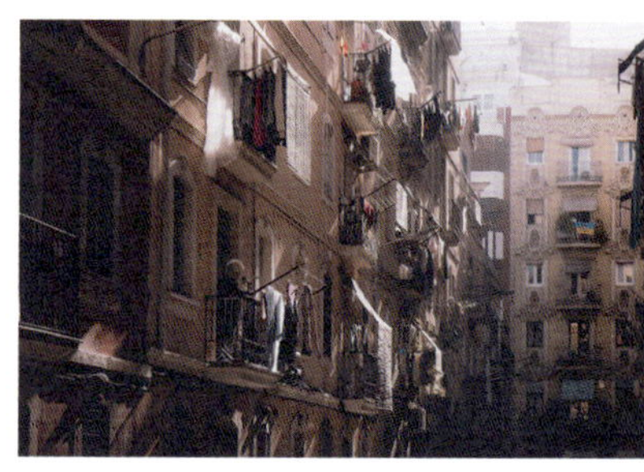
6-7 La Barceloneta

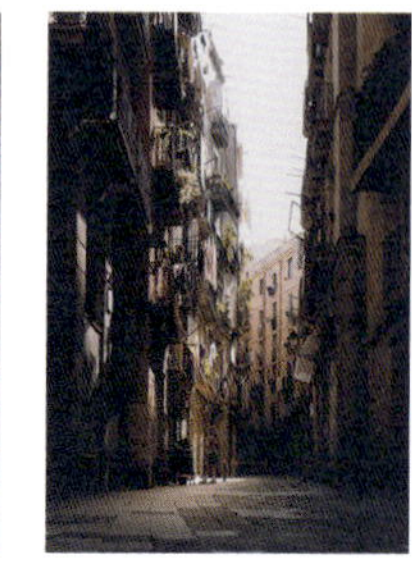
8 El Born

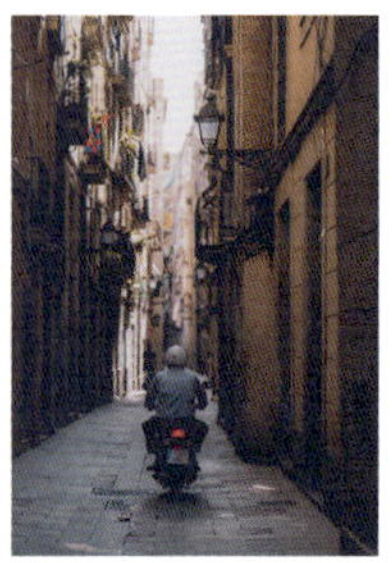
9 El Born

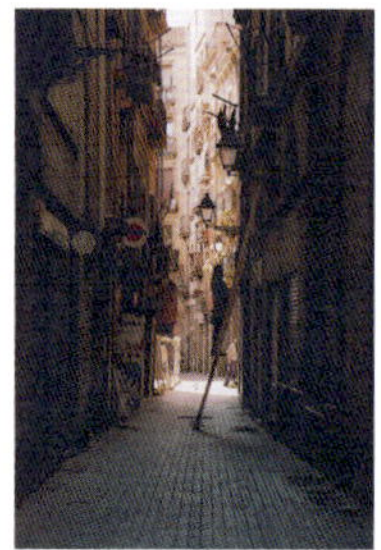
10 El Born

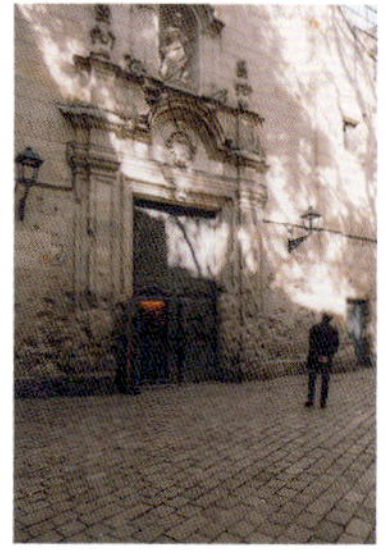
11 Gothic Quarter, Plaça de Sant Felip Neri

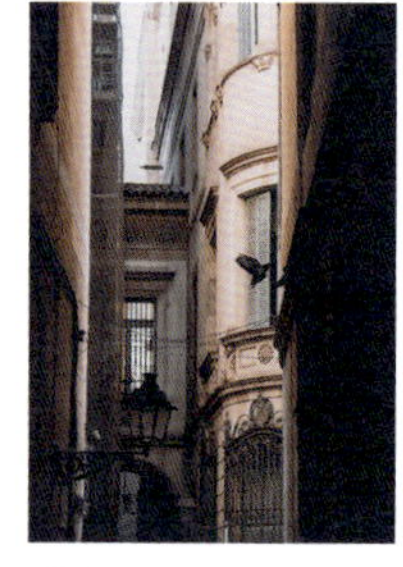
12 Gothic Quarter

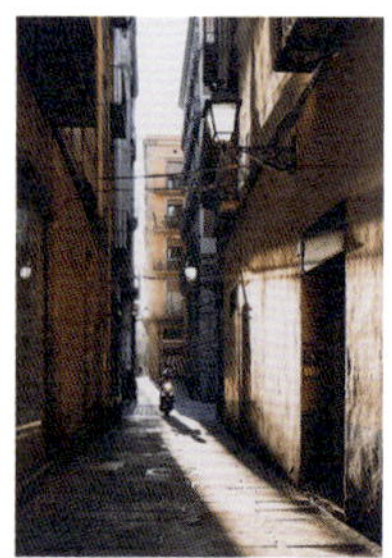
13 Gothic Quarter

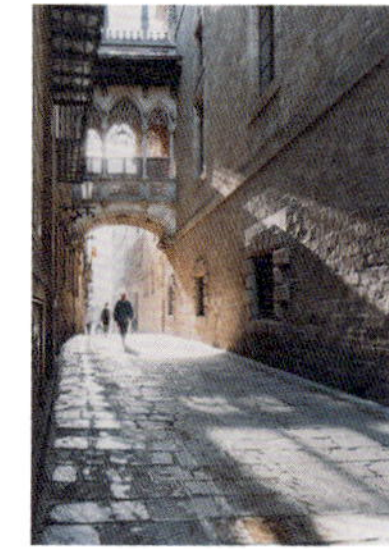
15 Gothic Quarter, Carrer del Bisbe

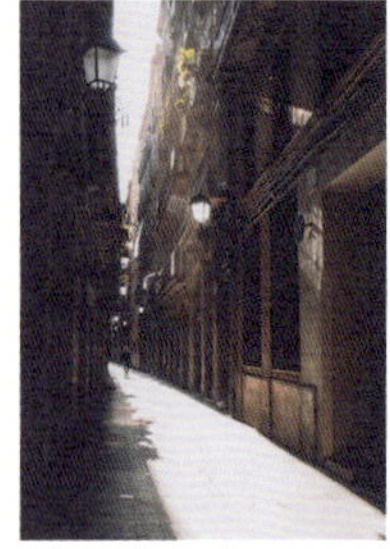
16 Gothic Quarter

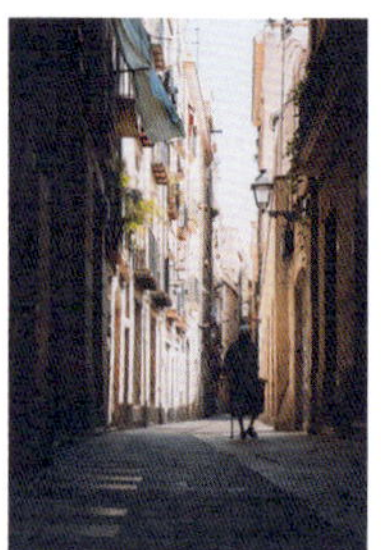
17 El Born

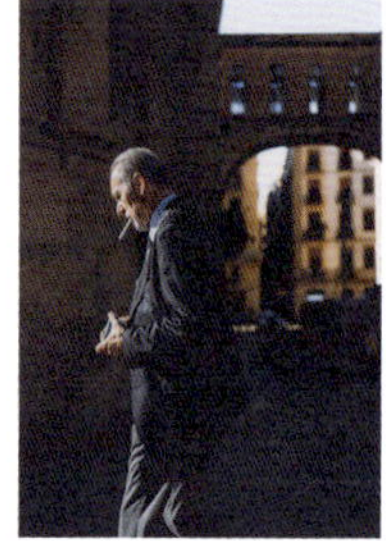
18 La Via Laietana

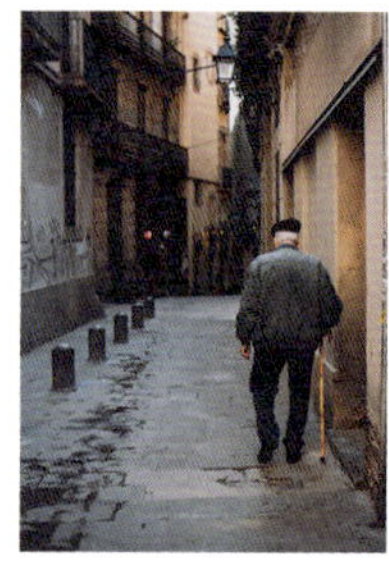
19 Gothic Quarter, El Call

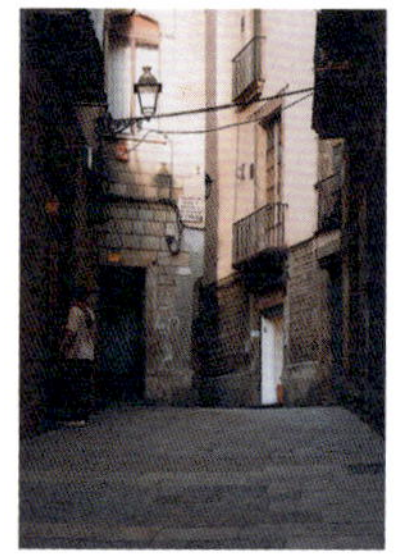
20 Gothic Quarter, El Call

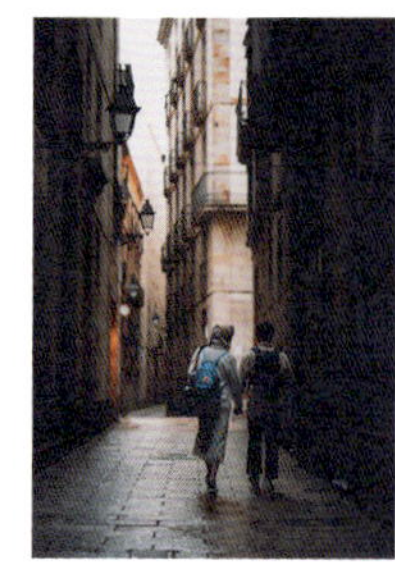
21 Gothic Quarter

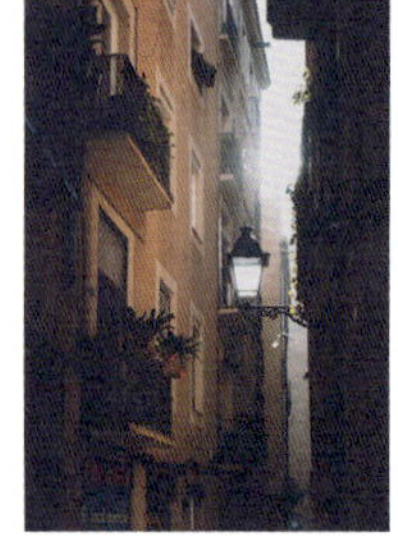
22 Gothic Quarter

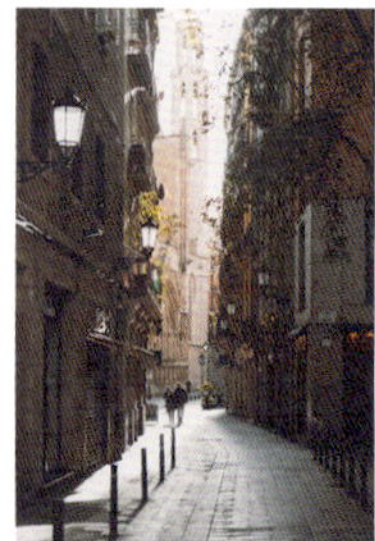
23 El Born

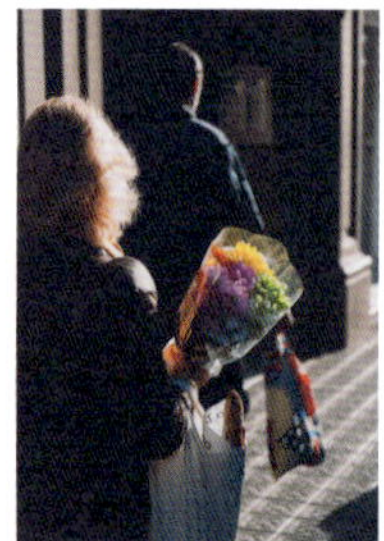
24 Via Laietana

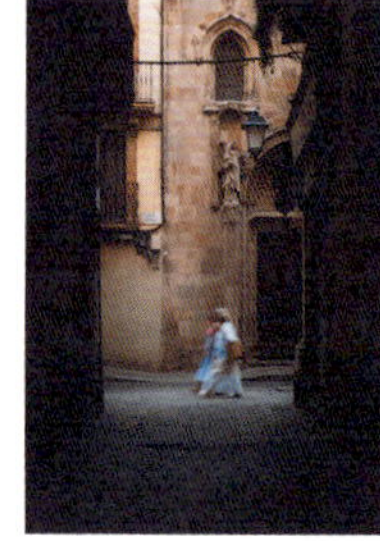
25 Gothic Quarter, Carrer de la Carabassa

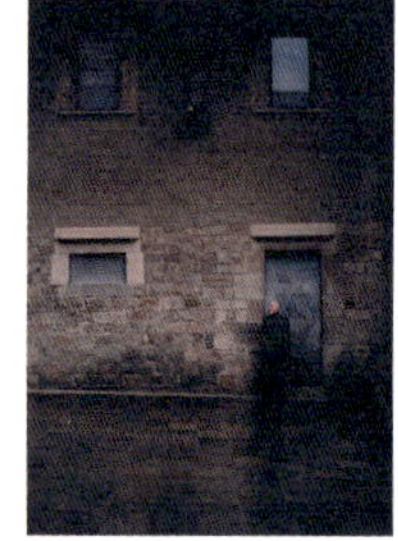
26 Gothic Quarter, Catedral de Barcelona

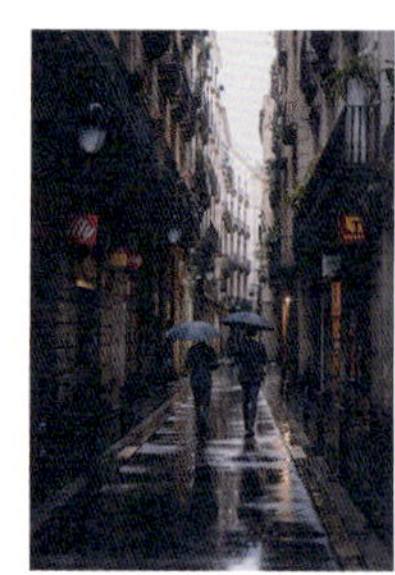
27 Gothic Quarter

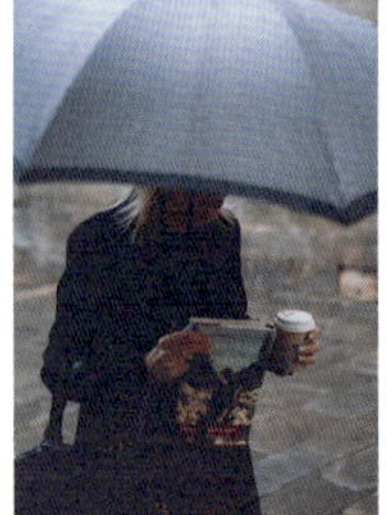
28 Gothic Quarter

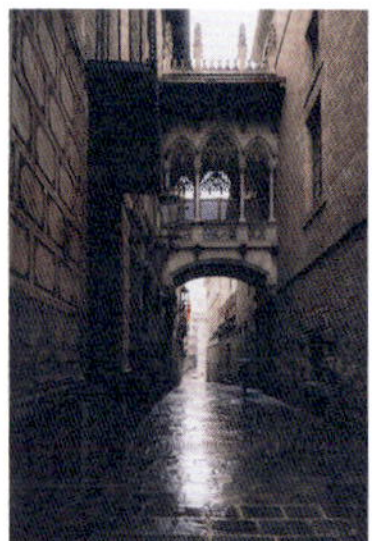
29 Gothic Quarter, Carrer del Bisbe

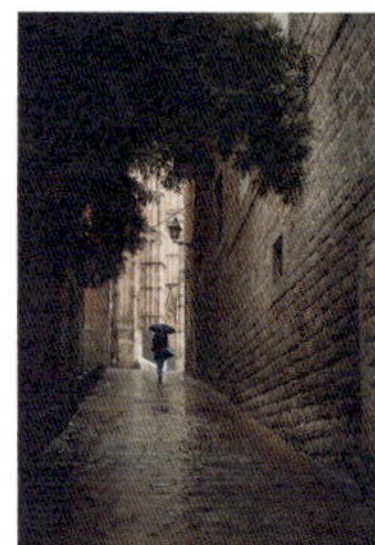
30 Gothic Quarter, Catedral de Barcelona

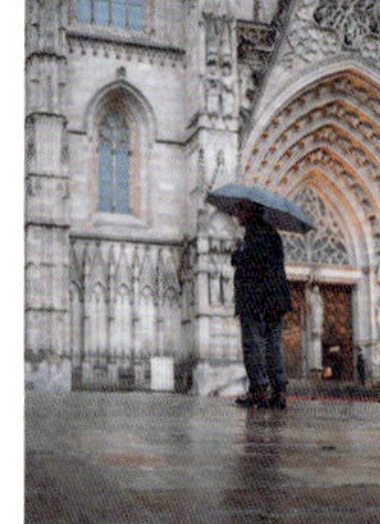
31 Gothic Quarter, Catedral de Barcelona

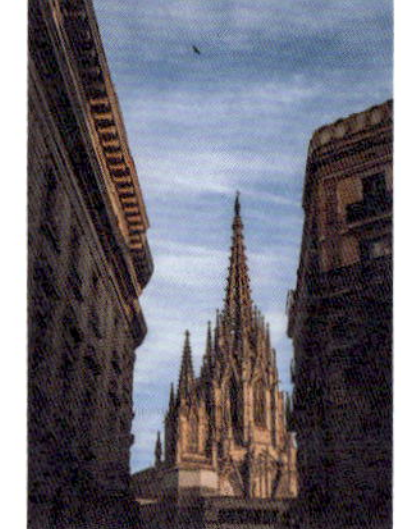
33 Gothic Quarter, Catedral de Barcelona

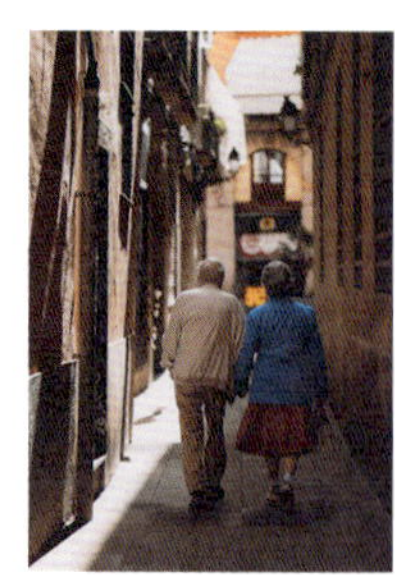
34 Gothic Quarter

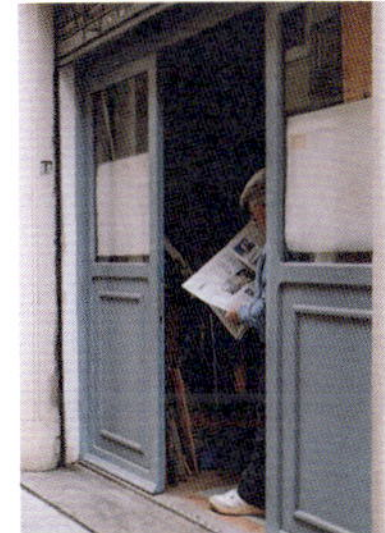
35 Vila de Gràcia

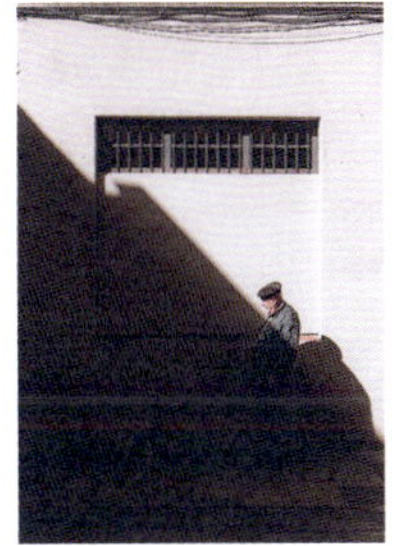
36 Gothic Quarter

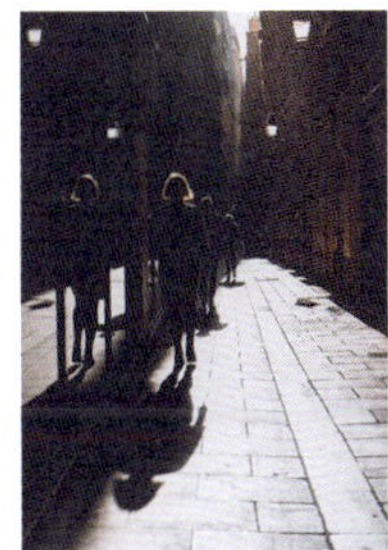
37 Gothic Quarter

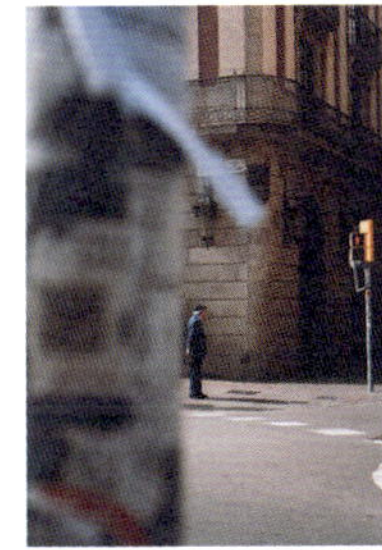
38 La Rambla

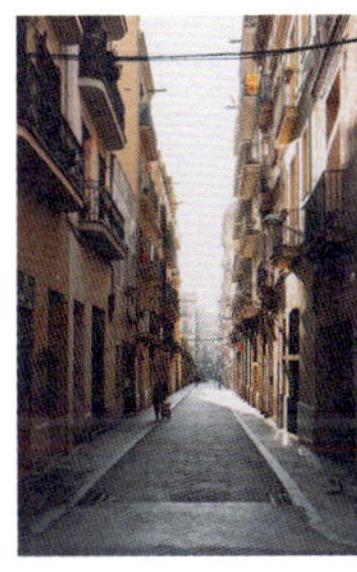
39 Vila de Gràcia

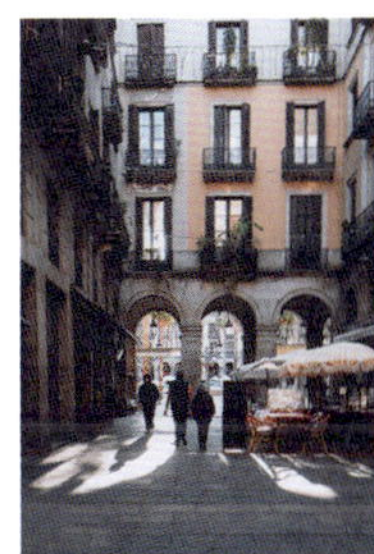
40 Gothic Quarter

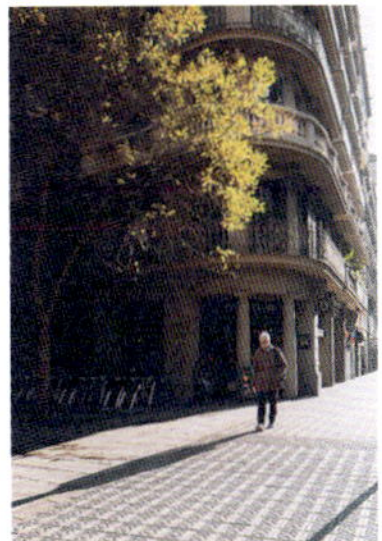
41 Via Laietana

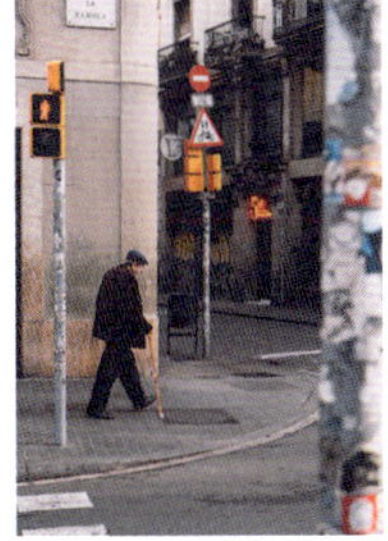
42 Gothic Quarter

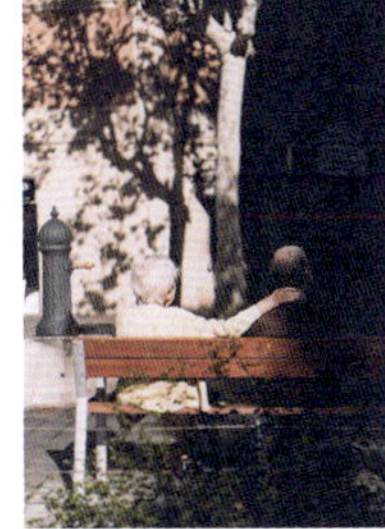
43 Sant Antoni

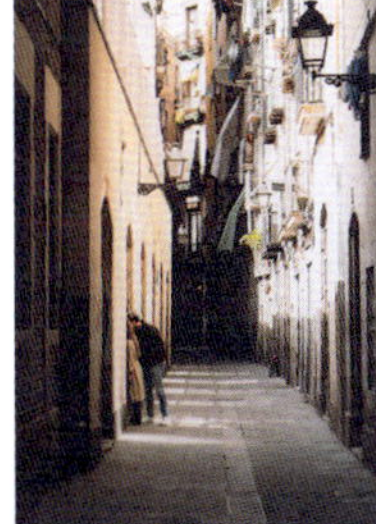
44 El Born

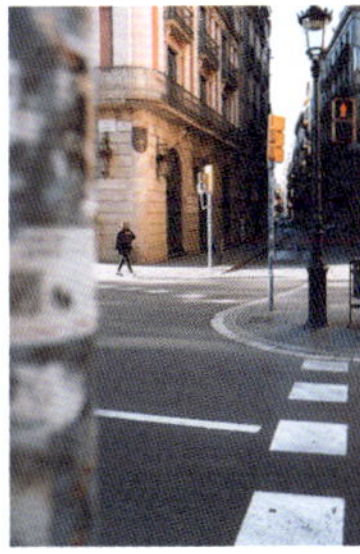
45 La Rambla

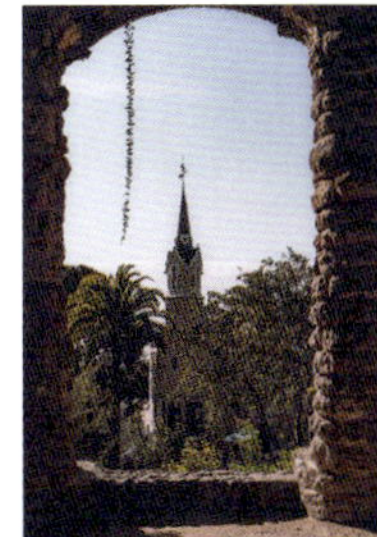
46 Park Güell

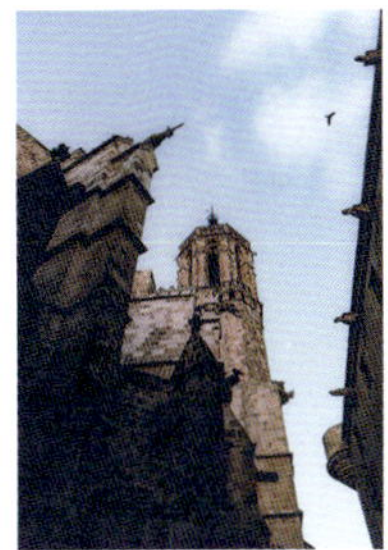
47 Gothic Quarter

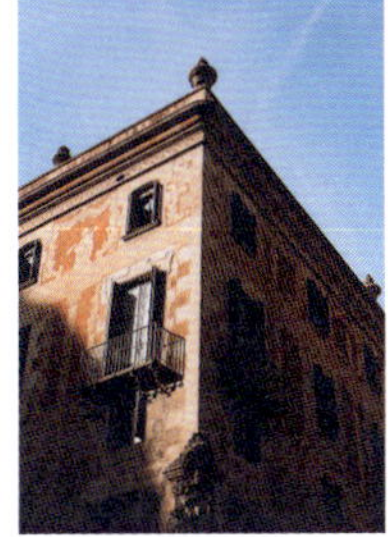
48 Eixample

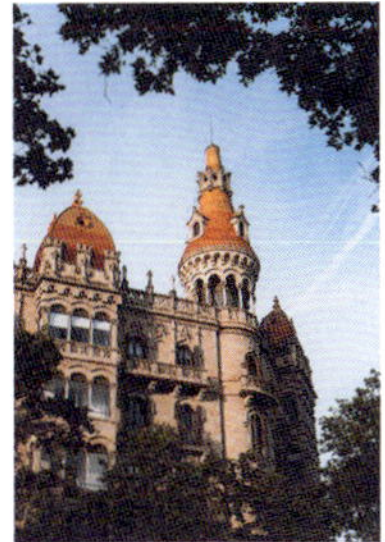
49 Eixample

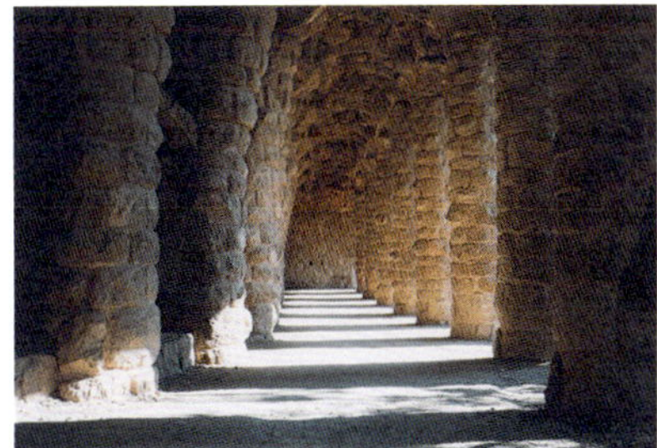
50-51 Park Güell

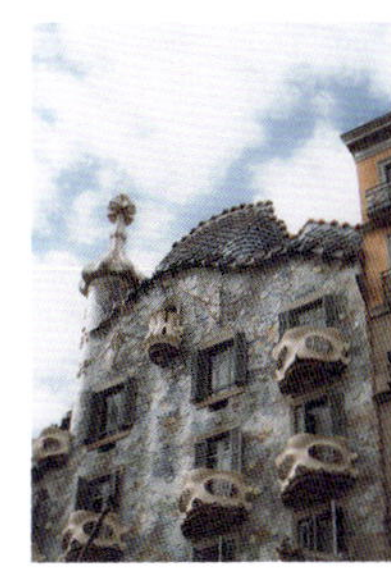
52 Casa Batlló

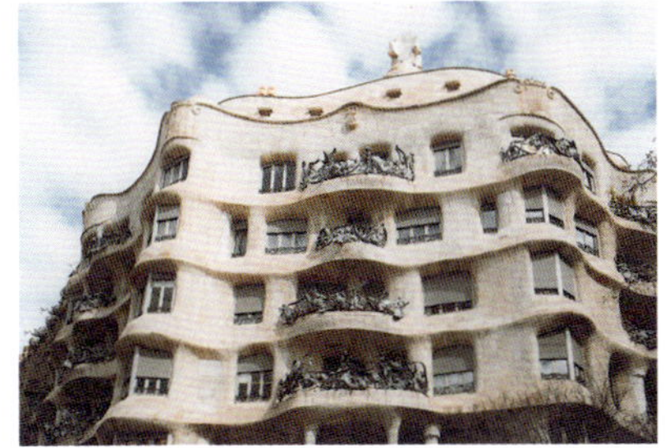
54-55 Casa Milà

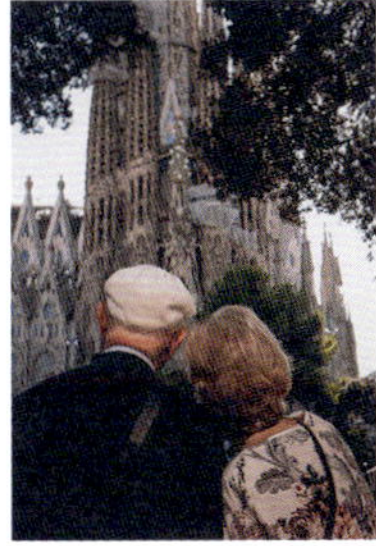
56 La Sagrada Familia

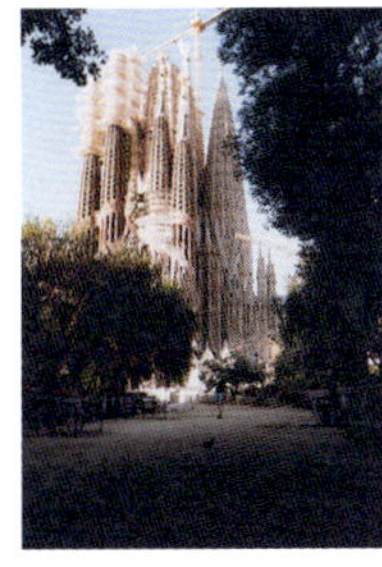
57 La Sagrada Familia

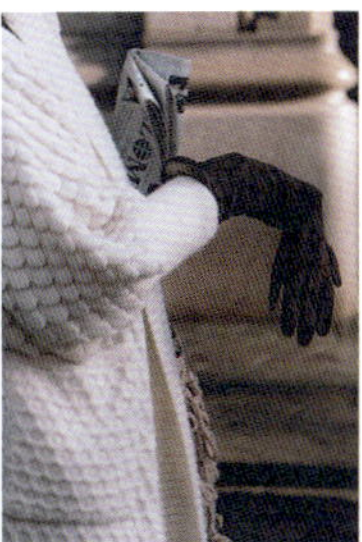
58 La Rambla

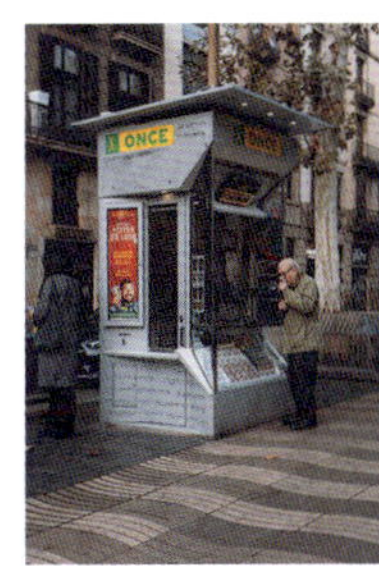

59 La Rambla

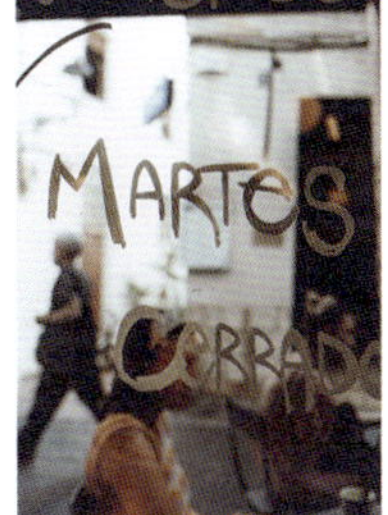

60 Sitges

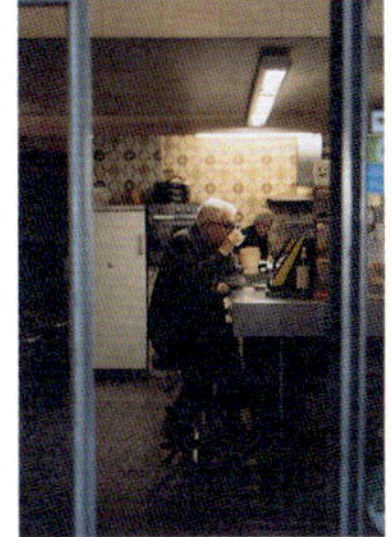
61 Gothic Quarter

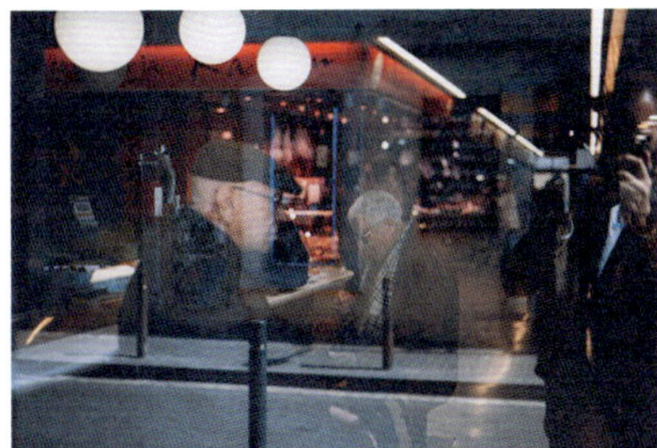
62-63 La Barceloneta

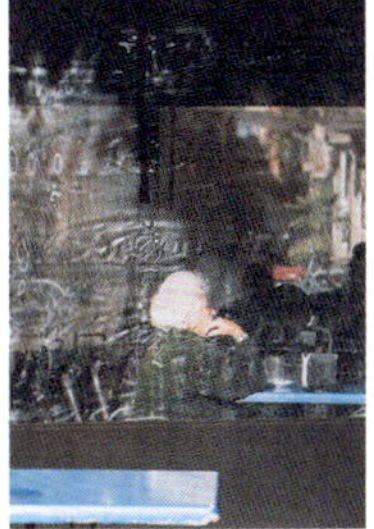
64 La Barceloneta

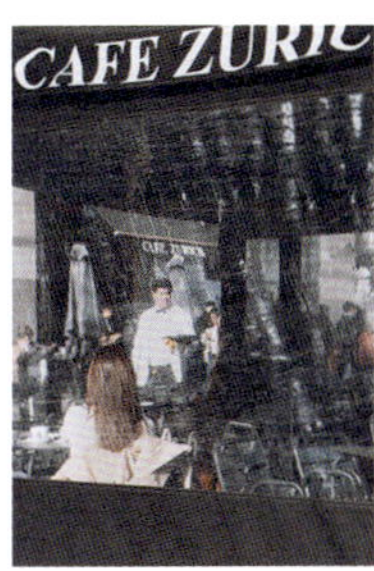

65 La Rambla

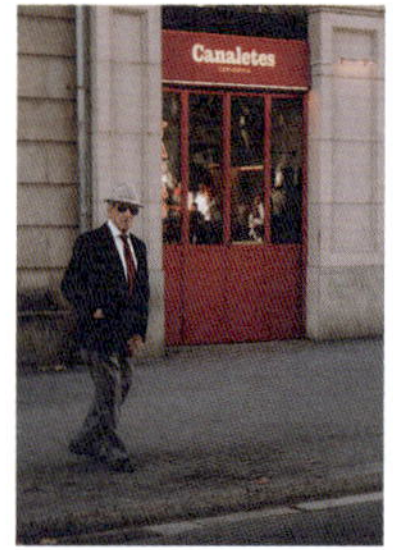

66 La Rambla

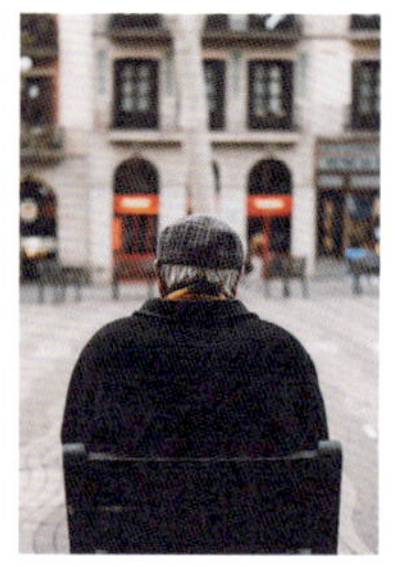

67 La Rambla

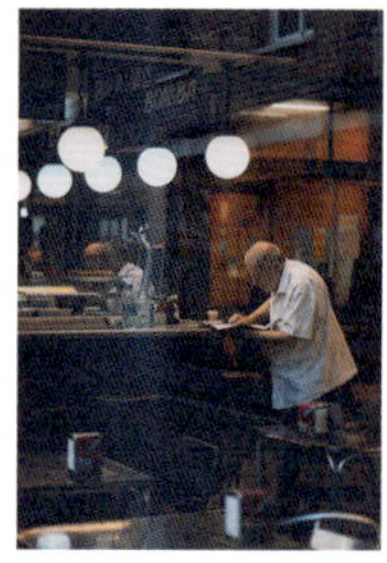

68 La Barceloneta

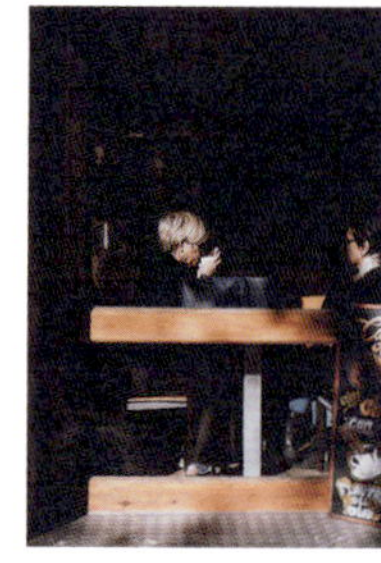

70 Eixample

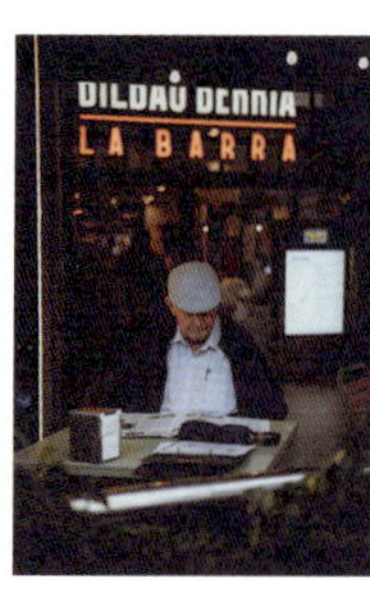

71 Gothic Quarter

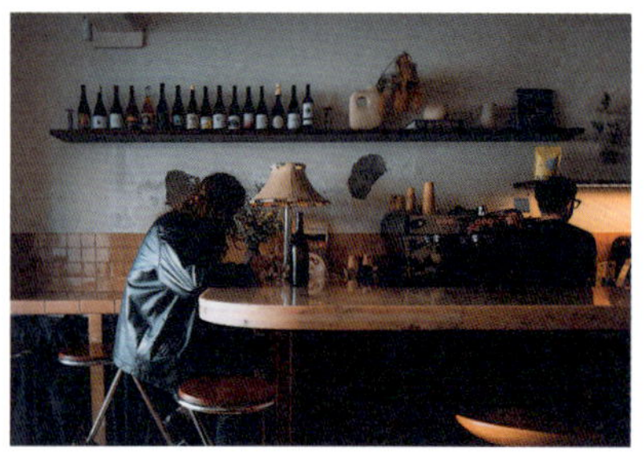

72-73 La Barceloneta

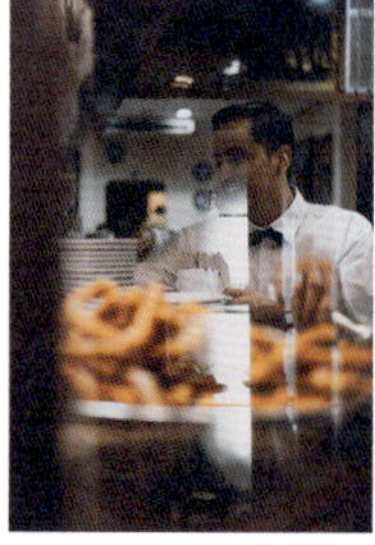

74 Gothic Quarter

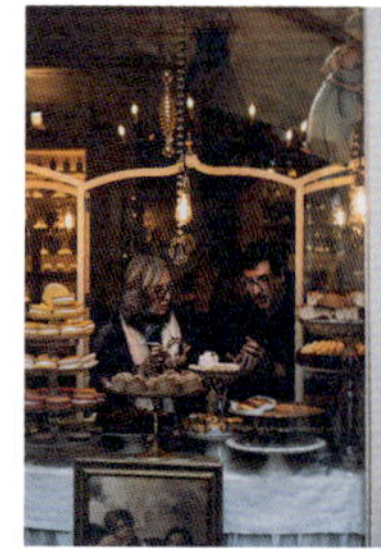

75 Gothic Quarter

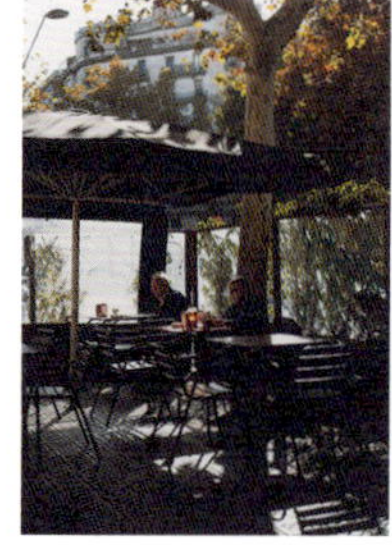

76 Eixample

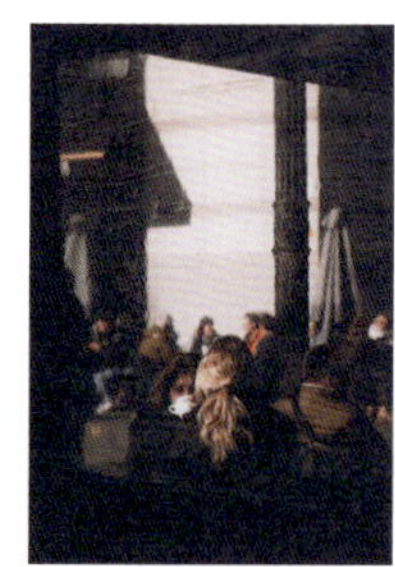

77 Gothic Quarter

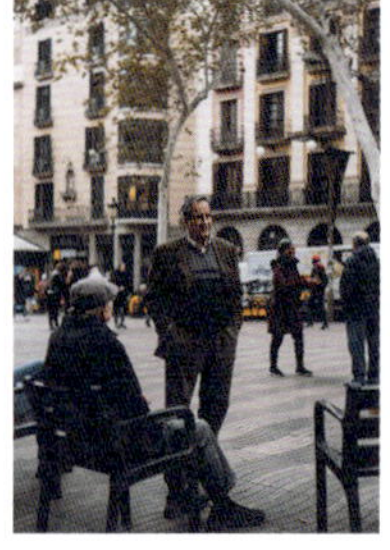

78 La Rambla

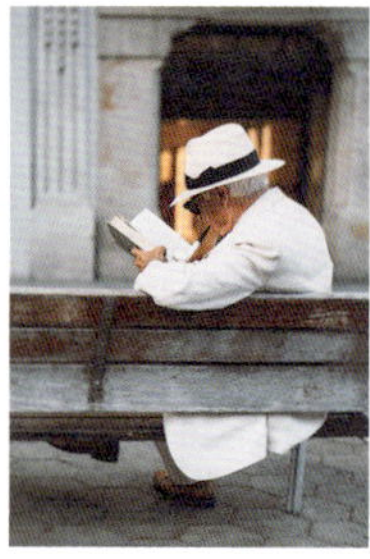

79 Eixample

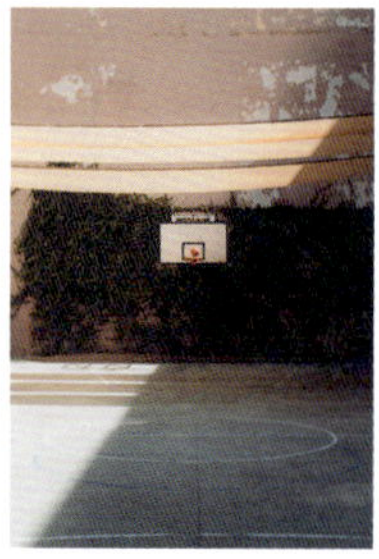

80 El Born

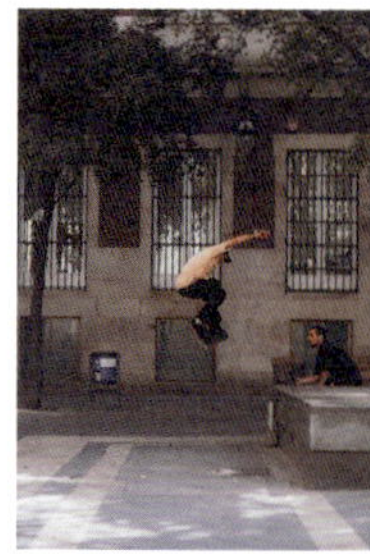

81 Gothic Quarter

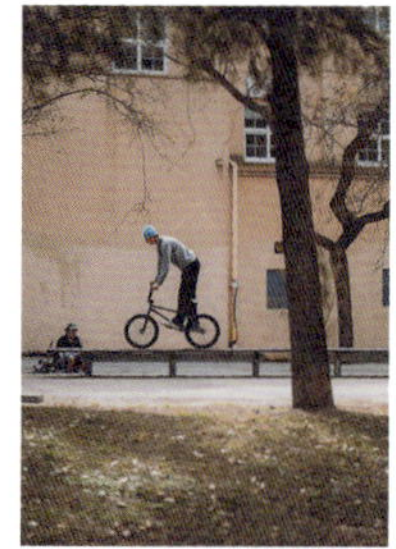

82 La Barceloneta

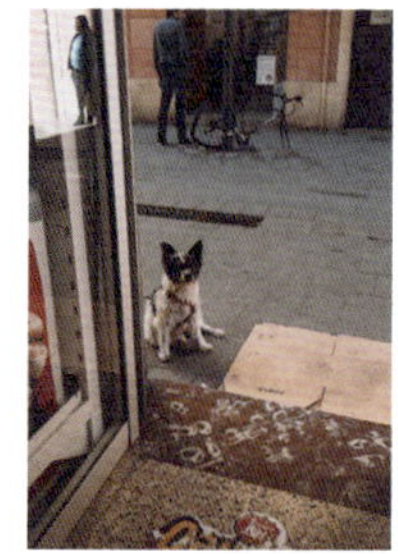

83 La Barceloneta

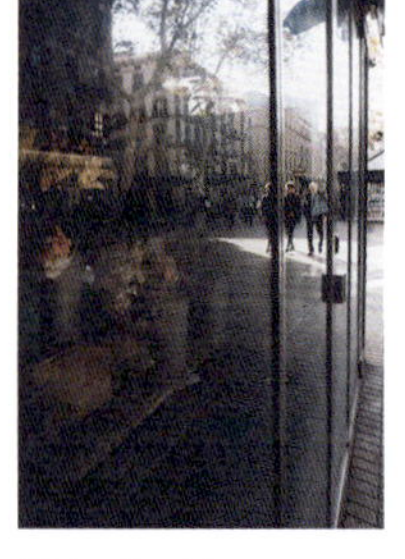

84 La Rambla

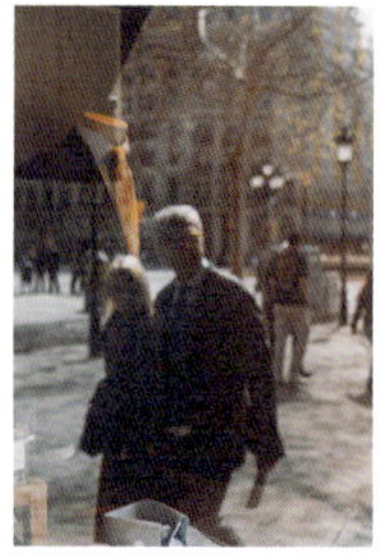

85 Eixample

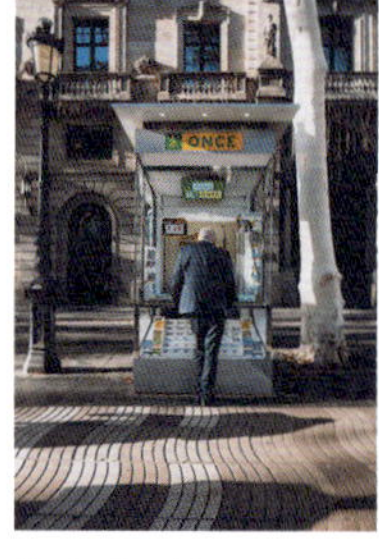

86 La Rambla

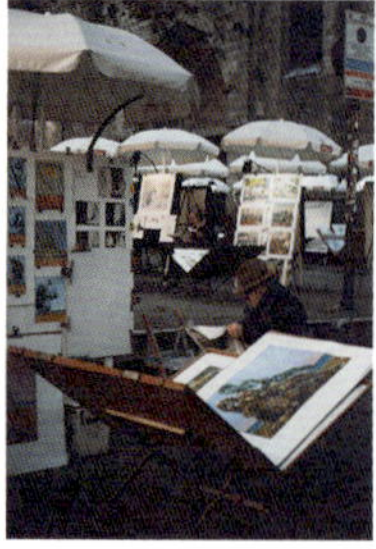

87 Gothic Quarter

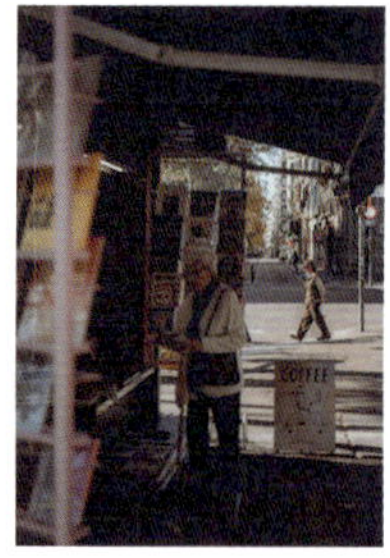

88 Eixample

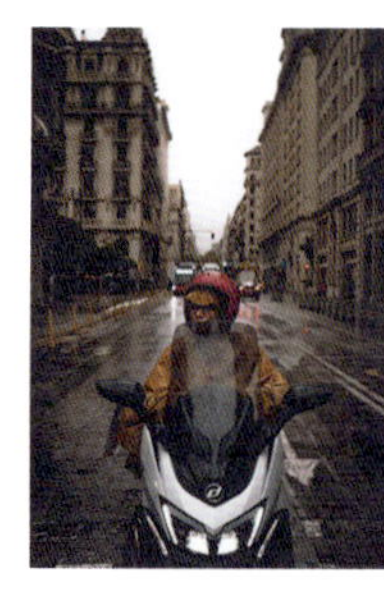

90 Via Laietana

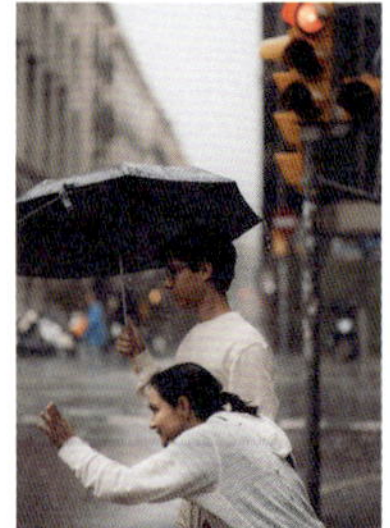

91 Via Laietana

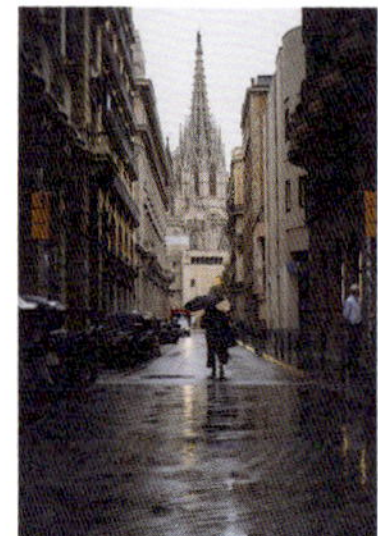

92 Gothic Quarter

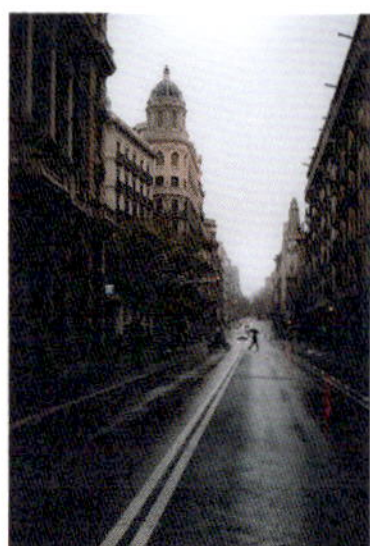

93 Via Laietana

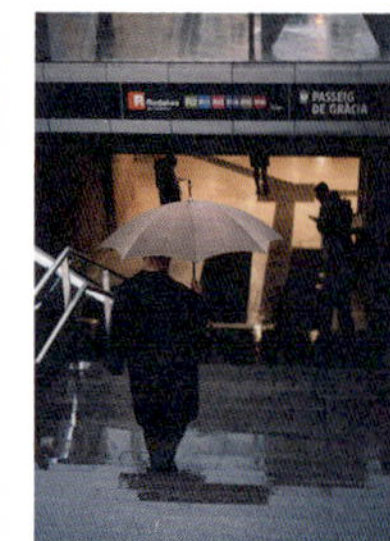

94 Eixample

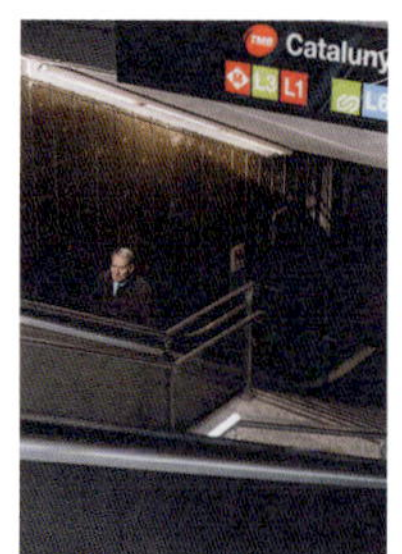

95 Plaça de Catalunya

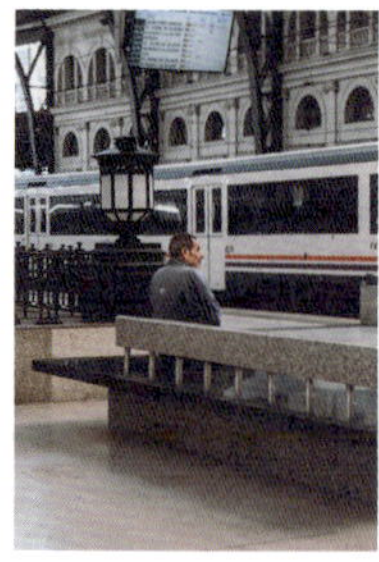

96 Estació França

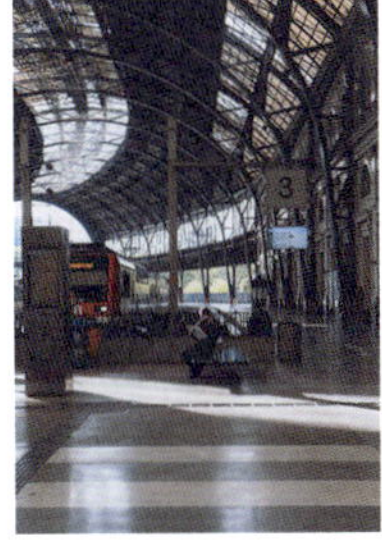
97 Estació França

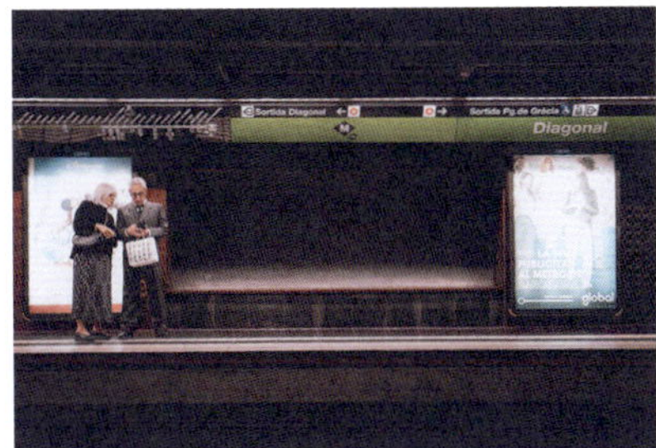
98-99 Eixample

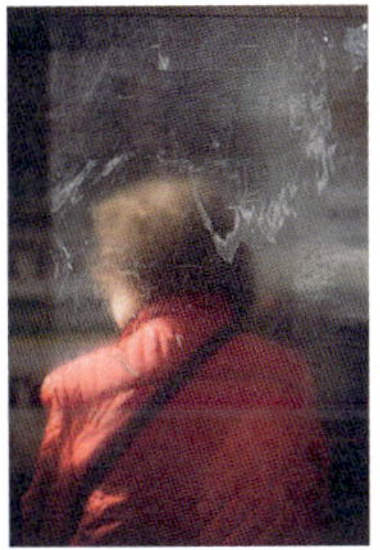
100 Eixample

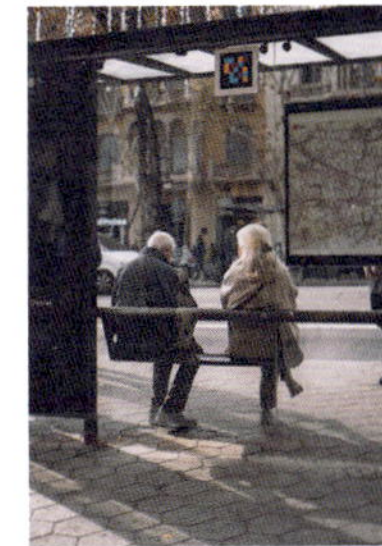
101 Eixample

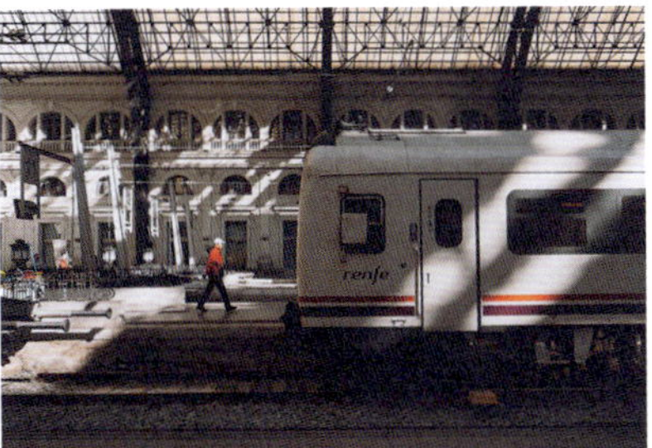
102-103 Estació França

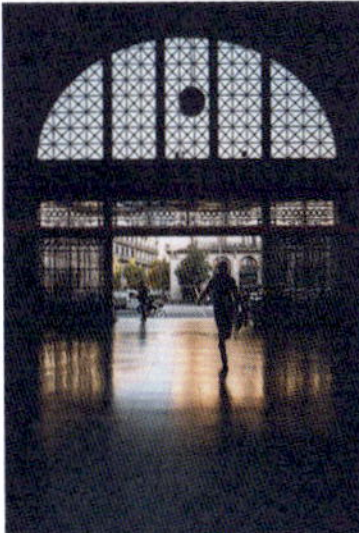
104 Estació França

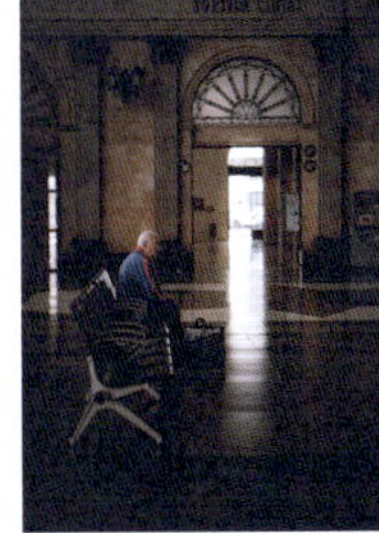
105 Estació França

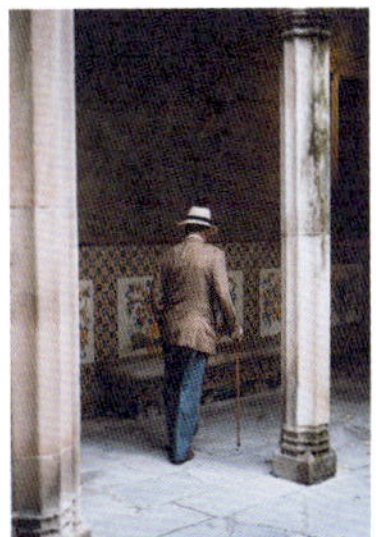
106 Gothic Quarter

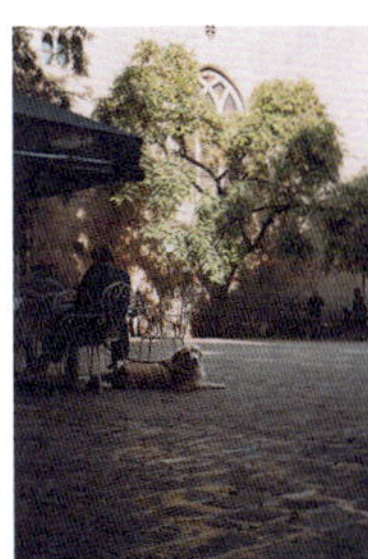
108 El Born

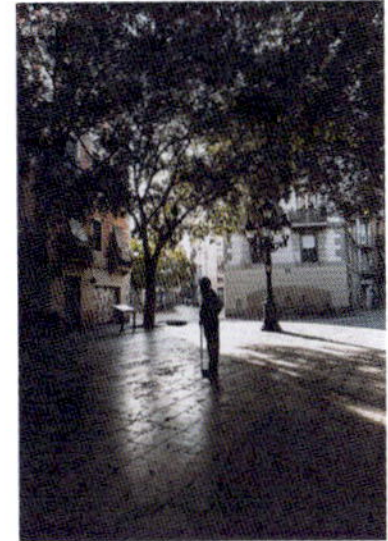
109 El Born

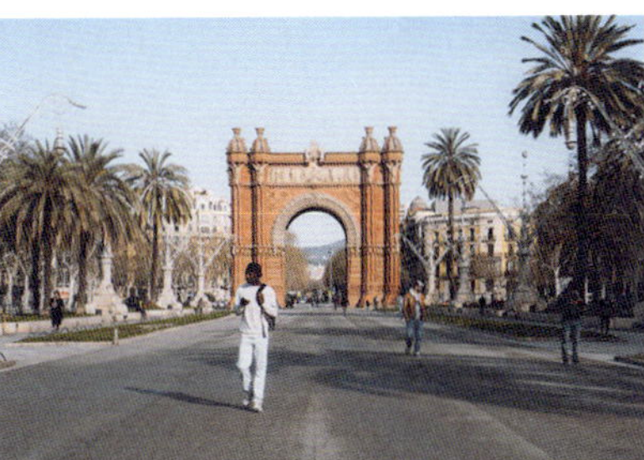
110-111 Passeig de Lluís Companys

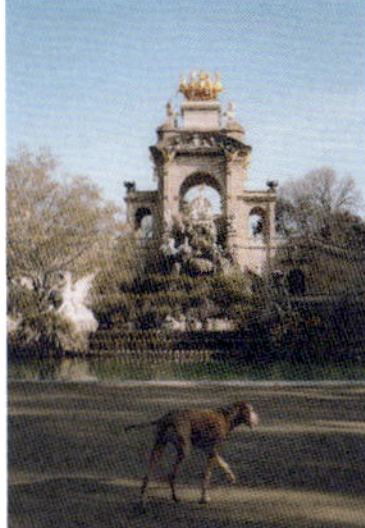
112 Ciutadella Park

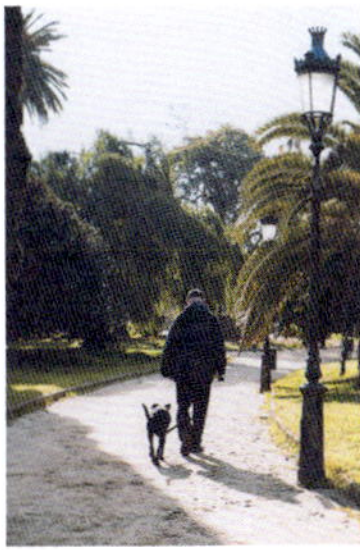
113 Ciutadella Park

114 Parc del Guinardó

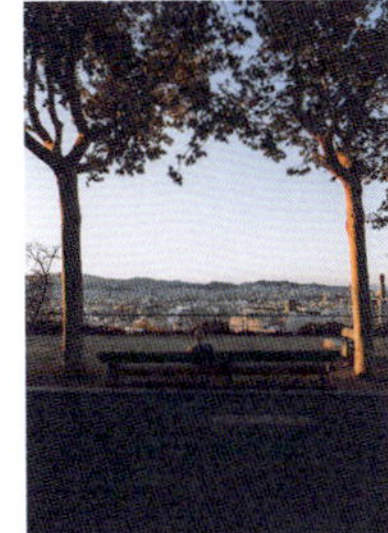
115 Montjuïc

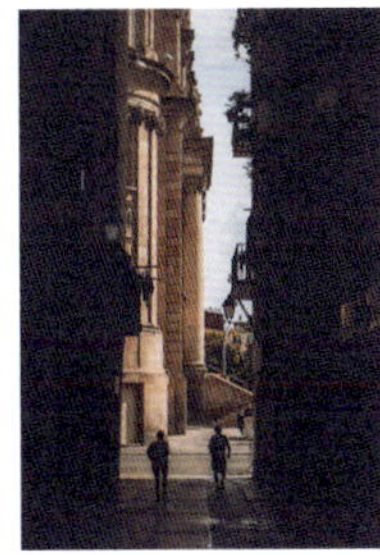
116 Gothic Quarter

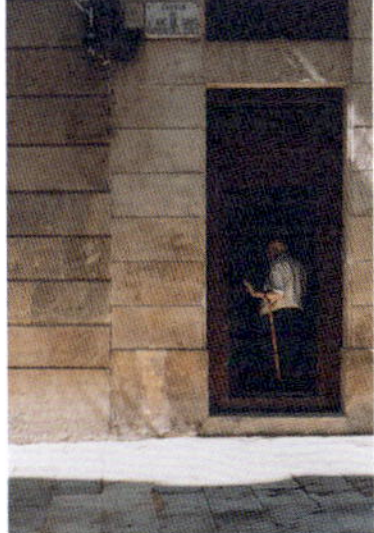
117 Gothic Quarter

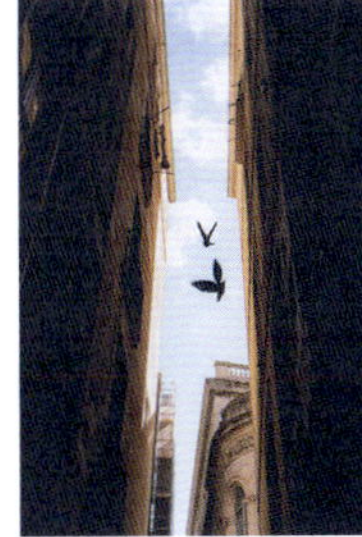
119 Gothic Quarter

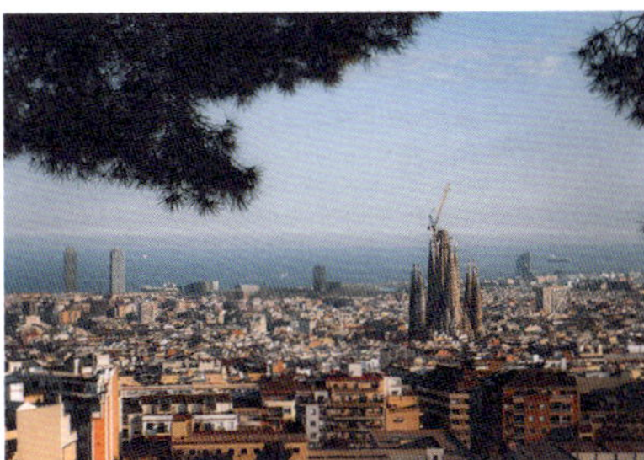
120-121 Parc del Guinardó

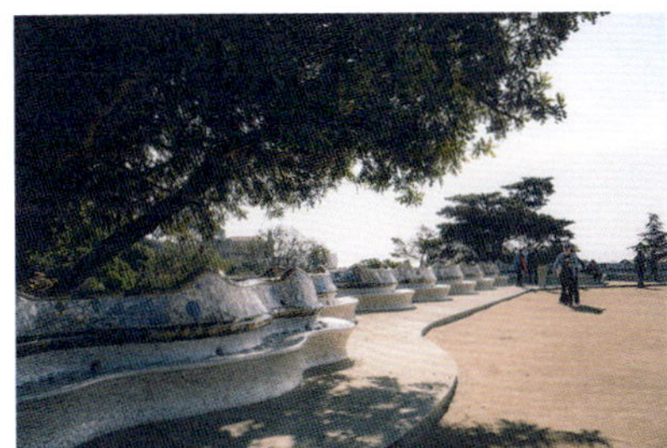
122-123 Park Güell

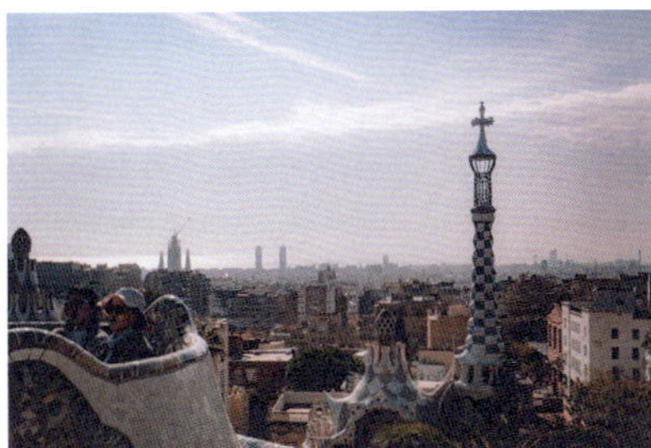
124-125 Park Güell

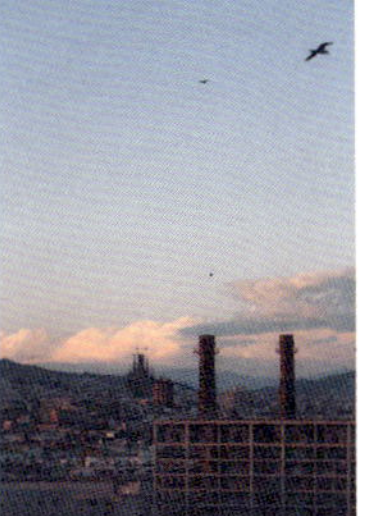
126 Montjuïc

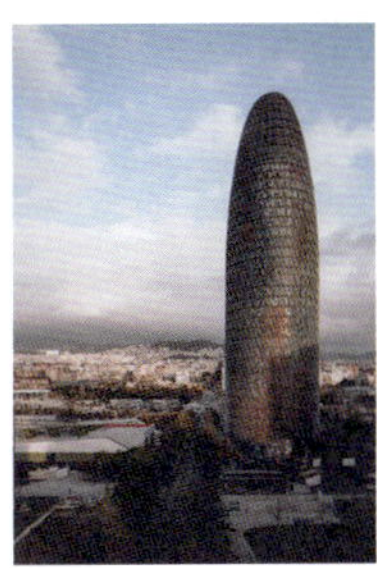
127 Poblenou, Torre Glòries

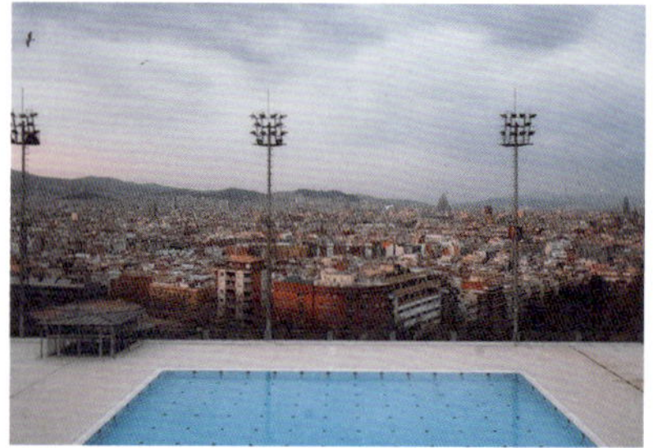
128-129 Montjuïc

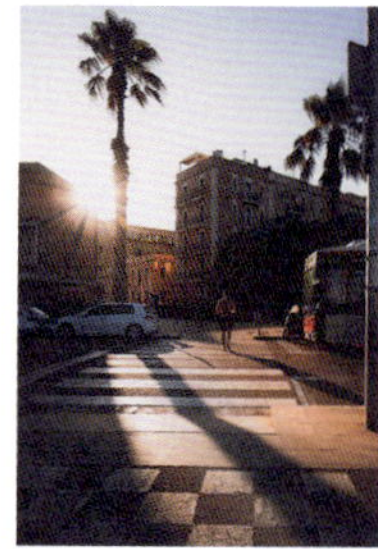
130 La Barceloneta

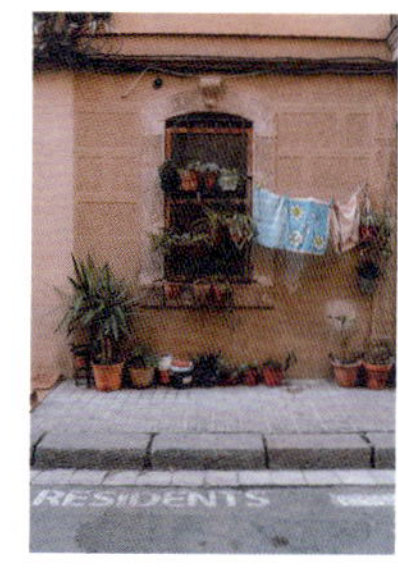

132 La Barceloneta

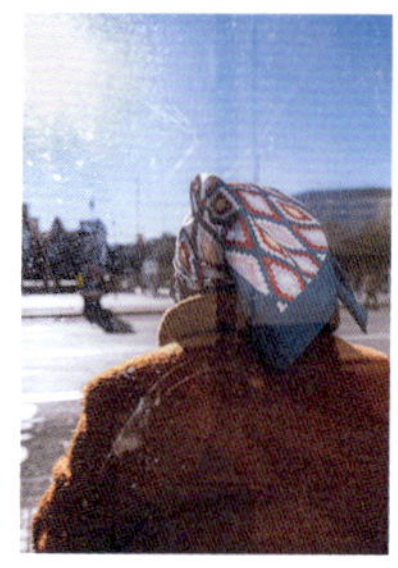
133 Eixample

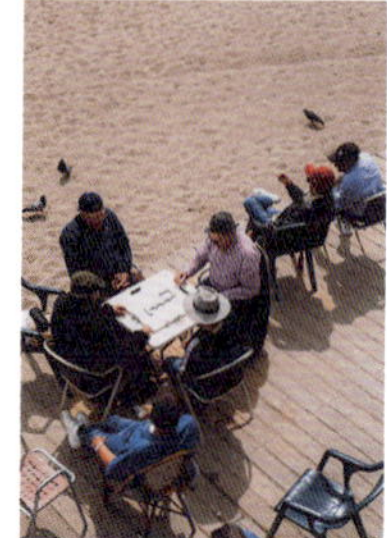
134 La Barceloneta

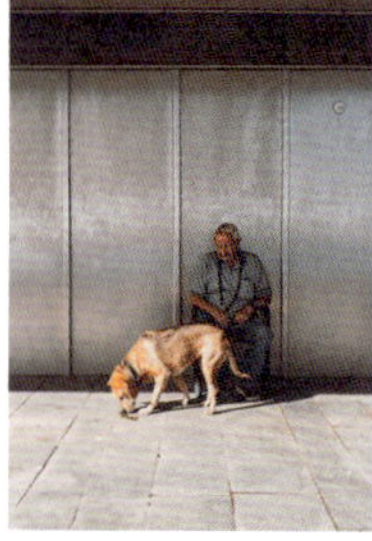
135 La Barceloneta

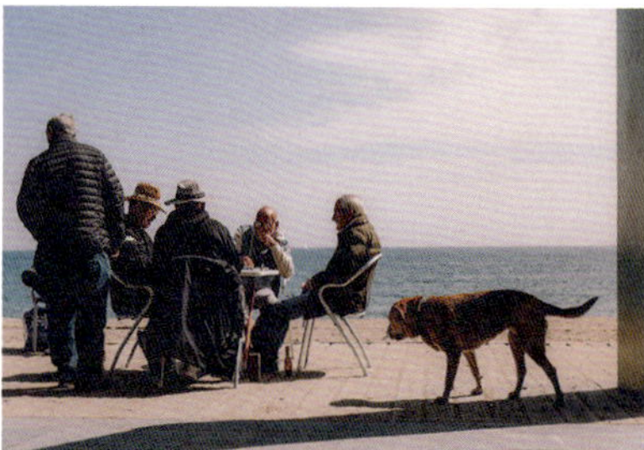
136-137 La Barceloneta

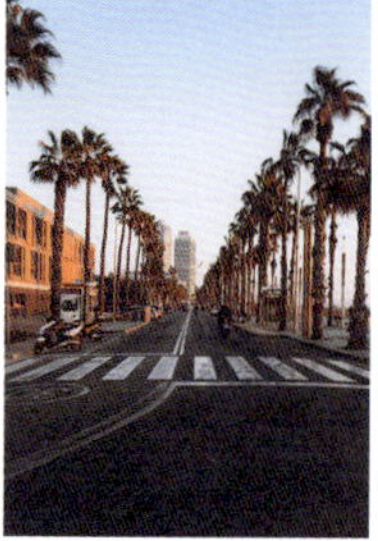
138 La Barceloneta

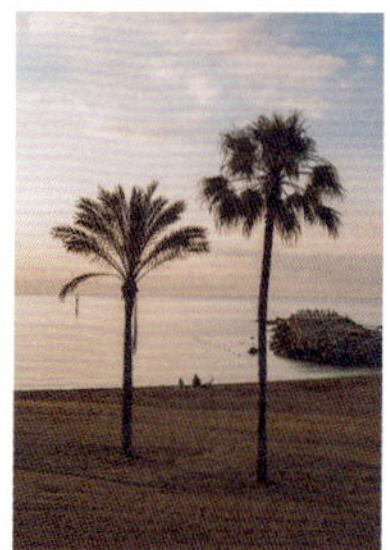
139 La Barceloneta

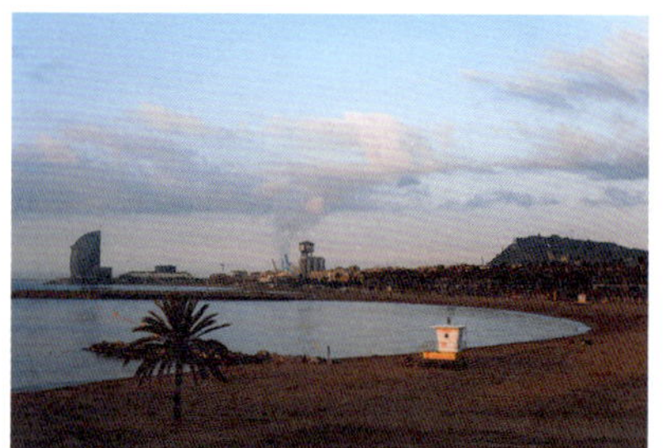
140-141 La Barceloneta

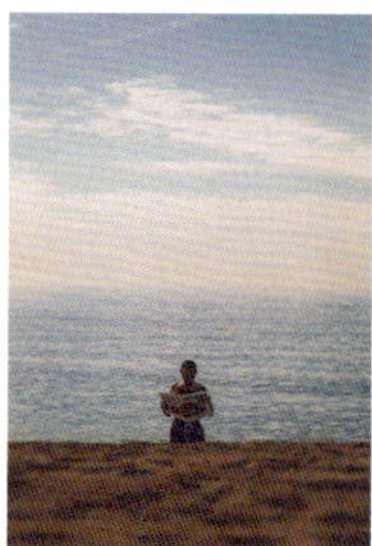
142 La Barceloneta

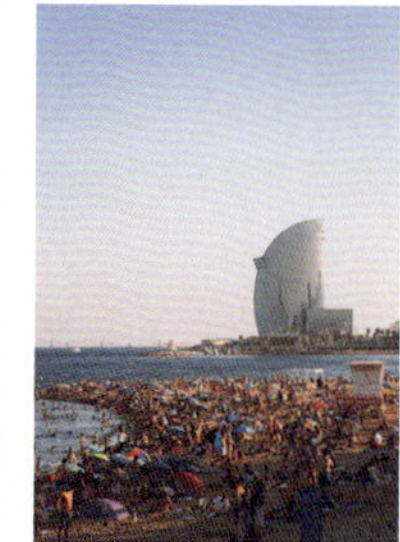
144 La Barceloneta

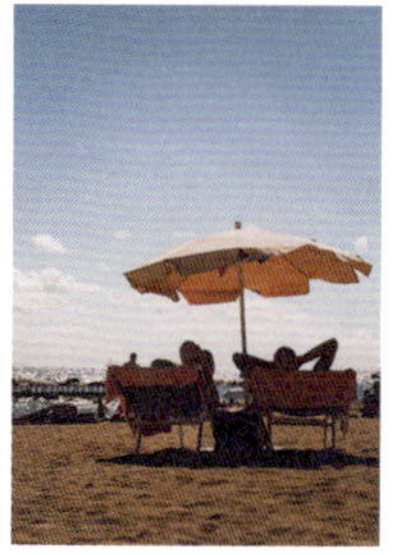
145 La Barceloneta

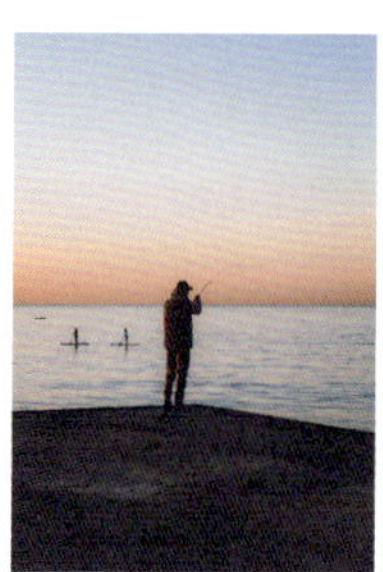
146 La Barceloneta

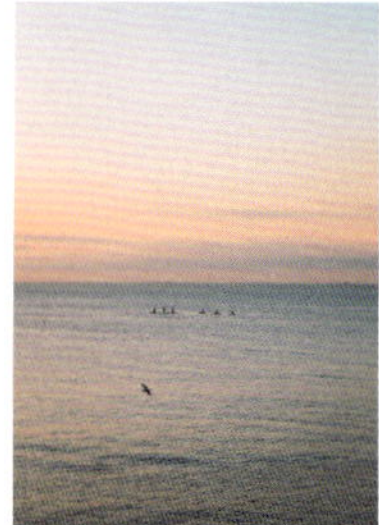
147 La Barceloneta

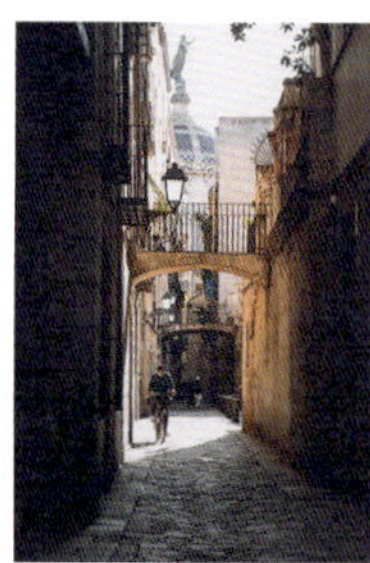
148 Gothic Quarter, Carrer de la Carabassa

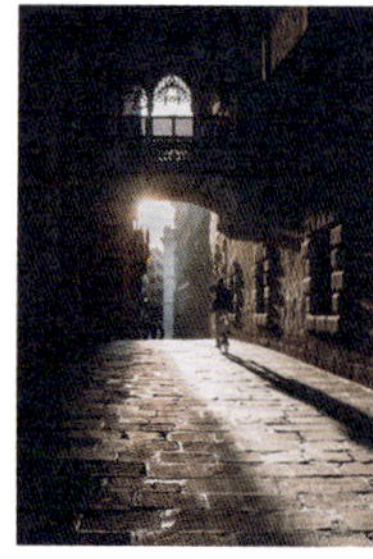
150 Gothic Quarter, Carrer del Bisbe

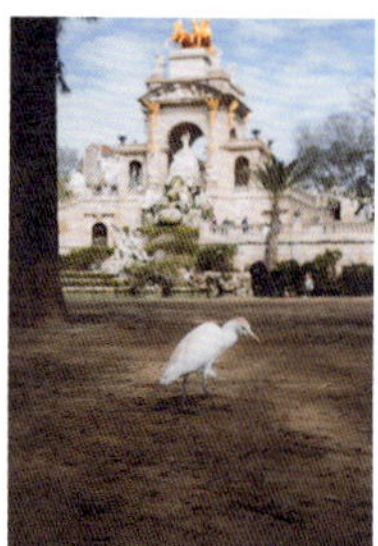
159 Ciutadella Park

LCCN: 2025940175
ISBN: 978-1-951963-50-7

Printed and bound in China
First printing, 2025

Trope Publishing Co.

Peter Jonker's photographs are available
for purchase. For inquires, go to trope.com
or email the gallery at info@trope.com

+ INFORMATION:
For additional information
on our books and prints,
visit trope.com

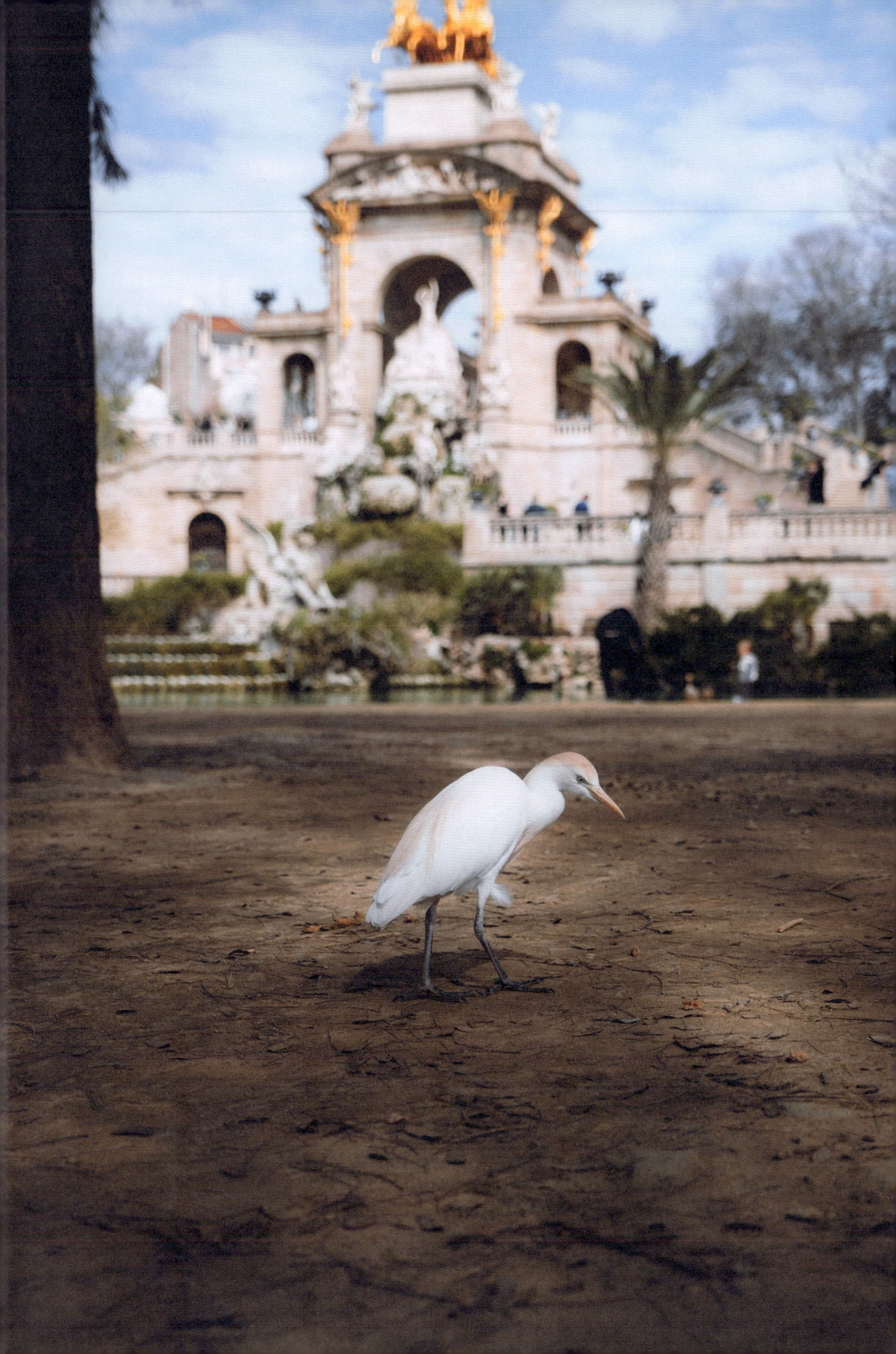